D1233389

NASDAQ

NASDAQ

A History of the Market
That Changed the World

MARK INGEBRETSEN

FORUM
An Imprint of Prima Publishing

To Walter and Alice

Published by Prima Publishing, Roseville, California. Member of the Crown Publishing Group, a division of Random House, Inc.

FORUM and colophon are trademarks of Random House, Inc. PRIMA PUBLISHING and colophon are trademarks of Random House, Inc., registered with the United States Patent and Trademark Office.

This book quotes the prices of certain stocks both in fractional and decimal form. Usually this is because the format used corresponds to the quoting convention used during the period illustrated.

Library of Congress Cataloging-in-Publication Data
Ingebretsen, Mark.
Nasdaq : a history of the market that changed the world /
Mark Ingebretsen
p.   cm.
Includes bibliography and index.
ISBN 0-7615-3560-8
1. Nasdaq Stock Market—History. I. Mark Ingebretsen. II. Title.
HG4574.2.I54   2002
332.64'273—dc21   2002016972

01 02 03 04 05 QQ 10 9 8 7 6 5 4 3 2 1
Printed in the United States of America

First Edition

Visit us online at www.primapublishing.com

CONTENTS

PREFACE

THINK FOR A MOMENT ABOUT WHAT THE SECRET IS BEHIND America's vast wealth. Many factors probably come to mind: the nation's culture, its resources, and the strength of its democratic traditions. But one of the reasons few of us consider is the strength of America's capital markets. Healthy financial markets empower companies to reach out to investors for the funds they need in order to grow. This book tells the history behind one of those markets: the Nasdaq.

Unlike the New York Stock Exchange (NYSE), which has long been the trading arena for America's largest and most powerful companies, the Nasdaq has always been the market for new and aggressive companies that seek to challenge the traditional ways of doing business. In that sense, as a market, the Nasdaq is the embodiment of the American dream.

The roots of the Nasdaq go all the way back to the 1920s, when rampant speculation during those boom times sparked the Great Depression but also led to the creation of institutions, such as the National Association of Securities Dealers (NASD), that were charged with preventing future abuses. From the 1930s on, the mandate of the NASD has been to bring order to the unique form of trading it was designed to oversee—the so-called over-the-counter (OTC) market. Shares of OTC stocks by definition do not trade on the floor of a brick-and-mortar exchange. Rather, they are bought and sold through an amorphous network of dealers and individual traders and investors. For that reason, OTC trading was uniquely suited to automation, which arrived in 1971, when the NASD's Automated Quotation System, the Nasdaq, made its official debut. It was one of the first real-time wide area networks. And it functioned much like the Internet does today, with users continually both updating and viewing information as stock prices changed and trades took place.

Like the Internet some 20 years later, the Nasdaq would become more than just a computerized network. It would span a vibrant, highly focused community. Inasmuch as this book discusses the history of the Nasdaq, it is also the story of that first online community, made up of a colorful cast—some brilliant, some admirable, some scoundrels—that have made and lost fortunes as a result of their trading on the Nasdaq stock market.

Because the Nasdaq is a network that moves vast amounts of money, it should come as no surprise that there have been and continue to be those crafty enough to exploit its shortcomings. Part of the Nasdaq story relays how some individuals and institutions were able to amass millions in this way and how the U.S. government has sought to deal with them.

Importantly, however, this is also the story of the people who have operated the Nasdaq market itself over the decades. At some point, it became clear to them that in addition to being a medium for trading stocks, the Nasdaq was also a business. Under their management, the Nasdaq emerged from relative obscurity to become one of the world's most recognizable brands.

A little over two decades into its evolution, the Nasdaq was able to merge itself seamlessly with the Internet. As a result, millions of Americans and countless millions more throughout the world were handed a window seat to the markets that a short time before was available only to Wall Street insiders. That window was the personal computer that sat on their desks. Little wonder, then, that the Nasdaq became a kind of global obsession. We reveled in stories of day traders who made and lost thousands in the course of a day just as we regaled in the tales of entrepreneurs, some barely in their 20s, who became multibillionaires in the space of hours when they took their companies public via the Nasdaq. Millions of average Americans profited as well. And as they watched their investment accounts expand each month and eagerly spent their new paper wealth, they drove up stock prices further still.

Ultimately, this is a story of how a stock market became a catalyst for a unique period in U.S. history—what now seems like a fabled time at the end of an old century and the dawn of a new one. And in that sense, the story of the Nasdaq is one that involves all of us.

ACKNOWLEDGMENTS

I WISH TO THANK ALL THOSE WHO GAVE SO GENEROUSLY OF their time in order to be interviewed for this book. In particular, I would like to thank those people associated with the Nasdaq with whom I spoke. Although this book was produced independent of any guidance or supervision from the Nasdaq stock market, the cooperation I received from individuals there was fundamental to making it possible.

PROLOGUE: TURNING POINT

STOCK MARKETS CAN BE VOLATILE ON FRIDAYS. THAT IS WHEN traders typically adjust their positions, particularly those that might prove vulnerable to weekend news. But by any reckoning, the sell-off on Friday, April 14, 2000, was extraordinary. At the end of the day, the Dow plunged 616 points to close at 10,307. However the real drama occurred on the Nasdaq. The Composite fell 355 points, or roughly 10 percent, to 3,321.

Some called it a natural correction. In fact, over the past three years, as the Nasdaq rose ever higher, periodic drops had meant only that the most aggressive speculators were selling. They could be depended on to buy the same wounded stocks again days later and ride them back up. Accordingly, on April 14, a few managers of Internet funds announced that they would soon be buyers, as Internet stocks had suffered especially.

Others were not so optimistic. Rumors swept through the markets that the "shorts" had failed to cover by the end of the day, an indication that they expected stocks to head lower still. Much of that expected selling was liable to come from day traders who owned heavily margined portfolios of technology stocks. Friday's meltdown topped off a week during which technology stocks went into a free fall. The Nasdaq, where many technology firms traded, had lost a quarter of its total market cap—well north of $1 trillion in wealth—during just five trading sessions. The Hambrecht & Quest Internet Index dropped more than 30 percent from its March high. Highly regarded MSN MoneyCentral columnist Jim Jubak pondered if the fall marked the end of "profitable tech investing."

By some quirk of fate, April 14, 2000, was also the day that the National Association of Securities Dealers (NASD), the Nasdaq market's parent, made public the results of a five-week-long voting process by the group's membership. The issue at hand was whether the NASD, a not-for-profit organization whose history stretched back to the Great Depression, should undergo a dramatic restructuring. Specifically, the NASD's leadership wanted to spin off the Nasdaq stock market and turn it into a private company. To some, this was a radical move. Throughout history, stock markets had been for the most part voluntary associations, like private clubs, created to support their members.

It could be said that most Americans at the time viewed with skepticism the idea that a trading market should be privatized. What would happen, for instance, if a stock market became a public company and its own shares of stock traded on that very market? The notion was confusing at best. Critics wondered how the interests of average investors would be looked out for—even though the Nasdaq restructuring plan did include mechanisms to ensure that the market would continue to operate fairly. Some NASD members who worked for the organization's smaller broker-dealers had also worried that a privatized Nasdaq would be dominated by a short list of huge financial firms. Lengthy negotiations over ways to distribute ownership had apparently resolved those fears. Even a last-minute effort to block the election results in a New York State court was denied by a judge. In the end, about 84 percent of the more than 4,000 NASD members voting had approved the plan in what was said to be a record turnout.

Officials at the NASD expressed their elation at the results. Privatization, they claimed, would do for the Nasdaq what it had done for innumerable other unwieldy, bureaucratic organizations. It would make it leaner, faster, and more accountable. "The members have spoken," said NASD Chairman and Chief Executive Officer Frank Zarb. "They have given the green light to spinning off Nasdaq—positioning it to be the most successful market in the world."

In many respects, at the dawn of the new millennium, the Nasdaq was already the most successful market in the world. Propelled by an aggressive new generation of high-technology and Internet firms, the Nasdaq Composite hovered at just over 2,000 at the start of 1999. In late December, it was touching 4,000. On New Year's Eve 1999, as an optimistic world readied to embrace the next century, their attention was focused on Manhattan's Times Square. The Nasdaq had a front-row seat to the event. Its newly completed MarketSite featured a 10,736-square-foot television monitor, the world's largest, arcing across the building's facade. The screen actually consisted of more than 18,000 light-emitting diodes (LEDs), each designed to last more than 10 years. It was easily the brightest light on Broadway.

As a not so subtle message, Nasdaq's leadership chose not to locate the MarketSite within the labyrinthine streets of lower Manhattan, so symbolic of the Old World of finance, a world that would always be dominated by the powerful New York Stock Exchange (NYSE). Rather, the Nasdaq's leaders had chosen Times Square, the crossroads of the world, the common man's entryway to New York. Like the Nasdaq, which had risen dramatically during America's new era of prosperity, Times Square had also undergone a stunning rebirth. A Disney-owned theater and shopping complex now stood in a place once overrun by drug dealers and porn shops.

For the Nasdaq market, the Times Square location also had a very practical purpose. "It's our public face," commented one Nasdaq official. For decades, nightly news reports showed the world the stereotypical image of a stock exchange. That image was of the paper-littered floor of the NYSE. The floor trading that occurred on the Big Board was a refinement of what traders had done for centuries: gather in one place to buy and sell shares from each other.

However, for nearly three decades now, the Nasdaq market had vastly improved on that process by placing participants on an electronic network, thus allowing them to trade from virtually anywhere in the world. The resulting network was in many ways similar to the Internet, which ironically had propelled the Nasdaq to its recent astounding growth. But while the Nasdaq had its online presence, it also needed a physical location so that its own visual sound bites could appear on the nightly news. The Times Square MarketSite was designed for that purpose. An entire wall displayed quotes of the Nasdaq's most actively traded stocks. This was the spot where commentators from the new cable financial networks stood, while a nearby window afforded the throngs passing through Times Square a view inside.

Yet at the start of the millennium, the MarketSite represented only a small piece of the Nasdaq and its parent organization, the NASD. Among the other components was the recently acquired American Stock Exchange and an independent regulatory arm, called Nasdaq Regulation. Actual trading on the Nasdaq occurs on what is one of the world's largest telecommunications networks. The main processing facility, which can handle a reported eight billion shares of daily volume, is located in a heavily guarded facility in Trumbull, Connecticut. A backup facility, tied into a separate electric power grid, resides in Rockville, Maryland.

During 2000, the year of the market plunge, the NASD took in more than $1.2 billion in revenues—small in comparison to the many billions earned by the Nasdaq's largest listed companies. But the figure belies the phenomenal influence that the NASD and the Nasdaq have on the world economy. You could think of the Nasdaq as a kind of ultimate Web portal to the brave new world of investing. Likewise, you could think of the millions that tuned into the market each day as world's largest online community. The community consisted of NASD's dealer firms, such as Knight Trading and Merrill Lynch; large money management firms, such as Vanguard and Fidelity; hedge funds; and independently owned trade execution networks, such as Instinet, Island, and Archipelago. Some 5,400 brokerage firms with 88,000 branch offices where 670,000 brokers worked also formed an integral part of the network. But that still would not take into account the fast-growing new financial media that included some 5,000 financial Web sites, major daily newspapers, and television networks like CNBC and CNNfn. And it would not include the millions of people worldwide who own Nasdaq-listed shares. An estimated 10 million Americans alone had opened online brokerage accounts that allowed them to trade on the Nasdaq network directly. As the market rose, so did efforts to bring more people into the community. The New York–based research firm Competitive Media Reporting estimated that advertising by brokerage firms alone jumped 95 percent in 1999 to reach an unprecedented $1.2 billion.

The size of this online community and the huge sums that went into promoting it all stemmed from the fact that at the turn of the century, millionaires were being created by the hour thanks to the Nasdaq. Their ranks included the young tech company executives who used the Nasdaq as the launching pad for their initial public offerings as well as the day traders and even the everyday investors who rode the prices of those shares skyward. Truly, it had been a long and glorious ride.

On April 14, 2000, the question on the minds of the newly wealthy and those who wanted to be was a simple one: Is it over?

CHAPTER 1

THE 24/7 GLOBAL EQUITIES BAZAAR

WHEN NASDAQ CHAIRMAN Frank Zarb stood before members of the National Press Club on June 13, 2000, he was a man on a mission. It was the same mission Zarb had been on for more than a year whenever he spoke before groups of politicians, investment advisers, the public, or whoever was willing to listen. A distinguished-looking man in his mid-sixties at the time, with short graying hair and an intent though friendly gaze, Zarb had been tapped to lead the Nasdaq and its parent organization, the National Association of Securities Dealers (NASD), barely three years before—a rough period for the Nasdaq, to be sure. It had been mired in a series of federal investigations and lawsuits over the trading practices of some of its members.

When Zarb took the top spot, many observers in the financial industry expected that because of the scandal these investigations had caused, he would choose to keep a low profile while he set about mending fences. But as it turned out, that opinion grossly underestimated a man who brought formidable experience and talent to his new job. Zarb had served as assistant secretary of labor in the Nixon administration, but he first came to the public's attention when President Gerald Ford appointed him energy czar. In the highly politicized atmosphere during the 1970s oil embargo, Zarb's job had been to slash through red tape and deliver gas to the pumps.

Following his stint in Washington, Zarb moved among several top Wall Street firms, serving as a partner with Lazard Freres & Co. and as head of Smith Barney. Now, at an age when most people would look forward to retirement, Zarb appeared determined to make his job at the Nasdaq the pinnacle of his career. Rather than simply laboring to heal the Nasdaq's sullied reputation, Zarb early on had formulated a grand vision for its future.

Standing before members of the National Press Club, he wanted his audience to understand how the Nasdaq might become the economic engine that generated trillions of dollars in new wealth and millions of jobs—not just in the United States but throughout the world as well. In Zarb's vision, the Nasdaq would be an online trading network that, like the Internet, never shut down. "I am more convinced than ever," Zarb told his audience, "that the stock market in the new millennium will be available to anyone, anywhere in the world 24 hours a day."[1] Which is to say, a day trader in Singapore could log on to her computer in the dead of night and trade stocks along with investors in North and South America. In the same manner, American investors could use the Internet to hunt for the stocks of vibrant start-up companies in Europe, Asia, and Latin America.

It was a radical vision, to be sure. Stock markets, despite efforts to the contrary, have always been closed-off, almost clublike organizations. Companies listing on one exchange have even been barred from listing on another. Typically, only the world's largest corporations have been able to list on more than one exchange. Stock of smaller companies, with some exceptions, has tended to trade solely in the companies' home nation. Being old boys' clubs, the world's markets had also set comfortable bankers' hours for themselves, oblivious to the fact that business continued long after they shut down for the afternoon. That has always been especially true in the United States. Regular trading on the New York Stock Exchange (NYSE) ends at 4 P.M. Eastern Standard Time, the hour when people in Los Angeles are just returning from lunch.

But on another level, trading has always followed the sun around the planet. After trading shuts down in New York, it quickly picks up in Asia. Hours later, the European exchanges open their doors. Then the action shifts to New York once again. Global financial institutions maintain offices in both hemispheres. Like tag teams in a wrestling match, their traders hand over responsibilities for buying and selling. Thus, these institutions could protect themselves if an international crisis in the Middle East occurred at 1 A.M. New York time and sent markets toppling in Asia. By contrast, individual investors have always been powerless to act. And all too often, they have woken up the next morning to find their portfolios decimated by a manic market.

Zarb's vision of a 24-hour stock market was at the very least an attempt to level the playing field. However, for a 24-hour market to work, it needed to be global. No single exchange had enough of a following to furnish the buyers and sellers needed to maintain fair prices. Unless the market was global, trading in the dead of night would be like attending an auction with only two or three other buyers. The bidding would tend to be erratic. But if Americans could trade in the dead of night alongside Asians and Europeans, collectively they would create a dynamic, competitive market.

The Internet Strategy

ZARB WAS CONVINCED the world was ready for a 24/7, truly global stock market. The Internet, he believed, had already paved the way. "We estimate overall Internet use worldwide will grow by another 60 percent on English-language sites," he told National Press Club members, "and will double in non-English sites, to a total of more than 160 million users worldwide." Zarb predicted that Japan, where the Nasdaq was poised to open its newest franchise, would have 120 million Internet users by 2004. Most telling of all, he said, the Nasdaq's own Web site had received 1.5 billion hits in the past year. "Thirty percent of those hits had come from outside the United States."

There was the proof. The world was beating a path to the door of America's most vibrant stock market. And thanks to the Internet, Zarb would be able to open that door to all comers. Zarb's hopes for the Nasdaq were perhaps more closely tied to the Internet than any organization on earth—and this at a time when every major corporation had rolled out an ambitious Internet strategy. Unlike some companies whose plans to become Internet-centered were at times forced and reactive, Zarb had good reason to be optimistic that his global online exchange would succeed.

Finance, as it turned out, appeared uniquely suited to the powerful new medium's ability to deliver highly complex information instantaneously. More important, the Internet enabled millions of users to manipulate that information—instantly and all at the same time. The simple act of checking one's portfolio was but one example. Only years before, prior to the Internet age, Americans checked stock prices in the newspaper while they drank their morning coffee. Now, it was suddenly possible to watch the value of an entire portfolio of stocks rise and fall as each transaction occurred. In the space of just two to three years, more than 10 million Americans had opened online trading accounts.

More than any stock market in the world, the Nasdaq was uniquely positioned to serve these newly empowered investors. It was, after all, the world's first online stock market and as such had been transmitting detailed financial information over a real-time network since the early 1970s. The name Nasdaq, in fact, is an acronym for National Association of Securities Dealers Automated Quotation System. Before the arrival of the Internet, Nasdaq information went out almost exclusively to market professionals. But now, average investors had access to much the same information. It was as if a potent drug had suddenly been unleashed. Millions logged on to the Internet each day and gleefully checked the value of their portfolios or watched how the prices of volatile Nasdaq stocks made and lost fortunes in minutes.

The Amazing Wealth-Creation Engine

BUT ZARB'S NASDAQ was intimately tied to the Internet in an even more fundamental way. By the late 1990s, thousands of start-up firms had built their business models around the Internet. It was widely believed that the new medium would shatter all the old ways of doing business. Shares of those companies traded on the Nasdaq. Investors bought into the Internet's promise and furiously bid up the shares' prices. Average investors were largely responsible for this buying frenzy. And as a group, they had propelled the Nasdaq to a phenomenal 86 percent rise during 1999. That gain in turn had helped create millions of jobs and was widely credited with producing the so-called wealth effect during the 1990s. As people watched in amazement while their investments grew, they themselves grew more optimistic about the future. And so they consumed more and further fueled the unprecedented prosperity.

True enough, at some point the Nasdaq's amazing wealth-creation engine would surely run out of steam. But what if that engine could be directed at other parts of the world? What if it could serve as the catalyst that turned complacent Japanese salarymen into zealous Silicon Valley–style entrepreneurs? Could it not do the same for young European entrepreneurs mired by the Continent's antiquated bureaucracy? And what if the Nasdaq could also assist bright, restless, entrepreneurial minds in Third World nations such as India and China and help them raise money for their new ventures?

Zarb told National Press Club members a story of his visit to China earlier that year to meet with Premier Zhu Rongji. At some point, Zarb broached the idea of opening a Nasdaq franchise in China. "Rongji turned to an aide and asked him, in Chinese, what he thought of the idea." Zarb recounts, "Then the premier turned to me and said, 'They're still studying it, but I think it's a good idea.'"

Thus, Zarb believed that if entrepreneurs in China and the rest of the world could collectively raise money to build their businesses and do so by tapping into the Nasdaq, the result would be a literal explosion of wealth. That, of course, is precisely what a stock market is supposed to do: create wealth. Companies wishing to raise funds to accomplish their aims have just two choices. They can turn to lenders for the cash. But that would force them to pay interest, which would siphon off profits. The alternative is to go to the equity markets and sell a percentage of ownership in the company in the form of stock. Aside from the underwriting costs and the regulatory expenses associated with being a public company, the money a company receives from a public stock sale is essentially free.

Investors can choose from among thousands of stocks. But they will naturally tend to purchase stocks of companies that they believe will be the most successful. And their collective buying will steadily raise the share prices of those companies. In that way, a stock market is a highly efficient mechanism for rewarding successful business ventures.

However, investors will risk their money to buy stocks only when they know that a buyer will be waiting for them when it comes time to sell. So a stock market, in order to be successful, must do two things well: It must make it relatively easy for promising new companies to sell shares to the public, and it must ensure there will always be buyers and sellers available to trade those shares. The term for the latter, of course, is *liquidity*. A market lacking in liquidity will quickly cease to exist.

Liquidity is seldom a problem when the shares of stocks being traded come from large companies because numerous buyers and sellers will always be waiting in the wings. Maintaining a liquid trading environment is far more difficult when the market contains thousands of tiny companies, many of which possess miniscule assets and erratic earnings. These, in fact, are just the sorts of companies that make up the Nasdaq stock market.

The Mother of Markets

THE NASDAQ'S SUCCESS stems from the fact that, as will be explained in chapter 2, buyers and sellers can be found for these companies' stocks. And indeed, the Nasdaq had become a formidable player on the global financial stage. In the space of three decades, it had arguably eclipsed the NYSE in importance. Zarb intended to build on this momentum.

When Zarb negotiated the buyout of the rival American Stock Exchange (chapter 15), Securities and Exchange Commission Chairman Arthur Levitt reportedly called the idea "unrealistic." The marriage of the two exchanges would give the Nasdaq access to options trading and a new financial instrument called exchange traded funds—literally index funds that traded like stocks—that would prove enormously popular in the years to come. Dissension among members of both exchanges at first cast doubt on the merger's outcome. But when Zarb pulled it off, Federal Reserve Board Chairman Alan Greenspan applauded the union. "This should have been done years ago," he said.[2]

In the months following Zarb's speech before the National Press Club, the Nasdaq announced a series of new partnerships and new ventures. In March 2001, for example, the Nasdaq unveiled plans to link up with the London International Financial Futures and Options Exchange. The venture was aimed at developing so-called single stock futures, a hot new derivatives product that would provide hefty leverage to traders of European stocks. In April, the Nasdaq announced plans to move its headquarters from Washington, D.C., to lower Manhattan. The new administrative center would follow the opening of the glittery Nasdaq MarketSite in Times Square. Both moves could be seen as open challenges to the NYSE, which had long reigned supreme in New York's financial district. Then in May, Nasdaq officials in the United States and Japan finalized the structure of the Nasdaq's Japanese franchise. During June, the Nasdaq made public details of its new trading platform for Nasdaq Europe. In addition to Europe and Japan, the Nasdaq had already launched a franchise in Canada, and it was forging ties with the financial communities in India and Hong Kong. Zarb told his National Press Club audience that Nasdaq officials were also looking closely at Latin America and the Middle East as sources of future expansion.

Its global reach notwithstanding, the core of the Nasdaq's operations remained very much in the United States. On any given day, more than 1.7 billion shares change hands on the Nasdaq National Market, the centerpiece of the Nasdaq empire. At times, volume on the Nasdaq is more than double the number of shares changing hands on the NYSE. If you added up the market capitalization of all the companies trading on the

THE 24/7 GLOBAL EQUITIES BAZAAR | 9

Nasdaq, which is to say if you added up the value of all the shares of stock from those companies, the total would come to more than $5 trillion.

That amount was less than one-third the NYSE's $17 trillion total market cap. But a closer look at the numbers revealed that the Nasdaq was truly a comer. The value of Nasdaq companies had grown from a mere $386 billion during the past 11 years. More impressive still, between 1995 and 1999, the Nasdaq's total market cap rose a mind-bending 257 percent. That market cap is divided up among the 4,800 companies that trade on the Nasdaq. This number, too, is more than double the number of companies listed with the NYSE. Many Nasdaq-traded companies, such as Microsoft, Cisco, and Oracle, rank on the short list of America's most powerful technology firms. Microsoft alone, for example, had a market cap of roughly $370 billion at the onset of 2002. Oracle's market cap during the same period was $83 billion. But in terms of size, these companies are the exceptions. Only about 15 percent of Nasdaq-listed companies have market caps north of $1 billion, and less than half have valuations of $100 million or more.

The Nasdaq is home to so many smaller companies (as will be explained in chapter 3) in part because its roots go back to the era when small-company shares traded informally among brokers. As part of its mandate, the Nasdaq makes it relatively easy for companies to list their shares. Before qualifying for a listing on the Nasdaq SmallCap Market, the anteroom for the Nasdaq's main-floor-level market, a company must possess a minimum of $5 million in shareholder equity. Some $15 million in equity is needed for a company to qualify for a listing on the Nasdaq National Market, the arena where Intel, Microsoft, and the other Nasdaq trophy firms traded. By contrast, the NYSE sets higher admission requirements. Companies need at least $60 million in equity to qualify.

While the high bar set by the NYSE is meant to ensure a degree of financial stability, the Nasdaq's relatively benign listing requirements have enabled it to attract a steady flow of fresh-minted firms. Roughly 89 percent of all U.S. initial public offerings (IPOs) during 1999 alone, for example, made their debut on the Nasdaq. Those IPOs raised a reported $51 billion for the companies fielding them. But investors in many cases reaped far more as prices of the newly hatched shares doubled, tripled, or quadrupled in a single day's trading.

America Inc.

THE ASTRONOMICAL RISE in the share prices of new tech companies illustrates just how fixated the investing public had become at the dawn of the millennium and how important, in turn, those companies had become to America's self-image. A few decades before, Americans, as well as people in the rest of the world, wondered seriously whether the planet's dominant stock market might soon reside in Tokyo or Frankfurt. Then, during the 1990s, when prices on the Nasdaq began their parabolic rise, a radical change in psychology occurred. No one talked any longer about the Japanese or German threat to America's steel or automobile industry, not when there were millions to be made just by buying shares of Juniper Networks or JDS Uniphase. Certainly no one talked about a threat to America's preeminence in the new world of the Internet and the new economy it promised.

By the 1990s, it became axiomatic that a new generation of American titans had arisen—equal in wealth, power, and vision to the Carnegies, Fords, and Mellons of the previous century—and were empowered, just as their predecessors had been, to mold a new American century. Shares of the companies founded by the earlier generation of American titans still traded on the NYSE. But the new generation, with well-known names like Bill Gates, Larry Ellison, and Mark Andreasson, eschewed the NYSE, with its industrial age roots. They had launched their companies on the nation's new electronic stock market: the Nasdaq. Long after their companies had grown and were actively courted by the NYSE, the new generation of corporate titans invariably chose to remain with the Nasdaq. To be sure, their motives for staying were due largely to the market's ability to promote trading of their shares (as will be explained in chapter 15). But companies also stayed with the Nasdaq because it had become synonymous with rapid innovation and growth.

The World or Nothing

NOT SURPRISINGLY, THE Nasdaq's allure quickly spread worldwide. Close to 10 percent of the companies listed on the Nasdaq are foreign in origin. In order for their shares to be listed, these companies must adhere to the same financial reporting standards as U.S. firms. And in many cases, those standards are more stringent than the reporting requirements mandated by their home governments. The companies put up with this for a simple reason: access to capital. No other stock market on the planet provided it so generously. During the height of the tech boom, "if you took a high technology company public, you would get a higher valuation on Nasdaq than on any of the European exchanges," notes Ian Jones, director of the U.K. venture capital firm Apax Partners & Co.[3]

Like their U.S. counterparts, non-U.S. companies trading on the Nasdaq have run the gamut from true global giants, such as Ericsson Telephone, Reuters, and Nissan, to start-ups, such as the Israeli networking firm AudioCodes Ltd. and Korean Internet service provider Korea Thrunet Co. "We're co-branding with our issuing companies," proclaimed a former top Nasdaq official.[4] By doing so, that official explains, the Nasdaq and the listing company were betting that their reputations would rise in tandem.

By listing with the Nasdaq, a company in turn—be it a start-up in a San Francisco loft or in a vacant warehouse in India—achieved instant credibility thanks to the co-branding. Indeed, the name Nasdaq has become one of the world's most widely recognizable brands. When the survey organization Response Analysis Corporation asked Americans to name the U.S. stock market that first came to their minds, a full 86 percent picked the Nasdaq. When the same question was asked in the United Kingdom, some 41 percent picked the Nasdaq versus 21 percent who named the NYSE.[5] Clearly, in addition to being a financial force to be reckoned with, the Nasdaq at the millennium had also become a powerful global brand—quite a feat for an organization that employs just over 1,000 people.

Yet, as Zarb spoke that evening in June, some in the audience were likely listening with more than the usual reporter's skepticism. Thanks to the crash that had occurred just weeks earlier, many had no doubt lost thousands. In the months ahead, of course, the market was destined to sink lower still, bottoming out in 2001, following the terrible events of September 11. However, the Nasdaq's decline had little to do with the economic uncertainty brought about by America's new war on terrorism. Rather it resulted from a sudden loss of faith in the very technology companies that had propelled it to highs of over 5,000 points. Yes, there had been abrupt corrections before. But the market had always quickly bounced back. This time, in the months before 9-11, there was a sense that things were different. The miraculous wealth-creation engine had stalled. And now it barely limped along. Suddenly, the Nasdaq no longer seemed like the path to assured wealth, even as it faced increasing competition from other stock markets here and abroad. Soon, some of the reporters gathered at the National Press Club that night in June would openly question whether someday it might even shut its doors.

CHAPTER **2**

HOW THE NASDAQ WORKS

THANKS TO ITS precipitous fall in April 2000, the Nasdaq would remain on the national front burner for months to come as people agonized over their vanished wealth and traders furiously bet on the short-term rallies and bearish nosedives that were to occur throughout the remainder of 2000 and into 2001. Day after day, television news reports and newspapers led with fresh tales of market carnage. You only had to follow the share price of Internet incubator company CMGI to see just how vicious that carnage had become. In January 2000, shares of the tech wunderkind were trading above $300. A year and a half later, a stock split and the dot-com bomb had reduced its price to just $3, wiping out billions in market capitalization in the process.

As one Internet powerhouse after another crumbled, a sense of doom overcame the markets. Aptly reflecting the sentiment of those dark months, a March front-page story in the Sunday *New York Times* led with this sentence: "The bull market, born in 1982 amid recession and concern that the American economy was terminally ill, is now being measured for its coffin."[1] Much to the confusion of average investors, many news reports featured wildly conflicting interviews with market gurus alternately predicting ruin or salvation. As happens during market panics, each prediction brought fresh salvos of buying and selling. The result of this new national anxiety was heightened trading. In 1999, as the Nasdaq shot upward during the tech stock peak, some 273 billion Nasdaq shares changed hands. During the 2000 meltdown, that number increased to nearly 443 billion.

Trading levels on the New York Stock Exchange (NYSE) were relatively stable by comparison. Some 204 billion NYSE shares changed hands in 1999 versus 262 billion in 2000.[2] The NYSE, in fact, held up well throughout the crash of 2000. The Dow traded mostly within a narrow range between 10,000 and 11,000. Dow component companies, NYSE officials were quick to point out, were after all the bedrock of American capitalism. They were not wing-and-a-prayer start-ups launched by overcaffeinated Generation Xers. The Nasdaq's downfall was inevitable. Or so they smugly proclaimed.

Yet even as average investors pondered this and worried whether their portfolios would ever recover, few understood how the stock market they had bet their future on actually works—in particular how the Nasdaq differs radically from the NYSE.

Deconstructing the NYSE

WHEN MOST OF us think of stock trading, we likely conjure up images of men and women shouting and rushing about on the NYSE floor. That is what we see on the news each night. So perhaps it is best to explain how the NYSE—a traditional stock exchange—works before beginning to describe the Nasdaq.

In fact, all the shouting on the NYSE floor results from hundreds of auctions taking place simultaneously. In a bit of understatement, perhaps, the NYSE is referred to as an auction market. Amid the pandemonium, it may seem hard to visualize how shares change hands. But the process is usually pretty simple. When you place an order to buy a listed share, which is how shares traded on the NYSE are referred to, that order first goes to your broker. From there it travels to your broker's representative on the NYSE exchange floor. It is the duty of this broker to get you the best possible price for those shares. However, the order is actually transacted by a person called a specialist, who stands inside what is called a trading post, right on the exchange floor. NYSE specialists work for large financial firms, such as Fleet Meehan and Speer, Leeds and Kellog. You could think of specialists as professional auctioneers who have purchased space on the exchange floor to conduct their business.

When making transactions, the specialist may match your buy order with someone else's order to sell a quantity of shares. This match may also occur automatically via an electronic network. Alternately, the specialist may sell you the shares from his or her own account. In almost every case, orders are funneled through the specialist. The fact that buy and sell orders nearly always go through a specialist is an important attribute of the NYSE. It means that all the floor brokers handling orders for a particular stock on behalf of their customers must meet at a central location. Everyone on the floor of the exchange can watch what everyone else is doing. And this, in turn, greatly increases the chances that the price a customer pays for stocks will be a fair one.

NYSE specialists have a monopoly on the trading of a particular company's shares. As a result of their unique position, specialist firms earn a lot of money from their buying and selling. They do this by making the spread. The spread is the difference between the price they are willing to buy shares for and the slightly higher price they charge to sell those same shares back to you.

Specialists operate a little like the people manning currency-exchange kiosks in airports. If you have ever visited one of these, you may remember how the currency trader posts the prices he or she is willing to accept to buy or sell dollars, rubles, and pesos. Buy prices are listed on one side of a chart, sell prices on the other. (The chart is usually erasable since prices frequently change.)

Likewise, specialists post the prices they are willing to accept when buying or selling stocks. Although the world of stock trading has its own unique lingo, the price that specialists promise to buy shares for is called the bid. The price they are willing to sell shares for is called the ask or sometimes the offer.

With shares of widely held stocks such as IBM or ATT, the spread—again, the difference between the bid and the ask—may be as little as a few cents. With shares of less frequently traded stocks, such as Winnebago Industries, the spread would probably be wider.

Remember that those pennies theoretically represent the profit a specialist makes on a single share of stock. With millions of shares changing hands each day, specialists have the opportunity to rake off millions of dollars in profits in the course of their work. In return for giving specialists the opportunity to make such large profits, the NYSE requires that they act as buyers and sellers of last resort. For investors large and small, this means that there will always be a buyer when they want to sell shares and a seller when they want to buy. From the point of view of the NYSE, the specialist's job is to ensure an orderly market. The specialists themselves, like everyone else, are in business to make money.

Ensuring an orderly market and making a profit at the same time entails a certain amount of risk. Specialists must remain tightly focused on every move the market makes, or else they will lose money. This can occur if a stock plummets in price and the specialist is caught holding too many shares that were purchased at a higher price. To help lessen this risk, the NYSE gives specialists a powerful advantage. Only they know how many buy and sell orders are stacked up awaiting execution at any given time.

Recent changes on the NYSE (see chapter 17) have made some of the information that specialists alone possessed available to the market as a whole. But the specialist still has access to the best information. And in any stock market, information is everything. Armed with information, specialists are able to predict where a stock will likely move in the short term. For example, the more sell orders outnumber buy orders, the more likely the stock will fall in price, until the imbalance is worked out. Conversely, the more buy orders outnumber sell orders, the greater the likelihood the stock will rise.

And that is where the second advantage the specialist possesses comes to bear, as it is the specialist—taking into account market forces—who can often set the price. That is a powerful advantage, considering that specialists have a monopoly on trading that particular stock.

So while the NYSE exchange floor would appear to be a highly transparent arena for trading (after all, everyone can see traders clamoring around the floor's many posts), until various reforms are initiated in 2002 there would remain a vast amount of important information that was withheld from traders. Even as those reforms become firmly entrenched, the specialists will continue to rule the NYSE, for the simple reason that each specialist is the most knowledgeable person on the planet when it comes to how the particular stock he or she oversees trades.

The Nasdaq Model

THE NYSE OPERATES more or less the way stock exchanges have been run for centuries. But the Nasdaq model is radically different. In fact, in the eyes of the Securities and Exchange Commission (SEC), the Nasdaq is not even considered an exchange.[3] Rather, it is a quote display medium. Recall from the previous chapter that the name Nasdaq is an acronym for the National Association of Securities Dealers Automated Quotation System. That acronym handily explains how the Nasdaq is organized. The National Association of Securities Dealers (NASD), is a membership organization composed of the brokers and other financial players that are allowed to trade Nasdaq shares. A nonprofit organization, the NASD supports the interests of its members and also enforces the organization's rules to ensure a just and fair trading environment. As you will see in the next chapter, its roots go back to the early 1900s, when the SEC searched for a way to oversee trading of smaller companies whose shares did not qualify for listing on the NYSE.

Another important task of the NASD—until recently when the two organization split—has been to supervise the Nasdaq. The Nasdaq is really a huge computer network, linking an estimated 300,000 terminals worldwide, many more if you count all the investors who access it via the Internet. The network takes the place of the NYSE's brick-and-mortar trading floor. As a result, the Nasdaq has no actual trading floor, unless you count the site in Trumbull, Connecticut, where the computers are actually located.

Instead of using specialists to serve as the central aggregator for all trades, as the NYSE does, it is the Nasdaq network that acts as a central conduit through which Nasdaq shares may be traded. There are a great many routes that a Nasdaq trade may take. However, each route can always be tracked via the Nasdaq network.

Best-Guess Prices

TO UNDERSTAND THE advantages of having a central portal through which all transactions are tracked and displayed, think back to the notion that Nasdaq companies in many cases have been those too small to qualify for listing on the NYSE. As a result, their shares were traded informally from one broker to another. For that reason, they were known as over-the-counter (OTC) stocks. Before the Nasdaq network came online, it was difficult to know what price OTC stocks were selling for at any precise point in time. And although it was always possible to buy or sell shares of OTC companies, the process was cumbersome, not to mention costly. It went something like this: You called your broker with an order to buy shares. He or she in turn made some calls to other brokers to see who might have shares available and at what price. The price quoted by each broker might differ substantially because, unlike the brokers gathered on the NYSE floor, these brokers were located all across the country.

As your broker called around the country to find the lowest price, he or she was aware that the brokers doing the selling were normally acting on orders from their own customers. In addition, the selling brokers would tack a hefty commission onto the prices their customers sought. Your broker would likely add yet another commission before delivering the shares to you.

When you wanted to sell the shares, you had to go through this awkward, expensive process all over again. Incredibly, this disorganized method of trading persisted until the Nasdaq's debut in 1971. Its effect, of course, was to stifle the development of smaller companies. Because of the hassles and high costs, relatively few investors were interested in buying small-company shares, the result being that relatively few small companies went public via the OTC market—at least compared to now.

In one bold stroke, the Nasdaq system brought speed and sanity to the byzantine process of trading OTC shares. It did this by becoming the central repository where all quote data on all the shares trading on the OTC market was stored. Now when you called your broker, he or she could look up the stock's symbol on a computer screen and tell you what the best bid and ask price was at that instant. The price was based on input from thousands of brokers and traders around the world who all had access to the same screen. When you agreed to the price, your broker made a few keystrokes, and the shares were yours. It was a huge breakthrough. Eventually, online trading would make this process even simpler. Instead of calling your broker, you could log on to the brokerage's Internet site and perform the transaction yourself.

Methods of the Middlemen

BUT THE NASDAQ had to provide more than just a means of displaying stock prices in order to smoothly facilitate transactions. It also had to ensure that a dynamic market existed for trading the shares you were interested in. No matter how small the company, there needed to be a seller willing to take the other side of your trade when you wanted to buy shares. Likewise, there needed to be a buyer always at the ready when you chose to sell.

To ensure that this always happened, the Nasdaq over the years has utilized several innovative mechanisms. The result is that the Nasdaq market is highly complex with many different players offering many different means of executing a trade. However, in all cases the trade is executed electronically and can be traced at every step along the way if necessary.

To understand exactly what happens, it helps to follow a trade you wish to make from start to finish. So let's say that you wish to buy 100 shares of Proton Energy (PRTN), a relatively small ($270 million market cap) maker of fuel cells that you read about recently. Proton Energy is also lightly traded. Average volume is just around 135,000 shares. Let's also say that you do business with an online broker. So instead of calling in your order on the phone, you place it yourself through the broker's Web site. You know that Proton Energy is a Nasdaq-traded stock because its symbol, PRTN, contains four letters.

By contrast, the symbols for NYSE-listed shares have three letters (WMT for Wal-Mart Stores, Inc. is an example), sometimes two letters (such as GE for General Electric), or in some cases just one letter (as with F for Ford).

Because you are a frugal and savvy trader, you decide to place what is called a limit order that is 2 cents lower than the best ask price of $8.15 per share currently being advertised. With a limit order, you specify the exact price you want to pay, whereas with another kind of order, called a market order, you automatically receive the best price available in the market at the time your order is entered. Placing a limit order is a form of negotiation. You are hoping that someone out there will meet your price.

Once you do enter your order, any of several things can happen. In some cases, the order may go to your broker's own trading room. There, traders employed by your brokerage check the prevailing price. They may then decide to sell you the shares themselves at the price you specified by your limit order. They might do this, perhaps, because they have a large inventory of PRTN shares that they bought at a lower price and that they now wish to sell off in order to lock in a profit.

Alternately, the traders working for your broker may send your order to a kind of wholesale broker known as a market maker. A market maker's role is similar to that of a specialist on the NYSE. It is the job of the market maker to help maintain an orderly market for a given security. And they are sanctioned by the Nasdaq to perform these duties. In exchange for providing an orderly market, market makers, like specialists, are allowed to profit from the bid-ask spread. But there is an important difference between market makers and specialists. Recall that NYSE specialists have a monopoly on the shares they trade. By contrast, on the Nasdaq several market makers might compete with one another to buy and sell a particular security. Usually they do this by broadcasting their best bid and ask prices over the Nasdaq.

Market makers on the Nasdaq compete for orders similar to the way several currency vendors might compete for your business at a busy international airport. Each dealer handles the same dollars, pesos, and rubles. But each might frequently change the price they will accept when buying and selling these currencies so as to gain a slight edge over their fellows while still profiting sufficiently from the spread.

In fact, several hundred market makers ply their trade on the Nasdaq. And, as with specialists on the NYSE, many work for subsidiaries of household-name firms, such as Merrill Lynch and Goldman Sachs.

But back to our example. Retail brokers like the one you used to place your order may have a special arrangement with one particular market-making firm. And so they will direct your order to that firm. If you had placed a market order with your broker and the broker had sent the order to a particular market maker, the market maker would have still been obligated to sell you the shares at the best price advertised in the entire market at that moment. But remember that you placed a limit order for the PRTN shares, and because it was a limit order, you specified the price you were willing to pay. Under the rules of the Nasdaq exchange, a market maker must either meet that price or else do one of two things: display your order as his own on the Nasdaq order book or else send it to the market at large.

If the market maker chooses the latter, the order will be sent to any of several electronic communications networks, better known as ECNs. ECNs are privately owned computerized trading networks that directly match buyers and sellers. Their creation has had a profound effect on the Nasdaq and on stock trading in general. Chapter 11 will cover this subject fully. For now it is important to know that because ECNs are totally automated, they can execute trades only when they find an exact match. In other words, the price you agree to purchase PRTN shares for must exactly match the price someone else is willing to sell those shares for.

If your order happens to be the highest-priced bid to buy PRTN shares at that moment, it will be the order that everyone on the Nasdaq sees when they enter the symbol for PRTN. In other words, until a better price comes along, your bid will lead the market. And when it is executed, it will be used to determine the overall value of PRTN at that moment.

But along with your bid, the Nasdaq network will simultaneously display other bids that are just off the best price. The effect is that you get to see your bid or whichever bid happens to be the best price at the top of the list along with those that are a penny or two off this price. These latter bids form a list below the best bid.

Besides the price, the Nasdaq network will also list the quantity of shares available at that price. The name for this display is Nasdaq Level II. (Level II often requires that you use a special kind of software or use a specialized type of broker. It will be discussed at length in chapters 5 and 12.) A Level II display, with its list of best bids and offers running alongside each other, is similar to the type of display a NYSE specialist sees. But instead of allowing only the specialist to see this information as had been customary on the NYSE, the Nasdaq makes it available to everyone willing to purchase the needed software and pay a small monthly fee to receive the quote data. The goal of the Nasdaq quote display system is to create what is called a transparent market—literally a market where everyone has a front-row view of what is going on.

The Great Electronic Casino

THE RATIONALE FOR using several market makers as opposed to a single specialist is that these market makers will compete for your buy and sell orders. And this will, it is hoped, bring the prices of shares down to the lowest possible level when you want to buy. Those same competitive forces should allow you to receive the highest possible price when you go to sell those shares. But market makers are not necessarily the only ones interested in your order. Day traders, brokers, and institutional traders are also tuned into the Level II screen. And they can snatch up your shares if they like the price. Now remember again that most companies that trade on the Nasdaq are small. On an average day, sometimes just a few thousand shares of their stock trade. When you are the one doing the trading, you know that there likely will be several who will compete for your order. And in addition to market makers, other traders will be able to see your order and act on it if they choose. Having multiple players is vital to ensuring a dynamic market for thinly traded stocks.

The end result is that a kind of video game takes place via the Level II screen for each Nasdaq-traded stock, with all the players watching as bids are entered and withdrawn while trying to decide whether they are tricks or traps or legitimate opportunities. All the while, traders collectively move billions of dollars on and off the table. If you consider the fact that nearly 5,000 stocks trade on the Nasdaq, then the entire network can be viewed as something like a giant electronic casino that is open for business each day and patronized by hundreds of thousands of investors and traders of all kinds. Day traders, traders who work for brokerages, market makers, and traders who serve mutual funds and hedge funds may buy shares piecemeal or buy them one minute and sell them the next in an ongoing melee that is totally silent and relatively anonymous. You may know that the market maker you are dealing with works for Knight Securities. But you cannot be sure whether he is intent on buying or selling inventory. And as for the other traders posting bids on the Level II screen, they could be professionals out to trap you or rank amateurs destined to lose money from their tactics.

As dynamic and efficient as it appears, the great electronic casino that is the Nasdaq does not always guarantee investors the best price. The staid NYSE system, as you will learn in chapter 17, actually manages to give investors a better deal in most cases. Indeed, at certain times in its short history, the Nasdaq system has been fraught with pitfalls. Over the years, unscrupulous traders and even some prestigious institutions have conspired against everyday investors. Just as Frank Zarb's vision of a global stock exchange described in the last chapter is an important part of the Nasdaq's colorful history, so too are these stories of nefarious dealings. As you will see in the next chapter, the Nasdaq's history stretches back to a time when markets were possessed by panic and fraud and politicians harangued over ways to fix them.

CHAPTER **3**

PIRATES ON WALL STREET

BY MOST ACCOUNTS, Joseph Kennedy was a bizarre
choice to serve as the first commissioner of the newly formed
Securities and Exchange Commission (SEC). In the wake of
the 1929 market massacre, President Franklin Roosevelt,
who made the appointment, had campaigned on promises
that he would reform the financial markets. When he tapped
Kennedy in 1934, some claimed that it was as payback for a
political debt. Roosevelt's opponents cried foul—and not
without reason. Years later, Kennedy would be best remem-
bered as the patriarch of one of America's leading political
families. But in the early part of the century, he stood toe to

toe with some of the most notorious stock manipulators of his day. Indeed, you could say that it was because of people like Kennedy that the SEC and subsequently the National Association of Securities Dealers were formed.

After the great crash, the public blamed high-stakes speculators for bringing the economy to its knees. They had a point. Greed on Wall Street raged unchecked during the turn of the century. And bright, ruthless market speculators were well equipped to fleece average American investors out of their savings. In 1919, when Kennedy set out from Boston to Wall Street, he was already a millionaire from stints at banking, shipping, and that hot new medium, motion pictures.[1] A man known for his perpetual owlish scowls, Kennedy's first job on the Street was as manager of the trading division of the investment-banking firm Hayden Stone. At the time, it was perfectly legal to trade on inside information or information companies kept secret from the public. Kennedy took full advantage of that fact. When he received a tip that Ford Motor Company was interested in buying a smaller firm called Pond Coal, he bought 15,000 shares of Pond at $16 per share. To finance the position, Kennedy managed to borrow roughly $216,000, or 90 percent of the stock's purchase price. When Ford inked the deal, the Pond shares naturally hit the roof. And Kennedy banked a reported $675,000 in profits, a hefty amount even for a trader today.[2]

But the great bull-market run of the 1920s had not even begun yet. In the years ahead, there would be many more lucrative deals for Kennedy and Wall Street mavens like him. Quite a few made their profits by managing so-called investment trusts, where thousands of Americans had placed their life savings. You could think of investment trusts as the ancestors of today's mutual funds. Launched first in Europe, trusts sold shares to the public in the same way that individual companies sold shares of stock. Trust managers then used the proceeds to buy stock in as many as 1,000 companies throughout the world. Thus, by buying into a trust, an average investor could create a diversified portfolio for relatively little money. It was an important benefit at the time. Single shares of stock often sold at triple-digit prices in the 1920s, effectively barring average Americans from owning more than a handful of shares of any particular company, much less a balanced portfolio. The latter was something that only the rich could afford.

But Americans in that booming postwar era did have money to invest. And shares of a trust seemed like a bargain. As it often turned out, however, the bulk of the trusts' true value had already been pocketed by the trust managers and their cronies—before the trust shares were even made available to the public. In his classic book *The Great Crash,* Harvard economics professor John Kenneth Galbraith describes how investment trusts proved to be such a lucrative financial product for their organizers. "Even in the United States in the twenties, there were limits to the amount of real capital which existing enterprises could use or new ones could be created to employ," he wrote.[3] In other words, although the economy at the time was expanding rapidly, there was still too much money chasing too few decent stocks. The result is always a kind of inflation of share prices—a classic market bubble.

The Market Becomes Unhinged

HOWEVER, THROUGHOUT MUCH of the 1920s, one factor had always managed to hold stock prices in check. Back then, stocks of large companies were normally seen as dividend investments. That is, people bought stocks for the dividend income they provided and not, as is so often the case today, because they expected the share price to rise. Dividend income tended to put a natural cap on a stock's value for a simple reason: As the stock grew pricier, its dividend yield actually decreased as a percentage of its purchase price. A lower yield made other competing investments more attractive. Put simply, if a dividend stock grew too pricey, no one would buy it.

However, a larger macroeconomic problem was also at work. America in the 1920s was awash with capital. And as Galbraith notes, the markets were prevented from absorbing all the capital that the newly well-off Americans of the era had to invest. Savvy financial mavens knew that boatloads of cash existed, waiting to be spent. But how to attract it? Investment trusts offered an ingenious solution. A trust could issue an infinite number of shares and invest the capital as it saw fit. Some trusts even bought shares in other trusts, effectively creating giant, multilayered houses of cards. As Galbraith explained: Trusts provided their managers with a way to separate price from asset value. Meaning: Share prices were no longer pegged to the normal measures of their worth, which until then had been the stock's dividend yield. The traditional yardsticks for measuring a stock's worth were being discarded. In the 1920s, pundits proclaimed that yield no longer mattered, just as in the 1990s their successors exalted that price earnings ratios did not matter. In both eras, these proved to be signs that a bubble was in the making.

As investors in the 1920s dove mindlessly into investment trusts, trading volume as well as the total market capitalization of the exchanges likewise mushroomed, wrote Galbraith. And as the share prices of trusts rose ever higher, they attracted more investors, creating a snowball effect as more and more investors piled on. The profits poured into hands of trust organizers.

Often the sponsors of a trust were investment-banking firms, Galbraith writes. And these firms were in effect manufacturing securities, which they could sell to a hungry investing public. Years later, their successors would do the same with IPO shares of Internet companies. Like those IPO shares that doubled and tripled in price during the first day of trading, shares of trusts also routinely sold at a premium to the stated value of their assets. In one example, Chancy Parker, head of a "fiscally perilous" investment bank, reportedly sold 1.6 million shares of a company called Seaboard Utilities to the public for prices between $11 and $18.25. He in turn had purchased the shares for $10.32. Other trusts had the stamp of the nation's most prominent investment banks, some of which still operate today. J. P. Morgan and Company sold shares of a company called United Corporation to a select list of cronies for $75. When those shares began trading on the over-the-counter (OTC) market a week later, the price rose to $94. By the late 1920s, a lengthy list of investment banks had entered the trust-peddling business. In 1928, some 186 trusts were thought to exist. During the early part of 1929, as the market bubble stood poised to burst, new trusts were forming at the rate of one per day.[4]

To its credit, the New York Stock Exchange (NYSE) did its best to shield investors from the dangers of overpriced trusts. It did not permit their trading until 1929. When trusts were allowed to trade on the Big Board, the NYSE required that its managers disclose the value and extent of the trust holdings each year. Given the trusts' inflated valuations, this was not something the managers relished doing. As a result of the NYSE's restrictions, many trusts traded on the American Stock Exchange or on the OTC market, the predecessor of the Nasdaq.

Dirty Pools

IN ADDITION TO trusts, another type of financial medium, called investment pools, was also common at the time. Pools were limited partnerships. Groups of investors pooled their money and appointed a manager to invest it. The arrangement is similar to the way hedge funds are organized today. However, in that unregulated era, many investment pools were created solely for the purpose of manipulating share prices for the members' benefit. Some pools even focused their efforts on shares of a single company. It was in this area that Kennedy reportedly excelled.

In his book *Toward Rational Exuberance,* author B. Mark Smith recounts one revealing story: In 1924, a colleague named John D. Hertz reportedly asked Kennedy for help. Hertz owned the Yellow Cab Company. And he believed that a competing pool of short sellers was intent on lowering the company's share price. Kennedy was recruited to organize a pool of investors who would buy the stock in order to prop up its price. Kennedy quickly dove into the task. He rented a suite at the Waldorf Astoria and ran his pool from there. Phoning his orders through brokers downtown as he watched the stock ticker, Kennedy over time succeeded in putting the bears at bay.

Rumor has it that when shares of Yellow Cab again fell a few months later, it was the work of Kennedy. Only this time he sided himself with the shorts.[5] These vicious wars, pitting teams of speculators against one another, were common at the time. With traders perilously overextended on margin loans, the price of losing a battle was often total ruin. Some pools worked similar to the way that certain infamous trading rooms and Internet chat threads would function decades later. A group of investors might bid up a stock by passing shares from one to the other. The pool manager might release bogus news to the publishers of tip sheets. Other traders who heard the news would watch as their stock tickers showed increased interest in the stock. Their appetites whetted by the stock's momentum, they rushed in to buy just when the price was highest. Pool members dumped their shares into this high demand. And the stock price fell.

During 1929, pools are said to have manipulated the prices of over 100 stocks that traded on the NYSE. The public was well aware of the goings-on. In fact, many people—particularly full-time speculators—believed that they could make money by trading in tandem with one or more of the better-known pools. Brokerage firms encouraged this belief by releasing tip sheets saying that at a certain hour General Motors or American Telephone & Telegraph would be "taken in hand."[6] The insinuation was that at the appointed time, a secretive, powerful group of men would jockey the shares among themselves in order to bid up their price.

Other traders believed that they could detect pool activity simply by watching the steady display of fresh prices coming off a stock ticker. Brokerage offices across the country were crowded with people anxiously watching as changing prices went up on a blackboard. Interest in the markets was so intense by 1929 that even ocean liners received stock quotes by radio. As they plied the North Atlantic, traders on board were able to buy and sell shares at all hours. Estimates vary, but somewhere between 600,000 and 1 million speculators were actively trading in the markets by 1929. By contrast, roughly 125,000 diehard day traders[7] were thought to be involved with the Nasdaq before the crash of 2000. Like their modern-day counterparts, many of the speculators during the 1920s gave up their day jobs in order to concentrate full time on the market.

What Goes Up . . .

AS THE MARKET rose daily to new heights, the pundits continued to paint an even brighter picture of its future. Mob psychology ruled, analysts would later say. Everyone seemed mesmerized by the madness of crowds. "The individuals composing the crowd lose their conscious personality under the influence of emotion and are ready to act as one, directed by the low, crowd intelligence," wrote Thomas Templeton Hoyne,[8] author of the classic book *Speculation: Its Sound Principles and Rules for Its Practice*. Thus, on October 16, 1929, just eight days before the final bubble, an economist named Irving Fisher wrote:

> Stock prices have reached what looks like a permanently high plateau. I do not feel that there will soon, if ever, be a 50- or

60-point break below present levels. . . . I expect to see the stock market a good deal higher than it is today within months.[9]

The stock of Radio Corporation of America epitomized the prevailing mania. Just as decades later people saw the Internet as the invincible new medium that would change the world, back in 1928 radio was the concept that sizzled. And RCA was the America Online of radio. At the start of 1928, RCA stock sold for about $85.25. By spring, it rose to $200. By fall, it hit $500. Eventually, it would reach a split-adjusted price of more than $573.[10]

Then the bubble burst. Even as the first hints of a crash took hold of the markets on October 24, speculators highly overextended on margin found themselves ruined. Those who jumped into the market to bargain hunt in the days following the crash were likewise blown out. In the space of just a few days, the panic spread, and shares of America's most powerful blue-chip companies crumbled like present-day dot-com stocks. Auburn Automobile plummeted 66 points; Otis Elevator dropped 45. On Tuesday, October 29, the board of governors of the NYSE met secretly in a crowded room underneath the trading floor and debated whether they should declare a halt to trading. In the end, fearing further investor panic, they opted to shorten trading hours instead. President Herbert Hoover declined to offer an encouraging statement about the markets despite pleas from his own staff. However, John D. Rockefeller—the Bill Gates of his day—was persuaded to announce that he and his sons saw value in the markets. And they were buying.[11]

But to no avail. The momentum at this point had become irreversible. Between September 1929 and June 1932, the NYSE fell by more than 86 percent. Making matters worse, many market players had bought stocks on margin. By using borrowed money to purchase their shares, they effectively doubled their losses. The teetering market gave the whole nation a case of the jitters. In Chicago, police rushed to a building on a false report that local mobsters with big stakes in the market were holed up inside and were refusing to pay their margin calls. A man was found face down in the Hudson River. In his pockets were margin-call slips. According to a popular joke at the time, two men reportedly jumped hand in hand from New York's Ritz Hotel because they had a joint account. Soon clerks at hotels throughout Manhattan were asking guests at check-in whether they planned on staying the night or jumping.

The resulting panic later spread to banks, which had engaged in speculation right alongside the investment pools. When crowds showed up at the doorsteps of the nation's major banks, the panic swept across the nation and then to the financial capitals of Europe. The result there and in the United States was a public that wanted blood. During the 1920s, an estimated 20 million Americans had some of their savings in the stock market. Collectively, their holdings totaled something like $50 billion. By the end of the decade, more than half of those securities were totally worthless.[12]

It Takes One to Know One

FEW ON WALL Street emerged from the crash unscathed. One who did was Joseph Kennedy. He boasted that he had clearly seen the end coming and reverted all his share holdings to cash, a fact that should not be surprising, coming from someone who had always been close to the action. By some accounts, Kennedy not only escaped the crash unscathed but may have cruelly profited from it as well. As the story goes, Kennedy and an infamous short seller named Bernard Smith allegedly worked together to drive other speculators to ruin. The speculators targeted by Kennedy and Smith were said to have had loans backed by inactively traded stocks. Employing their arsenal of investment-pool techniques, Smith and Kennedy reportedly found out who these people were. Then they shorted the stocks that they were using as collateral. Flooding the market with these additional shares forced the price down. As a result, the loans' collateral evaporated. The banks called in the loans, compelling the speculators to sell their stock at a loss. When they did, Kennedy and Smith were said to have been the eager buyers. And they reportedly used these shares purchased at fire-sale prices to cover their own short positions.[13] That is, they used these newly purchased shares to replace the ones they borrowed. In effect, they bought the shares for less than they sold them for and pocketed the difference—all in a day's work.

By 1929, Kennedy had reportedly made enough from stock trading to create a $1 million trust fund for each of his nine children. Little wonder that the patriarch reportedly once remarked, "It's so easy to make money in the market we'd better get in before they pass a law against it."[14] In his new role as head of the SEC, Kennedy would do precisely that: put people like himself out of business.

Kennedy was a man who always seemed to find the center of action, whether it was in movies or banking or on Wall Street. After the 1929 crash, he must have sensed that Wall Street would no longer occupy center stage. His next move took him to Washington, which was in the throes of coping with the beginnings of the Great Depression and where a newly elected President Roosevelt was promising to alter the very nature of government.

As one of the first steps, Roosevelt and Congress set about sifting through the carnage of the markets, trying to find what went wrong and where to lay blame. The result of the hearings were two landmark laws that would put the securities markets under government scrutiny more than ever before. In 1933, the Glass Steagall Act prohibited banks from speculating using depositors' money. The Securities Act of 1933 and the Security and Exchange Act of 1934 required that companies tell investors the truth about their financial situation and that those selling securities put the interest of their customers—that is, individual investors—first.

These were novel concepts at the time. Wall Street's attitude during the 1920s was that investors should watch out for themselves. And if they were not willing to do that, they should suffer the consequences. As the old gambler's saying goes, If you sit at a poker table and you don't know who the patsy is, you're the patsy. Roosevelt acted to change that. He convinced Congress that with millions of new investors flooding into the markets, it was unreasonable to expect that they should all be educated. Therefore, it was up to the exchanges, the companies whose shares traded there, and the brokers who acted as middlemen to look out for average investors. To make sure they did, the laws created a new federal agency called the Securities and Exchange Commission.

Heal Yourselves

EVEN SO, IN resource-scarce America of the 1930s, the SEC's power was sorely limited at first. In that era before wiretaps, traceable cell phone calls, and subpoenaed computer files, paper trails were nearly impossible to construct. So it was relatively easy to conceal any sort of fraud. Making matters worse, markets at the time were highly fragmented. Dozens of regional exchanges existed around the country. So fraud was not only untraceable but also apt to occur anywhere.

One reason so many markets existed was that the underdeveloped communications system at the time made it difficult for traders based in the hinterlands to move shares via New York. For example, before 1933 there was not even a direct phone line between New York and Hartford, Connecticut. Brokers in Hartford found it easier to organize their own exchange than to try to transact business in New York. But even when a phone line was installed, calling was often prohibitively expensive. In the 1930s, a three-minute long-distance call might cost $6 to $10, roughly equal to $50 in today's prices.[15]

Meanwhile, the NYSE monopolized the information flowing from its own exchange floor through its ticker, which was the only mechanism available that allowed people around the nation to keep tabs on their stocks during regular trading hours. No similar reliable method existed for tracking the prices of OTC stocks. And so their pricing—as you'll see in the next chapter—was often highly arbitrary. That made it even more difficult to prove that fraud had occurred.

As a first tentative step toward regulation, the Security and Exchange Act required that national exchanges be registered. Broker dealers—that is, firms that traded on behalf of clients and themselves—were also required to register. But in passing the two acts and forming the SEC, Congress realized that it lacked both the resources and the expertise to regulate the securities markets from Washington. The solution was to require the markets to regulate themselves. They were mandated to form what became known as self-regulatory organizations (SROs)—a strange concept, even today. The exchanges were, after all, membership organizations composed of broker dealers who had a strong vested interest in not being regulated. Decisions were made by member vote. And except for the enfeebled oversight of the SEC, those decisions could be kept quiet. By publicly policing themselves, they were being asked to act against their own best interests.

Nevertheless, the SEC proved itself successful at policing the exchanges. For example, abuses were said to be at their worst on the smaller and regional exchanges throughout the country. So when the SEC moved to investigate, its clout was quickly felt. The New York Mining Exchange, the Boston Curb Exchange, and the California Stock Exchange all closed their doors less than two months after the SEC's investigations commenced in 1935.[16]

Shorting the Shorts

AS THE INSTIGATOR of these investigations, Kennedy may have actually been in a uniquely advantageous position when he assumed the SEC chairman's post. Many no doubt preferred taking their medicine from insiders like themselves rather than from a zealous Roosevelt Democrat with little knowledge of Wall Street. In fact, widespread fear existed in the financial industry that the new regulations would bring about the Street's ruin. Some investment banks even threatened to quit underwriting new securities when the measures passed—a bluff, most likely—since new issues were one of the principal ways investment banks made their money. In any event, it seems that Kennedy was able to allay the worst of Wall Street's fears. But he was also steadfast in his duties. Having ruled the markets for 10 years, particularly as a short seller, it is perhaps not ironic that one of the first reforms he enacted was intended to curtail short selling. It was the so-called uptick rule.[17] It required that anyone wanting to sell a stock short wait until it traded up in price. Previously, short sellers in investment pools mercilessly drove down the prices of stocks by flooding the market with borrowed shares, in effect creating nonexistent shares. The uptick rule was intended to at least slow down a stock's descent.

Kennedy spent just one year at the SEC. During that time, he proposed other rules aimed at curbing abuses. Then once again the center stage appeared to be shifting. In 1937, he became ambassador to Great Britain, where the stirrings of war would soon engross that nation and later the world far more than the financial markets had a decade earlier.

Securities Dealers Organize

MEANWHILE, THE SEC'S regulatory responsibilities continued to grow. However, they were focused almost solely on the national stock exchanges, such as the NYSE. Left out was the vast, little-understood void of securities trading within the OTC markets. If listed shares on the NYSE and other exchanges had been subject to manipulation, those trading on the OTC market were often the results of outright thievery, the reason being that the exchanges at least made attempts to ensure a level playing field. Recall, for example, that when the NYSE had barred investment trusts of dubious value from trading on the Big Board, the trusts traded on the OTC market, where few examples of restraint existed.

Those in the business of trading OTC securities were keenly aware that flagrant abuses during the 1920s had marred their reputation—and perhaps scared off new customers. Even before the Securities Act passed in 1934, a league of brokers had been at work to develop some tacit standards for their industry. Likewise, a group of investment bankers also formed something called the Investment Bankers Code Committee. It was logical for investment bankers to take the lead in creating a conduct enforcement agency since this was the same group that enabled small companies to raise money through public stock sales. If all the companies were viewed by the public as frauds, there would be no buyers.

The problem was that the Code Committee had no legal authority. At first, it attempted to enforce its rulings by citing powers it claimed were granted to it by the National Recovery Administration.[18] However, the Supreme Court ruled against the committee in the case known as *A.L.A. Schechter Poultry Corp. v. United States.*[19]

Following this failure, the SEC and industry officials remained determined to create some kind of regulatory agency whose actions would carry legal authority. As a next step, they drew up plans for something called the Investment Bankers Conference Committee. However, it too failed to take root. In the largely uncharted waters of securities regulation, the committee's members feared that their work would also lack any legal clout.

A third attempt would prove successful. The SEC and financial industry executives created something called the Investment Bankers Conference, Inc. Then committee members and the SEC went to Congress, where they found a sympathetic ear in Senate Banking Committee Chairman Francis Maloney. The result was an addition to the Securities Exchange Act, section 15a,[20] the so-called Maloney Act, which gave such industry associations the right to register with the SEC and enforce a code of conduct on their members. This meant that they no longer could be arbitrary in making and enforcing the rules as they had perhaps been in the past. Now, being quasi-enforcement agencies, they had to behave as such.

It was a brilliant scheme on the SEC's part because it fostered an unlimited number of regulatory agencies while it delegated much of the nitty-gritty enforcement to them. The SEC's job then became to enforce the enforcers. As Senator Maloney described it:

Congress has undertaken to provide a mechanism whereby the securities business of the country may deal with the problems of technical regulation, leaving to the Securities and Exchange Commission what it is hoped will be the residual position of policing the submarginal fringe which recognizes no sanctions save those of criminal law.[21]

Enter the NASD

TODAY, THE SEC'S job is destined to become more complex as some private trading networks or electronic communications networks (ECNs; see chapter 11) seek to register themselves as exchanges. By doing so, they must create their own SROs. In the 1930s, however, the task may have been just as complicated, with so many regional exchanges in existence. But at least these exchanges possessed a singular address—the place where member brokers showed up for work. The world of OTC trading was largely one of phones and telegrams, of orders rushed across Manhattan or Philadelphia by messenger, and of brokers working as sole proprietors in small towns across America. What would compel traders of this ilk to join cooperatively to clean up their act? Money turned out to be the answer. The Maloney Act contained this intriguing provision:

> The rules of a registered securities association may provide that no member thereof shall deal with any nonmember professional (as defined in paragraph (2) of this subsection) except at the same prices, for the same commissions or fees, and on the same terms and conditions as are by such member accorded to the general public.

In other words, if you belonged to a registered securities association, you could trade with fellow members at the wholesale price while you traded with all others at retail—a marvelous incentive. It gave birth to a group called the National Association of Securities Dealers (NASD). Of the estimated 6,700 securities dealers plying their trade at the time, some 1,500 had signed up with the NASD just one year after the Maloney Act passed.[22] Now there was a way to at least keep tabs on the amorphous group of traders who handled OTC securities. They had to be registered, eventually they would be required to pass competency exams, and they had to submit to enforcement. For three decades, the NASD set about doing just that. Among its activities were conducting surprise raids on brokerages to make sure that they were following the rules. By 1945, the Nasdaq had 25,000 members.

But given the nature of OTC trading at the time, the NASD likely did little to help average investors receive the best possible price when they bought or sold their stocks. How did you know where to turn when you wished to buy and sell securities? And how did you know whether you were being taken advantage of? The broker in New Haven might charge several dollars more per share than the broker in Philadelphia. The Nasdaq system of collecting quotes and displaying them via a centralized computer network for all to see would not come until 1971. And until its launch, the OTC market would continue to be rife with abuse.

CHAPTER 4

THE WILD, WOOLY WORLD OF OVER-THE-COUNTER TRADING

EVEN AT AGE 38, Ross Perot had a penchant for using homey aphorisms whenever he tried to explain complex topics. So when he took his infant computer firm Electronic Data Systems Corp. public in 1968, he used a Texas cattleman's analogy to describe the process: "If you have 20,000 head and bring them to market all at once, the buyers know you have to sell, and you won't get much." But if you portion out the steers you sell a little at a time, chances are you'll get a better price.[1]

Perot was also a quick study. He had a country boy's natural mistrust of the fast-talking suits on Wall Street. Thus, for a long time he resisted the idea of taking EDS public. No doubt he feared losing control of the business he had launched with a cadre of crack former IBMers. But these were the so-called go-go years in the stock market. And computer companies like EDS, as well as firms involved even remotely in space exploration, were the equivalent of dot-coms in the 1990s. Throughout the decade, shares of new computer companies had flooded the over-the-counter (OTC) market. However, Perot's EDS was different. Unlike many start-ups of that day, EDS could show solid earnings. As a result, some 16 investment banking firms made the trip from lower Manhattan to the wide plains of Texas, urging Perot to let them manage the initial public offering (IPO). Various offering share prices were reportedly discussed, ranging from 30 to 70 times earnings. The 17th banker to visit Perot, Kenneth Langone of R. W. Pressprich and Company, dangled an offering share price that was roughly 100 times EDS's earnings of $1.5 million per year—a multiple worthy of any dot-com. What Texas boy could resist?[2]

Shrewdly, however, Perot allowed only 10 percent of EDS stock to trade publicly. He himself retained 72 percent ownership in the company. The shares hit the market at $16.50. By 1970, they had risen to $160, which put Perot's net worth in excess of a billion.[3] But he was just warming up.

Unlisted and Unwashed

DESPITE ITS SEEMINGLY inflated price, EDS would turn out to be one of the strongest companies to emerge during the 1960s go-go era, a time when life oozed back into the nascent OTC markets for the first time since the Roaring Twenties. During the years following the 1929 crash and World War II and its aftermath, the OTC was a quiet backwater. However, by the 1960s it had begun to explode with profits, though these went mostly to the broker-dealers who brought companies public and traded them on behalf of their clients.

This at a time when the financial markets in general occupied the back burner. During much of the 1960s, the nation's main focus was on the deeply divisive Vietnam War. To most Americans, the world of OTC trading seemed an even more far off exotic place than Indochina—and it too was perceived as being fraught with danger.

The term *over the counter* goes back to the early 1800s, and it refers to the actual countertops used by private banking houses to handle transactions.[4] Over the years, the OTC became the venue used to buy and sell just about any tradable financial product, from mutual funds, to bonds, to private placements. But strictly speaking, OTC referred to stocks not listed on one of the national exchanges, such as the NYSE or the American Stock Exchange, or on one of the many regional exchanges that existed at that time.

As noted in the previous chapter, the Securities and Exchange Commission (SEC) required these established exchanges to watchdog themselves. In the same manner, the SEC helped create the National Association of Securities Dealers (NASD) to oversee trading on the OTC—not an easy task, as it turns out, and for a fundamental reason: The brick-and-mortar exchanges had a physical floor where traders met to buy and sell on behalf of clients. Any abuses could be watched, theoretically. In contrast, the OTC was nothing more than an affiliation of trading firms that bought and sold on their own behalf and on behalf of their clients. It was an amorphous network of relationships as haphazard as the list of phone numbers on a broker's desk. Moreover, the OTC's center of gravity continually shifted from one place to another, wherever strong buying and selling were taking place.

Seeing the problem, the SEC attempted to define the OTC market this way:

Transactions in securities not taking place on an exchange are referred to as over-the-counter transactions. The over-the-counter markets, unlike the exchanges, have no centralized place for

trading. There are no listing requirements for issues traded. . . .
The broker-dealers vary in size, experience, and function; the securities differ in price, quality, and activity.[5]

Not very helpful, perhaps. The SEC goes on to admit that
"the diversity and lack of organization of the over-the-counter
markets have continually perplexed those seeking to study or
regulate them." During the early 1960s, so few people outside
the world of Wall Street understood how the OTC worked—
notably including those in Washington charged with regulating
it—that the SEC was obliged to conduct an enormous multi-
year study to educate Congress on how it operated. The study
involved some 65 people, half of whom were lawyers, economists, and similarly trained professionals. The three-volume
Special Study of the Securities Markets that was the end product of their work examined both exchange-traded securities
and the OTC. Little wonder it encompassed thousands of pages
of text and charts, and remains the most granular look at U.S.
financial markets ever attempted before or since. The study was
presented to Congress in 1963.

For starters, the *Special Study* revealed that trading firms
that worked the OTC basically broke down into two categories.
Retail brokers bought and sold company shares for their customers. Wholesale brokers acted in effect as warehouses for certain stocks. Some wholesalers may have handled only one or
two issues. Other, larger trading firms might make a market in
as many as 200. And some of the latter firms specialized in particular sectors, trading only bank or energy stocks, for example.

During the early 1960s, some 5,000 broker-dealer firms existed across the country. Roughly 3,300 of these traded exclusively on the OTC market, basically ignoring the NYSE and
other national and regional exchanges.[6] Many broker dealers
were sole proprietors. A guy in a small midwestern city, for instance, might buy and sell stocks on behalf of his acquain-
tances. In the course of his work, he would rely on a handful of
wholesalers who had assisted him in the past, just as a restau-

rant manager might rely on a few key suppliers for things like bread and produce. Thanks to this arrangement, it was seldom a problem obtaining buyers or sellers for shares of larger companies since ready supplies of these stocks could be easily located. And there was always someone buying.

But trying to find buyers and sellers for certain lightly traded stocks was a true challenge—maybe a little like attempting to find a taillight for a vintage Corvette. You made some calls and attempted to locate the desired number of shares. Never mind the price.

How Trades Got Made

ONE REASON SO many brokers chose to focus on the OTC was that unlike the regional stock exchanges and the NYSE, the OTC did not charge steep membership fees. Nor, like some private club, did it limit the number of members that could join. Equally important, a broker-dealer with some keen trading ability and a list of well-heeled clients could make a bundle trading OTC stocks. This is because many brokers acted much like retail storeowners. They bought stocks from wholesalers at wholesale prices and then marked them up, sometimes by as much as 25 percent. The public, as you will see in detail in a moment, usually had no way of verifying what the actual price of the security was. And even when prices were available, they were at times only best guesses or, worse, utterly fictitious.

Indeed, before the Nasdaq computer network brought some order to OTC trading, it is difficult to imagine how accurate price quotations were communicated at all, especially among such a large group of participants spread out over the country. The SEC study gives a clue of how OTC trading took place:

> The trader ordinarily sits at a desk from which he has one or more telephones or wires to other firms and sometimes to banks and other institutions. Some market makers have as many as 200

private telephone lines and wires to other firms. In firms with more than one trader, each trader is assigned a number of stocks in which he makes markets. He maintains a "book" or some other means for informing himself of the size of his positions in each security which he trades. In firms with only one trader or in which traders are permitted to trade only the stocks assigned to them, the trader may keep notations showing his current quoted bid and asked prices. In other firms, a quotation board is also maintained at the front of the trading room for this purpose, and changes in quotations are shouted to a clerk, who posts them on the board. . . . After executing an order, the trader notes the change in his inventory position and fills out a slip reflecting the transaction. The bookkeeping (or clearance) departments of both the buying and selling firms send a memorandum of the transaction, called a confirmation, to the firm on the opposite side.[7]

Traders at these wholesale firms acted much like day traders today, focusing only on extremely short term price movements. As the SEC's *Special Study* notes, "Many firms which make markets . . . have little information concerning the [stock] issuer's financial condition. They have no research or statistical departments, do not subscribe to investment or counseling service." Instead, the study observed, "wholesale traders concentrate on quoting prices in response to incoming orders."[8]

In 1962, there were some 1,200 wholesale trading firms, similar to the one just described, far more than the number of market-making firms that perform a similar function on the Nasdaq today. Like trading firms today, wholesalers were located throughout the country, begging the question, How could anyone know what a stock might be selling for over the course of a day?

Again, for many of the more popular OTC issues, this was not a problem. Enough shares changed hands hour by hour that professional traders could quote a more or less accurate price. But this was not the case for small, little-known, often new companies. And such shares made up the bulk of OTC stocks. Only one-third of all OTC firms during the period covered by the SEC's *Special Study* had assets greater than $10 million. How could the prices of these smaller stocks be tracked?

The answer was something called the "sheets." These were simply lists of stock quotes that subscribing broker-dealers received daily. The sheets contained quotes on as many as 8,200 stocks. But not just a single quote. Instead, they resembled something like the Level II quote display that electronic day traders use today (see chapter 5). The sheets listed representative bid and ask prices from major wholesale trading firms, sometimes listing them in order of price. But not always. With so many stocks and so many wholesalers making markets in these stocks, it is little wonder that the sheets could run 200 pages. And there were also regional editions. The Eastern Section was printed in New York on pink paper. (The term *pink sheets* is still used to describe listings of smaller OTC stocks.) The Western Section came out of Chicago on green paper. And the Pacific Coast Section was printed in San Francisco on white paper.

The sheets were published not by the NASD but by a private company called the National Quotation Bureau, Inc. Subscriptions cost $336 per year and were available only to investment professionals. The public was ostensibly barred from access, although savvy individual traders could obtain copies.[9]

Prices listed were supposed to represent tradable quotes at the time they were given. Most firms used them as a basis for negotiations during the trading day. In addition, wholesale trading firms were not required to post bid and ask prices and honor those quotes. If stock prices were falling across the board and someone called offering shares for sale, a trading firm could decline the offer.

Complicating matters further, the trading firms polled by the National Quotation Bureau were not always the wholesalers that did the largest volume of trading in that particular stock. In short, the lists were a far cry from the real-time accurate quotation data we take for granted today. Because the National Quotation Bureau was unregulated, some within the SEC and the NASD voiced concern about possible misuse. As one unidentified NASD official put it:

> In the last three or four years we have had an entirely new type of person entering the underwriting business. I do not think that their ethical concepts are the highest. I think they would not hesitate to use the sheets for their own purposes in maintaining their own markets. . . . I can also see certain dangers in certain types of trading houses getting control of the sheets. They could use the sheets for their own purposes.[10]

In other words, one wholesale trader, or more likely several acting in concert, could rig share prices. And, as you will see in a moment, this indeed happened. Meanwhile, the average investor in OTC stocks often had no more idea about whether they were receiving the best possible price than a used car shopper. Since they had no access to wholesale prices contained on the sheets, they relied on prices listed in their daily newspapers.

Don't Believe Everything You Read in the Newspaper

QUOTES APPEARING IN newspapers were compiled by a special NASD group called the National Quotation Committee, which gathered the information from subcommittees located around the country. While 8,200 stocks were quoted on the sheets, only about 3,000 made up the retail list. The *Wall Street Journal,* the nation's largest business newspaper, regularly published 1,400 of these. For decades, there was a dearth of information about many of these companies. Then in 1962, the NASD began requiring companies on its quote lists to promptly disclose developments "which may affect the value of the company's securities or influence investors' decisions."[11]

The National Quotation Committee divided stocks into national and regional lists. The national lists were composed of larger, more heavily traded companies. Regional lists were composed of companies of interest mainly to investors within a particular region. There was also a weekly list.

Both then and now, the quotes coming from the established exchanges that appear in newspapers are typically end-of-day prices. That is, they show the price of the last trade before the exchange officially shuts down for the night. Investors ideally can read the previous day's final quote with their morning coffee before the start of trading and then decide how the stock will move from there.

However, back in the 1950s and 1960s it was impossible to know where the last trade of a particular OTC stock occurred. It might have taken place in a large wholesale trading house in New York or Chicago or via a phoned order from a broker working out of a corner store in Florida. In the latter case, it could take several days for information about the trade to reach the markets. Consequently, newspaper quotes of OTC stocks were intended to give only an idea of a stock's trading range. If you wanted a timelier quote or the price of a stock not compiled by the NASD, you had to call your broker.

But your broker might not have the current information, either. So he (brokers were almost exclusively men at this point) would in turn call around to several wholesalers. Often, brokers had special relationships with certain wholesalers, which allowed them to receive a kickback of, say, 5 cents a share for any orders sent the wholesalers' way. In theory, when a broker accepts your order, he has a responsibility to find the best possible price for you, the customer, since the broker is acting on your behalf. As a practical matter, this was close to impossible with OTC stocks in the days before the Nasdaq, given the sheer number wholesalers and brokers who might be

trading a particular stock. It would be about as difficult as trying to obtain the best possible price of gasoline by calling
around to the hundreds of filling stations found in any large
city. Add a wide array of commissions and markups charged at
the time, and the resulting price was likely far removed from
what savvier traders could obtain.

At the same time, because of the OTC market's fragmentation, even wholesalers were often unsure about prevailing prices.
And their uncertainty led to wide spreads in the prices they
quoted. In short, the OTC was hardly efficient by today's standards. This often manifested itself in heightened trading costs.

Market Mayhem

AS BADLY AS the OTC may have functioned in the course of
normal trading, it broke down completely whenever markets
panicked. This is exactly what happened in May 1962, when
the Dow dropped by roughly 25 percent. Trading had been
brisk during the preceding months. As a result, wholesalers had
large inventories of stocks on hand to meet the demands of retail traders. Then at the beginning of the year, wholesalers sold
off their inventories bit by bit as bearish sentiment mounted.
Some firms ceased trading the more speculative OTC stocks.
Others reduced the size of orders they would handle. The reduced liquidity drove prices down further.

One of the catalysts of the drop, interestingly, is that investors had been led to believe that America's young president,
John Kennedy, was friendly toward business and the markets.
But that opinion changed in April, when Kennedy locked horns
with the steel industry over alleged price fixing. Rumors circulated that he had remarked to aides in private, "My father always told me businessmen were sons of bitches!"[12]

At any rate, stocks tumbled on the NYSE on May 28. Prices
on the OTC followed suit, and many wholesalers protected

themselves by quoting spreads that represented 30 to 40 percent of the bid price. (In contrast, spreads of heavily traded Nasdaq stocks today may be as little as a penny.) Panicked, a few wholesalers said that they would accept buy orders only when they knew that retail sell orders were waiting. Many firms ceased trading altogether, virtually drying up liquidity among a long list of stocks.

Analyzing what went on that day, the SEC put some of the blame on the fact that wholesalers were not able to see what their colleagues were up to. Some commenced predatory trading against each other. But whatever the causes, the system had clearly failed. And any retail investors who sold into the panic likely lost a great deal of money as a result.

Go-Go IPOs

BUT IF THIS fledgling OTC system broke down when the going got rough, in good times it proved exceptionally adept at doling out untold scores of IPO shares to retail investors—though not always to their benefit. Unlike the markets decades later, when follow-on offerings and tracking stocks became common, large companies during the 1960s were more apt to raise cash through debt financing (namely, bonds) than with stocks.

However, IPOs of small companies proliferated. Seasoned market watchers warn that the end of a boom is imminent whenever a flood of new issues hits the market. And this was the case as the OTC market rose and then corrected at the beginning of the 1960s and once again at the decade's end. Likewise, analysts say, the new issues associated with each boom are always pegged to current market fads. Just as tech stocks and dot-coms led the rise and fall of the Nasdaq during the 1990s, during the 1960s investors could not get enough of stocks in companies that had even the remotest connection to aerospace and electronics. This was the era when NASA was leading the free world's race to the moon.

Even companies possessing little more than a name suggesting that they were part of the great space race found eager buyers. In 1962, for example, shares of Welch Scientific Company hit the market at $28. By the end of the day, they had reached $52. The investors who received calls from their brokers may have believed that they were buying into a company that would let them share the journey to the moon. In fact, the Skokie, Illinois, firm manufactured laboratory equipment. However, besides its techy sounding name, one of the reasons Welch's price shot up so quickly was that the offering consisted of only 545,000 shares.[13]

Indeed, limiting the offering price was just one tactic in the arsenal used by an ad hoc industry that at the time was devoted to bringing new companies public. The OTC, because of its diffuse structure, proved highly suited to bolstering the price of a fledgling young company. Wholesale traders on the OTC routinely bought and sold from each other, just as they took the other side of retail trades. This continual buying and selling helped support the stock's price. In contrast, on the brick-and-mortar exchanges, the specialist holds a virtual monopoly on the wholesale market for the shares he trades. With the exception of trading taking place through certain third-party brokerages and through the regional exchanges, the specialist on the NYSE or the American Stock Exchange was the only game in town. Therefore, unless buyers and sellers approached the specialist, invariably no activity took place. As one financial observer of the period noted, "It sometimes happens that securities actively traded over-the-counter lose their activity and marketability when listed on an exchange. This, when it results, is because over-the-counter houses do not usually trade in the securities as before."[14]

Some OTC-traded companies that grew large enough to qualify for listing on the NYSE or American Stock Exchange even requested that they be allowed to return to the OTC so that their shares might trade on heavier volume once again. Decades later, this advantage of OTC trading would be cited as the reason why large companies such as Intel and Microsoft choose to remain with the Nasdaq, even as the NYSE has strongly lobbied them to switch.

In past decades, there were other powerful reasons why companies chose to debut on the OTC. Listing requirements, for all practical purposes, were nonexistent. This saved companies the onerous task of having to come clean about their performance. The SEC looked at a sampling of OTC-traded companies during the 1940s and 1950s. It found that only half published adequate annual reports. Some refused to furnish even a rudimentary profit-and-loss statement. And 25 percent did not disclose any information.[15]

If you owned a small company in those times and you wanted to go about your business without meddling from your investors, clearly the OTC was the place to be. Moreover, scores of promoters stood ready to help take your company public. Writing at the time, financial historian John Brooks described the IPO mania this way: "Goaded by stock underwriters eager for commissions or a piece of the action, owners of family businesses from coast to coast—laundry chains, soap-dish manufacturers, anything—would sell stock in their enterprises to the public."[16]

The SEC's *Special Study* similarly vilified new issue underwriters, saying that "a number of public offerings made appear to have been the result not of any genuine corporate need for funds, but rather of calculations by promoters that a large profit could be made by satisfying investors demand for new issues."[17] To many, the charge might sound eerily familiar. Recall how Internet IPOs in the 1990s put millions in the pockets of investment banks and huge cash reserves in the kitties of newly minted firms (to be spent later on Super Bowl ads). In addition, like the 1990s-era spin doctors molding the image of freshly formed Internet companies, those of the 1960s knew the importance of a good name. As the SEC charged, "Some companies with prosaic names were rechristened in order to give the impression correct or not that they had some connection with electronics, in much the same way Hollywood starlets are renamed and glamorized to satisfy the public's craving for romance."[18] Evidence suggests the methods used to locate IPO-worthy companies and unleash their shares on the public were in some cases even more advanced than they are today. Broker-dealers maintained networks of scouts, called finders, whose job it was to locate companies ripe for a public offering. Finders, even for that time period, received a fairly modest salary of $35 per week. The main lure consisted of stock options in any company they persuaded to go public. Law firms and wholesale trading firms also acted as finders, right alongside investment banks.

Advertising was also used. One ad that appeared in the *New York Herald Tribune* in 1961 read like this:

THINKING OF GOING PUBLIC?
Discuss the matter with Edward & Hanley's underwriting department. There are many reasons for firms to arrange a public offering of securities . . . and many advantages. Raising capital for expansion is only one. Prestige is another. In addition, there are estate benefits, incentives for employees, and the possibility of other company acquisitions.[19]

With competition fierce to find ripe IPO candidates, all too often due diligence fell by the wayside. As a result, the SEC leveled a charge that again may sound familiar: "Many of the companies offering stock to the public through such firms had no history of earnings, no plant, no product and management with no experience in which the company claimed to be engaged."[20] For example, one company, Transition Systems, Inc., possessed a product called an All-Purpose Correlator, a highly versatile machine. According to some of the stock's promoters, it could "detect cancer, heart disease and oil." In fact, no such machine existed.[21]

Once suitable companies were located, the IPO grooming process began in earnest. To be sure, many of the companies, such as Perot's EDS, were legitimate. But undeniably, many were not. And philandering and abuses were common. Financial firms took advantage of their relationship, with the soon-to-be-public companies loaning them money at high interest rates, overcharging for services, and adding these fees to their already high commissions on the eventual sale of stock.

Setting the price of that sale, when it occurred, was always a well-thought-out process. As one broker described it, "We believe . . . that you can offer a stock at $20 and it can go to $35. But you could very well offer that same stock at $28 and it would go to $26."[22] As a result, many IPOs were deliberately underpriced so that they could produce an initial pop when they debuted. Investors would see this quick rise in the stock's price and falsely believe that they were buying a stock with the potential to rise even more. The underwriters, naturally, had a vested interest in seeing the shares rise past their offering price since many deals gave them options to purchase even larger quantities of shares at the initial offering price or in some cases below the offering price.

Sales of new stock were often handled by an ad hoc syndicate formed by trading firms and retail brokers for the express purpose of trading that one stock. In the months after the issue debuted and sales cooled off, the syndicate might disband. In many instances, the final link in such syndicates consisted of "boiler rooms," where traders, sitting in rows of desks, hyped the stocks to unsuspecting investors over the phone.

To make the stock's story appear even more attractive, unscrupulous traders might convince wholesale trading firms to issue false bids for the stock. These bids would then appear on the sheets. Underwriters were also known to plant blocks of shares in dummy accounts, thus reducing the number of shares available for sale, which would tend to raise their price.

Indeed, the best way of controlling the price usually was to control supply. Underwriters accomplished this in several ways. Shares were often pledged to key clients, but with the stipulation that they must not be sold. If the customers did attempt to sell, the brokers might deliberately ignore their orders. Clients were led to believe that they could not sell their shares until the actual stock certificates were delivered. And it might take months before they received them.

Win Some, Lose Some

DESPITE EDUCATING ANYONE willing to pore through its three bound volumes on the nefarious ways of the markets in that era, the SEC's *Special Study* would directly lead to a landmark event in the history of finance. Among its recommendations, it called for a computerized network that would allow brokers to immediately ascertain the price of virtually any security trading on the OTC markets. Only by knowing the correct price and only by possessing a central domain from whence to find it could some order be made of the chaotic and little-understood OTC. The result, as the next chapter reveals, was the National Association of Securities Automated Quotation system: the Nasdaq.

It would debut just as the markets were forced to pick themselves up off the floor once again. Widespread philandering in the markets, of the kind that the *Special Study* described, inevitably ushers in a crash. And this is precisely what would happen as the 1960s came to a close. Inevitably that fall is preceded by a stratospheric rise in the price of many stocks. By 1970, thanks to his EDS shares, Ross Perot had a net worth on paper of $1.5 billion. He promised to allocate most of that money to "the improvement of American life." And he focused his attentions on charities such as the Dallas school system and the city's Boy Scout troops. Perot also spent considerable money and energy in efforts to gain release of U.S. war prisoners in Hanoi. Convinced that the American capitalist system could allow one individual to make a difference in the world, Perot was willing to entertain even far-left ideas for reform. In one account, a group of radicals asked him to help underwrite revolution in 1969. Perot's quick mind processed their request in milliseconds. "How long will it take, and what will it cost?" he asked in his typically raspy voice.

A year later, in May, Perot found himself in a meeting with an EDS client. At about one o'clock, he called down to an associate, Tom Marquez. When Perot asked, "What's new?" Marquez told him that his stock had dropped by 50 or 60 points. He had lost an estimated $450 million, more than any American in history had ever lost in a single day.[23] Oddly, there had been no news about EDS that day. Earnings had doubled since the previous year, and despite a recession environment they had risen 70 percent from the previous year during the first quarter of 1970. It was a typical case of a high-flying OTC stock crashing and burning. And even with the new Nasdaq system in place, there would be many more like it.

CHAPTER 5

MACHINES TAKE CHARGE

NINETEEN SEVENTY GREETED the financial markets much the way 1930 or 2000 had. There was a dismal recognition that the 1960s go-go era was gone for good. The Dow, which remained the only popular measure of market performance at the time, had flirted with the 1,000 mark just two years before. In the first months of 1970, it tumbled below 700. The more volatile OTC stocks, as is typical, often fared worse. A *Business Week* article at the time ran through a litany of reasons for the plunge that should sound eerily familiar to anyone who suffered through the 2000 tech wreck: So-cal led story stocks, the overhyped electronics and aerospace firms that had fueled the 1960s boom, fell the hardest, hurt by an oversupply of weak new entrants that swamped the market. Those who had championed the story stocks, the high-flying money managers then called gunslingers, likewise fell from grace. Many were said to be in a state of shock over the vast wealth that they and their clients had watched evaporate. As one analyst commented, "There are a lot of bright young money managers walking around with blank stares on their faces. They can't believe that a stock is only worth what someone will pay for it."[1]

Despite their losses, many individual investors tenaciously held on, just as they would in the months following the 2000 crash. Analysts looked for a final surge of panic selling that would signal the market's capitulation and establish a bottom. Instead, the market inexorably stairstepped downward in a classic bearish pattern of progressively lower lows and lower highs. Volume also diminished. Little new buying took place. Economists worried that a decline in people's portfolios would cause consumer spending to drop, deepening a recession that many suspected was at the nation's doorstep.

This relationship between the stock market and the economy was called "the Pigou effect." Better known today by the more pleasing term "the wealth effect," the Pigou effect got its name from British economist A. C. Pigou. His theory was that people's spending habits are more likely influenced by their perceptions of their net worth and not so much by their current income levels. And with fund manager portfolios down by as much as 30 percent, Americans' perceptions of their wealth had suffered a very real setback.

It was not hard to find other reasons to feel gloomy about the economy. Inflation had crept up to 6 percent. (It would, in due course, climb much higher.) Corporate earnings had fallen 13 percent. The nation remained gripped by social unrest. The Vietnam War had spread into Cambodia, and students at Kent State University protesting against the war had been fired on by National Guard troops.

Wall Street firms, meanwhile, were caught up in a crisis of their own, as lower trading volume severely cut earnings. Twenty firms that did business on the New York Stock Exchange (NYSE) reportedly closed their doors or merged in the first three months of 1970. In all, some 120 firms shut down in the wake of the 1968–1970 financial crisis.[2] Prominent firms, such as F. I. du Pont and Blair & Co., sought partners as a way to firm up their wounded bottom lines. Over-the-counter (OTC) market-making firms and NYSE specialists were said to be hurt most by the slump on the Street since their wholesale function demanded that they maintain large inventories of stocks. As buyers disappeared, the value of that inventory had progressively fallen.

Financial firms responded to the crisis by cutting broker commissions, which predictably enraged their rank-and-file brokers. Some threatened to unionize. Angry rallies were held. A financial reporter noted that "except for the preponderance of mod suits and sideburns, gatherings of the Association of Investment Brokers over the last few weeks have resembled strike-vote meetings of angry Teamsters."[3]

The larger problems plaguing the brokerage industry were less visible to the public. Some firms faced severe capital shortfalls as a result of the market crash. Back-office processing had gotten bogged down—a problem that was only exacerbated by massive layoffs of clerical personnel. Congress wanted to know whether the NYSE had knowledge of its members' precarious financial shape and, if so, why the Big Board had allowed those firms to continue trading.

Graduation Day for the OTC Market

IT WAS IN this tumultuous environment that the National Association of Securities Dealers (NASD) Automated Quotation System, the Nasdaq, commenced operations on February 8, 1971.[4] Incredibly, in that era of moon landings and push-button-launched intercontinental ballistic missiles, the arrival of the Nasdaq marked the first time that dealers across the country were able to see something close to real-time quotes of the OTC stocks they bought and sold on behalf of their customers. "Nasdaq is graduation day for the over-the-counter market," proclaimed then NASD President Gordon S. Macklin.[5] True, but the Nasdaq was a long time in the making. Many of the hurdles it had to overcome were not so much technical as political.

The Nasdaq's origins harked back to the gargantuan *Special Study of the Securities Markets* by the Securities and Exchange Commission (SEC; see chapter 4) presented to Congress in 1963. Concluding their exhaustive analysis of the OTC market, the study's authors saw automation as a way to rein in the many abuses they had uncovered and narrow the canyon-like spreads and mark-ups customers at the time were paying for OTC stocks. The SEC's recommendations painted a highly accurate picture of what financial markets would look like in years to come:

> Automation has only slightly touched the over-the-counter markets, present uses being largely concentrated in servicing back office operations. Recent rapid advances in technology now offer the prospect of major new applications in over-the-counter markets in the handling of quotations and otherwise.
>
> It appears to be technically feasible to use a central computer to record and report interdealer quotations for some or all over-the-counter securities on a continuous basis. In addition to providing a method for instantaneously determining best quotations, such a system might provide wholly new means of matching buy and sell orders and even accomplishing their executions in some circumstances. The same system might be used for reporting and storing actual transaction information, thus for the first time making price and volume data available on a current and continuous basis.[6]

Note that the SEC envisioned a system that would handle both executions and quote dissemination. As you will see in chapter 17, some 30 years later the Nasdaq would work very hard to link its quote dissemination network with a mechanism that funneled trades through a single conduit they called Super-Montage. Over the decades, Nasdaq officials came to realize that their market's very survival depended on that pairing. Likewise, in the early 1960s, when the SEC study authors hit on the idea of using automation to untangle the OTC market, their solution seemed uniquely suited to the times. Automation had already become an American buzzword and was becoming pervasive in American society. "Do not fold, spindle, or mutilate" was a phrase known to anyone who had received a water bill or paycheck printed on an IBM punch card.

Yet a computer network designed to merge mail was one thing; a continuous real-time system that received input from hundreds or perhaps thousands of users and fed data back to an equally large number was pushing the existing technology, especially when something as hypertense and fragile as the securities markets was concerned.

On the other hand, automation of a kind had been a factor in the securities industry since the stock ticker began transmitting NYSE prices in 1867.[7] (Stock prices had previously been relayed by messenger.) The industry had always been the first to embrace new technology if it looked as if that technology might provide its users with an edge. The *Special Study* authors could point to several successful examples of automated quote delivery systems already in existence in the early 1960s. At the time the study was written, some brokerage firms had also taken steps to automate their back-office operations. And automated systems had been set up to monitor compliance by branch offices. Even retail customers at some brokerage houses could receive quotes of some OTC stocks right at the broker's office. At least three companies—Teleregister Corp., Scantlin Electronics, and Ultronic Systems Corp.—dispensed quotes in both listed and OTC securities to more than 600 subscribing brokers.

Quotes entered into any of these systems were transmitted via Western Union. A customer calling up a quote could see only the latest bid or ask price. No system at the time informed users which dealer firm was supplying a particular quote or the number of shares available from the dealer at that price. These early systems had other severe limitations as well. The Scantlin system, for example, supplied only the bid price, or the price that people were willing to pay for a security. The OTC quotes available from all three suppliers might be updated only a few times each day. And not all dealers were willing to pass along their quotes to these suppliers. Thus, the picture of the market painted by these early quote delivery systems remained vastly incomplete.

Seeing the possibilities, however, the SEC study authors solicited advice from brokers as well as officials at computer manufacturers and data processing firms. At one point, they asked officials at Univac, a division of Sperry Rand, what it would take to build a quote delivery and execution platform. The requirements outlined by the SEC might appear modest by today's standards. The system should be capable of processing 200,000 quote changes per day and execute 100,000 trades; 2,000 broker dealer firms would make heavy use of the system, and another 3,000 would use it occasionally. Univac executives crunched the numbers and advised the SEC that a computer system up to the task would probably lease for $24,000 per month. The cost of dedicated phone lines or some other transmission medium would be extra.

Clearly excited about the prospect of automating the securities markets, computer industry executives convinced the *Special Study* authors that a system with then-undreamed-of capabilities might be built:

> Some described a system which would select the best bids and offers, execute orders, and clear transactions. Transmitting and re-

ceiving units would be installed in the offices of all subscribing broker-dealers. Wholesale dealers and other broker-dealer sub-scribers could enter quotations (and size of market) for central in-dexing under the appropriate security and could interrogate the computer to determine the highest bid and lowest offer, selected by the computer, together with the number of shares bid and of-fered at such prices.

This would enable a broker-dealer to execute at the best pre-vailing price or, if he chose, to enter his own limit order in the hope of bettering that price. Thus, in their view the principal bar-rier to the crossing of public orders—namely lack of central loca-tion—could be overcome by use of a single central computer.[8]

Thus, the Nasdaq, which did not have an exchange floor, could now possess one. Thanks to a central computer, it would become, to use today's terminology, a virtual exchange, a move that might put it on par with the NYSE for the first time. Those interviewed by the SEC also correctly foresaw that such an au-tomated system might be a boom for the then-arcane field of technical analysis, where traders use information about past buying and selling patterns to forecast a stock's performance. One analyst said that extracting price and volume data on a particular stock for use in constructing a "report" might take as little as an hour.

The Rewards of Ambiguity

TODAY, THE DATA needed to perform technical analysis usu-ally can be accessed in seconds or less by anyone with an Inter-net connection. Yet three decades later, some aspects of the SEC's original proposal remain unrealized. For example, listed shares are not broadcast with the same granularity as the Level II display affords for OTC shares. And certain electronic com-munications networks (ECNs) provide more options than others in the types of orders they accept and execute. Which is to say that no single, centralized transaction system yet exists for U.S. markets.

Putting aside for the moment arguments over whether such a system would, in fact, be desirable, the reason none exists is mostly to do with politics and self-interest and very little to do with any technical hurdles. In fact, resistance to having an automated quotation system arose almost immediately. And the source, the SEC insinuated, was the NASD's own member firms.[9] Since accurate, up-to-the minute quote data were difficult if not impossible for the average retail investor to obtain, NASD member firms were able to hide their markups. The *Special Study* authors charged:

> In these circumstances, the [current quote reporting] system encourages the handling of purchase transactions on a principal "riskless" basis, with increased cost to the customer, and provides no basis for evaluating the quality of executions. Moreover, the NASD and many of its members have consistently opposed the release of wholesale quotations to the general public, yet institutions and other favored investors have gained regular access to the sheets through NASD members.[10]

The SEC study then voiced a good point. The NASD as a self-regulatory organization was ultimately responsible for the reliability of OTC quotes and trades. Therefore, the study's authors said that "the task of regulating and policing wholesale quotations might be eased considerably if the NASD itself were to operate the system."[11]

The NASD board of governors did discuss automation at its May 1961 meeting. Notes from that meeting attest to the group's wariness:

> The Board . . . should attempt to steer this period of change, not only to promote the advancement and modernization of our industry but also to predetermine that the end result is controllable.

Otherwise we may well see leadership fall into the wrong hands and thereby lose our ability to supervise.[12]

Ironically, that is precisely what happened decades later as ECNs gave investors numerous alternative trading networks: The NASD lost considerable control.

Building a New Board

WHATEVER THE REASONS, concerted action on an automated OTC quote delivery platform moved at a snail's pace for five years following the *Special Study*'s completion, much like the 175 other recommendations made by the *Special Study* authors in 1963. William Carey, the SEC chairman who ordered the study, had proposed that the recommendations be relayed to Congress in the form of legislative proposals. But in the end, despite prodding from Congress itself, he chose to work directly with the NASD and the other exchanges to bring about the study's recommended reforms.[13] Indeed, in 1964, Congress voted to expand the NASD's original mandate by amending the Securities Exchange Act of 1934. As a result, instead of having the reforms of the *Special Study* foisted on it, the NASD was given broader new enforcement powers that specifically allowed it to take action against members who violated its rules.[14]

Interestingly, other changes to the NASD that resulted from the *Special Study* appeared focused more on the organization's structure and governance than on actual disciplinary actions against member firms the SEC had accused of abuse. According to the NASD's own documents, the study recommended that the organization hire more staffers to deal with disciplinary matters. This would free up the board of governors to concentrate on broader issues. The Special Study also urged the NASD to become "more truly a national organization." As a result, the NASD added "Governors-At-Large" who might work for large financial firms. Although some came from other professions.[15] This innovation likely deepened a conflict within the NASD that had existed since its earliest years. Namely, it gave larger financial institutions increasing representation on the NASD's board, alienating the group's smaller firms. Prior to the change, NASD's governing structure was organized more along regional lines, similar to many organizations. "The way the NASD was originally designed spread the governance power throughout the country," explained Gordon Macklin who in addition to serving as president of the NASD, became Nasdaq's first chief executive officer from 1971 to 1986. Before making the move to NASD headquarters in Washington, Macklin had served on and then chaired a district committee covering Ohio and Kentucy.[16]

The Long Arm of the NYSE

WHILE THE NASD was modernizing its structure, a fierce struggle over order flow was developing between the NYSE and rival regional exchanges as well as nonmember broker-dealer firms that made up the so-called "third market" in listed securities. Third-market trading of listed shares was similar to OTC trading; brokers and their customers dealt directly with one another and notably without an exchange serving as a facilitator. That conflict would pave the way for a new market, the Nasdaq, that would provide listed companies with a truly national alternative to the NYSE.

The power struggle arose largely because the NYSE refused to grant membership to institutions, such as insurance companies, banks, and mutual fund managers. There was blatant self-interest in this refusal. Institutions traded thousands of shares and were the major holders of securities at the time. Granting membership privileges to institutions would have enabled them to trade commission free, depriving the NYSE's current members of millions in commissions. As members of the NASD were wont to do, NYSE member firms often voted in conflict with what would prove beneficial to their ultimate customers—in this case, the mutual fund–owning American public, who would have benefited from the removal of commissions. The Big Board proved zealous in maintaining its monopoly. It had the power to shut off the flow of quote data to firms that it believed had violated the NYSE's rules, forcing those firms to in effect trade blindly.[17]

But holding millions of dollars of the public's savings gave the institutions some clout as well. And they were not about to be bullied by the Big Board. One financial services firm, Jefferies & Co., a division of mutual fund giant Investors Diversified Services, reportedly prepared a suit against the NYSE on antitrust grounds for denying it membership.[18] Other large institutions sought a way around the NYSE trading floor by purchasing seats in the nation's regional exchanges. These exchanges were located throughout the country in places like Philadelphia, San Francisco, and Chicago. In addition to trading shares of local companies, the regionals also did a fair amount of business in Big Board stocks. Some regionals, like the Pacific Exchange in San Francisco (recently merged with the ECN Archipelago, see chapter 11) and the Philadelphia Exchange, have adapted well to modernized trading practices, and they continue to thrive today.

In the 1960s, membership in a regional exchange cost as little as $16,500, many times less than a seat on the Big Board.[19] Seeing institutions as a major source of new business, the regionals crafted ways to lure them as members with lucrative incentives. Some regionals, for example, allowed nonmember brokers to trade commission free. This practice greatly benefited institutions that were members of that regional exchange because it enabled them to reward a broker that sold their mutual funds and other products—the reward being commission-free trading. The member institution would in effect handle the trade for the brokerage as a kind of perk. Prodding from the SEC put an end to the practice in December 1968. And some undoubtedly saw the hand of the NYSE in the move.

The SEC ban forced the regionals to find other value-added services to entice high-volume traders. In 1970, the Midwest Stock Exchange fell on one solution. It created an automated trading system that was eons removed from anything else available at the time. And it debuted months before the Nasdaq. Like the order-routing systems administered by some ECNs nearly three decades later, the Midwest Stock Exchange system first sent limit orders from its members to the exchange itself. If an execution did not occur within a minute, the order was relayed to the larger market. The network was also able to automatically settle trades. That is, it was able to ensure transfer of shares from seller to buyer while also expediting payment.

The Fight over Displaying Listed Share Quotes

THE NASDAQ SYSTEM, as envisioned by the SEC, would be even more ambitious since it would link together far more participants and present each individual dealer's bid or offer as well as the number of shares each dealer was willing to trade. In addition, part of the original plan was for the Nasdaq to display quotes of at least some listed securities, that is, shares traded on the NYSE and the regionals. To the NASD's smaller member firms, this undoubtedly was a tantalizing idea. Many could not afford Big Board membership, so their trading was confined to the OTC market. If an active market in NYSE shares could be created through NASD dealer firms and brokers, the NYSE might even become irrelevant. Those charged with planning the Nasdaq held onto this idea until just months before the Nasdaq system launched. In June 1970, a provision allowing the Nasdaq to include listed shares was submitted to the SEC for approval as part of the NASD's revised bylaws. But soon afterward, powerful interests within the NASD quashed the idea.

So what was their gripe? On the surface, including listed shares seems a small matter. The Nasdaq was not designed as an execution platform after all. It only displayed quotes. Therefore, in theory at least, no order flow would be stolen from the NYSE. But the NYSE had its own quote delivery system for which it held a monopoly. And even up to the start of the 21st century, it was not as granular as the type of quote data the NASD planned to provide. The NYSE quote system displayed only the best bid or ask price and their respective quantities. The Nasdaq, by contrast, would give a clearer picture of the depth of the market since it showed bid and ask prices from all its dealers. What the NASD's smaller member firms hoped for the NYSE deeply feared, namely, that armed with an alternative quote delivery system those non-NYSE-member dealers might be empowered to trade among themselves, especially their large orders, thus bypassing the NYSE specialists.

The same fate would befall the American Stock Exchange, which was also an auction market that made use of specialists, modeled after the NYSE. The perceived threat prompted complaining letters from the presidents of both the American Stock Exchange and the NYSE. The letters requested that listed shares be excluded from the Nasdaq.

In late October, NASD Chief Executive Officer Gordon Macklin reportedly telephoned the association's executive committee for their take on the controversy. All six committee members were reportedly against the idea of including listed shares. Critics later complained that the committee members' veto arose because all six were "partners or officers" of NYSE member firms.[20]

Criticism of the executive committee decision poured in from several fronts, including *The Bank Stock Quarterly*. "In view of the dominance of the NASD board by New York Stock

Exchange members, it is not surprising that they [the Big Board] so quickly carried the day inside the NASD's own command post on this issue."[21] The *Quarterly*'s readers were likely already upset with the NYSE over the Big Board's one-time practice of excluding banks from membership. Another critic, Donald E. Weeden, whose third-market trading firm Weeden & Co. competed directly with Big Board specialists, charged that the NASD executive committee decision "is a blatant example of how far the NYSE is willing to go to maintain its position."[22]

Despite this criticism, Macklin informed the SEC that the Nasdaq would not display quote data on listed shares. Today, Macklin remembers well the delicate politics of the time. While NASD member firms were committed to the success of the Nasdaq, he says, they did not want that success to come at the expense of the Big Board. Furthermore, Macklin says that the controversy threatened to delay deployment of the Nasdaq system, which the OTC market sorely needed. "It was not our primary mission" to trade NYSE stocks, he says. "Our mission was to take care of companies that were primarily listed in our market. Our target company was not General Motors it was Intel."

Nevertheless, smaller NASD member firms were outraged. One of those firms, Dallas-based broker-dealer Gaston Shumate, reportedly filed a class-action suit against the NASD for excluding listed shares. The action further illustrates a perennial conflict within the NASD membership that surfaced at particular moments during its history. Smaller NASD member firms complained that their larger counterparts dominated decision making.

Bowing to pressure from many smaller firms, NASD's board of governors agreed to consider the issue at a meeting it held March 1971. But by that time, however, the Nasdaq was already up and running, and listed shares had been excluded.

Significantly, despite complaints from various quarters, the SEC voiced no objections to the Nasdaq's exclusion of listed shares. Had the SEC pressed the point, trading in securities might have turned out quite differently in the succeeding decades. The Big Board at the start of the 1970s might have faced the kind of fragmentation of order flow that the Nasdaq was to face with the debut of ECNs in the late 1990s. Whether or not the display of competing quote data was desirable at that time is open to question. Price differences in the quotes displayed on the Big Board and the Nasdaq would have existed. And this might have led to arbitrage plays between the Nasdaq and the NYSE, for example, and perhaps even the kind of programmed trading that helped bring about the crash of 1987—all at a time when fledgling, new automated-trading systems were ill equipped to handle fast markets.

That said, there can be no doubt that the SEC was aware that the NYSE maintained a de facto monopoly on its own quote data, just as the SEC must have been aware that the NASD executive committee vote had likely arisen out of its members' allegiance to the Big Board. Still the SEC chose to do nothing. Two decades later, in an abrupt reversal of this position (see chapter 8), the SEC would charge the NASD board with consistently voting its own self-interest. And as a remedy, it would force the board to include more outside members.

The Devil Is in the Details

THOUGH LISTED SHARES would not be a part of the system, the Nasdaq did nevertheless rock the world of OTC trading to its core and forever change the way securities were traded throughout the world. Indeed, much careful planning was required to create such a revolutionary system. That planning began in earnest when a NASD Automation Committee formed in 1966 to sketch out the system's general parameters. Later the NASD hired a consultant to help firm up the systems specifications. Bids were submitted in 1968,[23] and defense contractor

Bunker Ramo Corporation won the right to develop the Nasdaq. Work began that same year. In an interview, Macklin explained the reasons behind the choice of Bunker Ramo. When the specifications were finalized, estimates of the system's cost reached $20 million. While at the time, Macklin says, the NASD's annual budget was somewhere between $5 and $6 million. Bunker Ramo offered to lease the system, giving the NASD the option to purchase it. And that was the only way the NASD could have afforded it.

The UNIVAC 1108 mainframe computer that was used to run the Nasdaq was housed in a well-guarded facility at Bunker Ramo's headquarters in Trumbull, Connecticut. The system was designed to handle up to 20,000 securities,[24] more securities than currently traded on the Nasdaq, the American Stock Exchange, and the NYSE combined. When it was first tested on February 8, 1971, the network included 500 proprietary terminals supplied by Bunker Ramo.

As Macklin recalls, the system pushed the technology envelope for the time:

The difference between the Nasdaq system and other networks is that it was online in real time. People were interacting with each other. Since this was a real-time interactive system it needed a lot of additional capabilities that most record keeping systems didn't have and didn't need.

The Nasdaq provided three levels of service. The first level of service was so-called Level I quotes, which cost $10 per terminal. Level I quotes were similar to quotes that might appear in a newspaper. That is, they were meant to convey a representative quote, not the real-time price of the stock. Level I service was intended for brokers buying on behalf of their retail customers. Some 30,000 brokers reportedly signed on. In 1980, representative quotes were finally replaced by the highest bid to buy and the lowest offer. Soon after, because traders now had access to more timely information, spreads narrowed on nearly all Nasdaq stocks.

The next tier up, Level II service, was modeled after the printed "sheets" that brokers formerly subscribed to. Just like the sheets, Level II service consisted of quotes from participating market makers. However, rather than being arranged haphazardly as was the case with the sheets, the Nasdaq Level II display listed quotes in order of price. In each case, the bid and ask prices had been entered into the system by market makers themselves. Level II service was geared to large traders who worked for mutual funds, pension funds, and the like. These high-end users paid up to $450 per month for the service. (In 2000, the cost of Level II quotes had dropped to $10 per month.) Because these traders handled a large volume of shares, it was important for them to see the market's depth, that is, the prices offered by the complete list of dealers posting prices at which they were willing to trade a stock. In the course of filling their orders, these institutional traders might buy 5,000 shares from one market maker at a certain price and then pick up an additional 1,000 shares from another market maker at a slightly higher price. Level II proved a powerful tool for doing just that. The quantities listed on the buy-and-sell column of the Level II display also gave clues to the stock's near-term price movements. If the number of shares that bidders wished to buy exceeded the number offered for sale, the price could be expected to rise in the short term, for example.

Level II afforded users an unprecedented amount of near real-time market information. Nevertheless, Nasdaq dealers still maintained a powerful advantage. Thanks to the Nasdaq system, only they could enter or retract orders. At the time, limit orders submitted to these dealers by their customers were not displayed for all in the market to see, as would be the case years later. Rather, they were invisible to all but the market maker who received them. Thus, other market participants were deprived of crucial information since often a limit order for a large quantity could trigger a price move. Another important advantage dealers possessed was that only they knew whether the order they were fielding was genuine or whether it was a ruse meant to convince traders that more shares were available to buy or sell than might actually be the case.

Entering or retracting orders into the Nasdaq system required Level III service, which was available only to market makers at a cost $500 per month per terminal. The Level III display was otherwise similar to Level II.

Unlike the Midwest Stock Exchange's automated system, the Nasdaq as yet had no means of actually executing orders. That was still done over the phone. Consequently, although price discovery was greatly sped up thanks to the Nasdaq system, actual trading remained a slow, cumbersome process, one that was built on relationships and that favored trading firms with fast private phone lines. This would remain the case for 13 years after the Nasdaq's initial debut.

Toward an Open-Source Trading Platform

BUNKER RAMO WOULD actually own the Nasdaq system under a five-year agreement negotiated with the NASD. In 1976, the NASD purchased it for $10 million. The system was then relocated to a building NASD purchased that was across the street from Bunker Ramo's facility. Nasdaq users were at first limited to eye-squinting terminals provided by Bunker Ramo. A newer-generation Harris terminal debuted in 1980 and offered some sorely needed improvements, including a larger screen. Users could also split the screen in two and follow two stocks at once.

More dramatic changes would occur in the mid-1980s as personal computers brought about a revolution of their own in the United States. In 1986, the Nasdaq Workstation debuted. Rather than requiring a dedicated terminal, the Workstation was a software program that could be loaded onto a DOS-powered personal computer. The software itself provided greatly expanded functionality that would serve as a model for the day-trading software (see chapter 12) in the years to come.

Users could create a customized list of up to 30 stocks they wished to follow. They could also receive alerts when those stocks reached specified price or volume levels. Users were also able to monitor automated trade executions and could program their systems to closely follow a particular market maker's trading—an important feature since in many cases one market maker served as the ax, or principal trader, for a particular stock. Prices quoted by that market maker were quickly echoed by other market participants who believed the ax to be especially knowledgeable. All the information on the Nasdaq Workstation appeared in color, and quotes were updated continuously, saving users from having to submit a new request each time they wanted a refreshed quote.

In 1994, Nasdaq debuted its Workstation II, with the familiar Windows-like interface of customizable screens and menus. Customers could also opt to create their own front-end platforms, incorporating increasingly sophisticated software tools to forecast a stock's price and speed execution.[25] This open-source platform led directly to a plethora of after-market software development firms and day trading brokerages. The trading software these companies devised (see chapter 12) were each armed with innovative features designed to let their customers outgun the competition. And in many cases they outperformed the technology used by Nasdaq dealer firms.

But even during its first years of operation, the Nasdaq's front-end quote display system indeed sparked a revolution in trading. Never had so much information been available merely at the touch of a screen. What Nasdaq's designers had launched in 1971 was in many ways a precursor to the Internet.

Thousand of participants were linked together adding and requesting information from the Bunker Ramo's "servers," just as Internet users interact today. And as with the Internet, a kind of community instantly arose around the Nasdaq. Pockets of users would congregate around the trading of a certain stocks, then migrate to other stocks, in much the way Web surfers migrate from one interactive site to the next. According to Macklin planners were confident it would boost volume. But just as important, it would make it easier for small companies to raise money. It all seemed eons removed from the paper-littered trading floor of the traditional brick and mortar exchanges.

> In order to have liquid markets you didn't need to have professionals standing face to face yelling at each other. You could centralize the information in the system, and consequently any dealer could compete regardless of where he or she was located. What we did with the Nasdaq was to create a trading floor that was 3,000 miles long and 2,000 miles wide. The whole capital raising process throughout the country has been geometrically improved by the Nasdaq.

This was the message Macklin took with him when he sold the idea of the Nasdaq to dealer firms that were wary that their profits would shrink. The Nasdaq, by finally making the OTC markets transparent, would prompt more mutual funds and individuals to participate. This would pump up volume. And that increase in volume would make up for any losses stemming from a reduction in stocks' spreads.

Still much work needed to be done with the upstart electronic network not only on viewing the information but also acting on it, that is, allowing executions to take place as rapidly as quote data were delivered. Macklin and his NASD colleagues envisioned a day when the system would link up seamlessly with the back-offices of brokerage firms, allowing the entire trade, from the initial order to the final clearing and settlement to take place via the network. To that end, in 1982 the Nasdaq launched what it called the small-order execution system (SOES). It allowed orders to execute automatically against the prices broadcast by Nasdaq dealers instantaneously. But it was a simplistic and flawed system compared to what was to come. As you will see in the next chapter, the Nasdaq's attempts to fix the SOES led to the first generation of day traders.

CHAPTER 6

THE 1980S: NERD KINGS, ROCKET SCIENTISTS, AND SOES BANDITS

APOCRYPHAL STORIES ABOUT Bill Gates can be found all over the Web and elsewhere. But one of the better-known tales goes something like this: Around midnight, the software mogul shows up at a convenience store near his suburban Seattle mansion to buy a carton of ice cream. When Gates gets ready to pay the cashier, he fumbles around in his pockets for a 50-cent coupon he thinks he brought with him. People in line grow impatient. Finally, a guy standing behind Gates—who apparently does not recognize him—angrily hands Gates 50 cents and says something like, "Pay me back when you get your first million." Incredibly, Gates actually accepts the guy's money, even though the software mogul was worth something like $3 billion at the time.[1]

By some accounts, Gates's wealth in the 1980s was growing so fast that the simple act of stooping down to pick up a hundred-dollar bill was not worth his time. Thanks to Gates's enormous holdings of Nasdaq-listed Microsoft stock, his wealth would eventually surpass that of Brunei's kinky sultan—not bad for a guy who reportedly spent his Harvard years playing high-stakes poker and who would go without bathing for days at a time. Gates became undisputed leader of one of the strangest generations of American business tycoons, nearly all of whom grew their wealth with the help of the Nasdaq. These were the nerd kings, the brains behind the personal computer revolution. Their companies sparked the first major rally in the Nasdaq, which set the stage for the outlandish Internet stock surge a decade later.

Known to be ruthlessly competitive and often wildly eccentric, nerd kings were known to shape cultlike organizations after their own image. Also of that generation was Oracle founder Larry Ellison. The database software tycoon made no bones about his company's out-for-blood culture. Ellison reportedly once led his employees in a chant of "kill, kill, kill," following a strategy session aimed at besting one of Oracle's competitors. "I want them on their knees," Ellison is said to have shouted, "begging for mercy, confessing their every sin." At business meetings, he quoted Genghis Khan. "It's not enough that we win," he said. "Everyone else must lose."[2]

Luck sometimes played a critical role in the nerd kings' success. Compaq's founders, for example, reportedly sat around a table at a House of Pies in Houston to work up a business plan for a computer company that would succeed by besting the margins of then industry giant IBM. Ideas that the three founders had previously discussed reportedly included a Mexican restaurant, a company manufacturing disk drives, and a key chain that would beep on command if it got lost.[3]

And then there is Apple's Steve Jobs, whose now legendary visit to Xerox's Palo Alto Research Center forever changed the way personal computers are used. During that visit, Jobs was shown a roomful of startling innovations devised by Xerox's brain trust. To date, none had been brought to market. Had they been, it is likely that Xerox, not Microsoft or Apple, would have grown to dominate the personal computer industry because they eerily foretold the innovations that competitors would develop in the years ahead. Among the most impressive things that Jobs saw was a first-generation graphical user interface that allowed all programs to share a common control panel. The Xerox interface inspired Jobs to create the Lisa, Apple's business computer. Lisa's high price caused it to bomb, but Jobs and Apple got it right with the less expensive Macintosh.

Such perseverance often comes at a price. Jobs reportedly was widely known within Apple for his bouts of nastiness aimed at keeping the troops fired up and forever on edge. According to one account, he would wander from office to office, deliberately badmouthing certain employees, just to gauge people's reactions. "I think Jeff is s——t," he might say. "What do you think?"[4] Yet like Gates and Ellison, Jobs rose to demigod status among his employees and customers. And also like his cohorts, he was prone to moments of sheer brilliance and uncanny luck. Despite resistance from Apple's management, Jobs insisted that the company make a $2.5 million investment in a fledgling company called Adobe Systems. Jobs desperately wanted Adobe's state-of-the-art graphics-oriented printer-interface software, seeing it as the perfect complement to the MacIntosh's high-end graphics capabilities. Six years later, Apple sold its Adobe stake for $89 million.[5]

Jobs and his team did not always get it right. Ultimately, the Mac would be soundly trounced by the Windows operating system, though it need not have been so. The Mac's inspiration, a Xerox-developed computer called the Alto, had built-in networking, something that Jobs saw no need for. Once personal computers developed reliable networking software, the gap between them and Apple grew irreparably wider.

The Boom Begins

TO ROBERT X. Cringely, author of the book *Accidental Empires,* where this story appears, it made perfect sense for Jobs to demand mindless commitment from his employees, just as it made perfect sense for Gates to shamelessly accept the 50 cents offered by a stranger. Success meant everything to the nerd kings of the computer world. And no amount of success would ever be enough, or, as Cringely writes, "Nothing is enough to prove to Bill Gates and to all the folks like him in the personal computer business that they are finally safe from the bigger, stronger, stupider kids who used to push them around on the playground."[6]

Like so many revolutions, the rise of the nerd kings began as an act of youthful rebellion. In this case, that rebellion focused on reviving capitalism in its purest form, with the help of the personal computer. An earlier generation wrote music. The nerd kings wrote code. And just like gang-speak serves as a communications barrier in urban areas, to these suburban white kids, code was the perfect means of separating themselves from the tired old world of their elders. Speaking in Basic or C++, no authority figures could hope to understand them.

According to Cringely, this paranoia, this rebellion at authority, led directly to the creation of a new generation of American corporate behemoths, like Microsoft, Compaq, Apple, and others. And indeed, these companies were marvels in the sense that unlike the Internet companies and debt-burdened Internet infrastructure companies that would emerge a decade later, they produced a profit.

And they were largely responsible for propelling the Nasdaq to previously unimagined heights. As is normally the case with sustained market booms, the first phase takes off on firm footing. Microsoft, for example, went public in March 1986. Unlike the Internet initial public offerings (IPOs) that were rushed to the market 10 years later (see chapter 13), Microsoft had already aptly proved itself to the investment community when its stock first went on sale. "We didn't grasp his profound understanding of business strategy," Alfred Berkeley III, who is currently vice chairman of the Nasdaq, says of Gates, whom he has known for many years. While a partner with the financial firm Alex Brown, Berkeley helped put together Microsoft's IPO. Berkeley was also advising the Nasdaq on ways to utilize new technology at the time, and Gates was at the time invited to take part in these discussions.[7] Microsoft's IPO came 11 years after Gates and Paul Allen had developed Basic, the programming language that ran first-generation microcomputers, and three years after the debut of Windows. The offering raised a relatively modest $61 million with its opening price of $21 per share. In September 1987, Microsoft stock was selling for $114 when the company opted for a two-for-one split. Weeks later, the crash of 1987 lopped 30 percent off its value.[8]

Crème de la Crème

ONE OF THE reasons that stocks such as Microsoft enjoyed such success is that they were highly tradable; that is, they were liquid, even when the firms were still small but especially as they grew larger. Their liquidity was due largely to a restructuring that took place within the Nasdaq market. In 1982, the Nasdaq debuted its National Market System (NMS; the name was later changed to Nasdaq National Market [NNM]). Arriving more than 10 years after the Nasdaq itself revolutionized how quotes were delivered to traders, the NNM added certain crucial refinements that investors take for granted today. For example, information on the price and volume of each trade reached investors just 90 seconds after an execution took place. Previously, this information became available only after the close of trading. The NNM was intended to finally put the over-the-counter (OTC) market on par with the New York Stock Exchange (NYSE) in terms of the quality of information. The quality of the companies whose shares traded on the NNM also was meant to equal the venerable blue-chip firms listed on the Big Board. Accordingly, companies that traded via the NNM were required to maintain higher standards of corporate governance than a run-of-the-mill OTC-traded firm. In addition, NNM companies already had to be among the most actively traded on the Nasdaq. About 40 companies made the cut when the NMS debuted. By the end of the decade, the NNM included some 2,587 companies.[9]

The NNM debuted during Gordon Macklin's tenure as Nasdaq's chief executive officer (see chapter 5). And while he and others at the Nasdaq worked to upgrade standards, reporting procedures, and quote display for NNM companies, they also asked newspapers to devote more space to Nasdaq quotes. Over the years, Macklin lobbied various groups with the goal of putting Nasdaq companies on equal footing with exchange-listed shares. As he explains:

> We had to get the cream of the Nasdaq automatically approved for margin accounts, rather than have a separate filing. We had to ultimately get the larger Nasdaq companies automatically approved by state securities regulators. The established exchanges had exemptions in most of these areas. So we had to build in the same luxuries and services that the exchanges had. Our goal was to make the listing decision based on whether the single specialist system was or was not preferable to the competing dealer system.

Put another way, if regulators and the investing public could put aside their preconceptions about trading in dealer markets versus NYSE-styled floor trading, Nasdaq's larger companies that met NNM standards could acquire some of the panache that NYSE firms enjoyed—a good way of keeping them within the Nasdaq fold. At the same time, they would enjoy the added liquidity that came from trading in a dealer-style market such as the Nasdaq as opposed to an auction market such as the NYSE. In fact, a dealer market was ideally suited to trading shares of hitherto unknown companies. And it is a key reason that many of the Nasdaq's behemoth companies, such as Oracle and Intel, chose to stay with the Nasdaq despite fierce lobbying by the NYSE and the lure of prestige wrought by a Big Board listing.

Here in a nutshell is why: Whereas an auction market routes orders through a single specialist, a dealer market theoretically encourages competitive buying and selling between a group of dealers and professional traders. The more trading, the more liquidity, naturally. And added liquidity again, in theory, tends to bolster a stock's price. This is because people will readily pay more for something that they can quickly sell, should they choose, at close to its purchase price.

Companies trading on the OTC had long enjoyed this dealer-market advantage. The arrival of the Nasdaq and then the NNM heightened this advantage by providing real-time quote information. The result, thanks to the NNM, was that the burgeoning creativity of the new breed of tech entrepreneurs could be matched by a trading mechanism that was uniquely designed to reward their efforts with higher stock prices. This created a powerful ripple effect. The stock performance of companies like Microsoft convinced anyone with an idea or the capital to back it that a mechanism existed to reap sizeable rewards in very short order. In other words, wealth through stock ownership became a clearly defined and dependable exit strategy for those who labored to build start-up companies as well as those who funded them: They could field an IPO. The success of these companies encouraged still more entrepreneurs and it created a huge support industry of venture capitalists and investment banks to nurture them along. The result was an amazingly efficient wealth-creation machine the likes of which had never been seen before.

Brave New World?

DURING THE 1980s, the average American profited indirectly from the rising Nasdaq and other markets through mutual funds or pension funds. While ownership of individual stocks was hardly pervasive, mutual funds came into their own during the 1980s, growing from some $95 billion at the start of the decade to over $1 trillion by 1990.[10]

But the real profits in this era were won by professional traders—the high-flying leveraged buyout specialists as well as global financiers like George Soros who could rock markets with their huge bets. There emerged during that period a cadre of megatraders who understood the frightening leverage provided by derivatives, such as options and futures. As financial author Gregory J. Millman revealed in his book *The Vandal's Crown: How Rebel Currency Traders Overthrew the World's Central Banks,* in the hands of the right person, derivatives were to the financial markets what nuclear weapons were to warfare. And during the 1980s, derivatives began trading in increasing amounts in exchanges in Europe, Asia, and the United States.

The megatraders were joined by yet another new breed of trader, the so-called quants (quantitative analysts). Quants were also known as rocket scientists. Financial geniuses all—at least in the ethereal realms of financial theory—rocket scientists tended to be shy, brooding, academic types, notably lacking in the killer instincts that many professional traders possess. Nevertheless, brokerages desperately sought out leading rocket scientists from the nation's top universities, knowing that the survival of their business depended on having their talents on board. That is because rocket scientists, like megatraders, understood well what few of the officers or traders at these houses did, namely, the absurdly complex relationship between stock or currency prices and the prices of their respective derivative products. More important, the rocket scientists knew how to program computers to exploit these relationships, a practice that became known as programmed trading.

The new breed of traders were further empowered by the fact that the Nasdaq and other world markets were becoming increasingly intertwined, even as the systems linking them together were new, somewhat fragile, and largely untested—all the more reason that those systems could be exploited by those smart enough to understand how they worked.

The result in several instances was havoc on a grandiose scale. The 1980s was characterized by a series of dangerous financial shocks that reverberated around the world and with frightening speed. They included the Mexico debt crisis, the Continental Illinois Bank crisis, the Ohio savings-and-loan crisis, and the stock market crash of 1987. Each debacle came about in an environment where the old rigid checks that had once reined in the world's financial systems were fast giving way to something far less predictable and controllable.

Things Become Unhinged

THE OLD FINANCIAL systems first began unwinding in 1971, the very year the Nasdaq debuted. Nineteen seventy-one was the year that President Nixon led the industrialized nations in abandoning the Bretton Woods Agreement, which had maintained order in the financial system since World War II. The United States would no longer make dollars convertible into gold at a fixed exchange rate. Thus, other world currencies linked to the dollar would no longer have a predictable, agreed-on value.

Instead, they would be allowed to float up and down in relation to one another. Their value would be based largely on the perceived fortunes of each country at a particular moment. In an era dominated by the Cold War and frequent Mideast crises, a nation's fortunes could change rapidly in the eyes of the market.

Yet by March 1973, all the world's major currencies had adopted floating exchange rates, which introduced yet another variable into the world's already volatile equities markets. Since a company's assets were denominated in its home currency, the value of those assets as reflected in the stock price would move somewhat in tandem with the denominating currency.

Unfortunately, this major sea change to the financial system came at a time when rising oil prices as well as severe price rises in other commodities and real estate led to a protracted period of higher inflation that reached double-digit levels in 1979. Inflation only amplified the destabilizing effects of delinking currencies to gold. Under Chairman Paul Volker, the Federal Reserve mounted an aggressive anti-inflation campaign from 1979 to 1982 that eventually succeeded in reining in inflation. The savings-and-loan crisis was collateral damage.

Stocks also declined as money flowed from equity markets into debt instruments. Little wonder that while stocks churned, money markets yielded a virtually riskless 18 percent annual return. Companies strapped with draconian interest payments saw their earnings wither. The result was that during 1981–82, the United States experienced its worst economic slowdown since the 1930s.

Pennies from Heaven

BUT AS OFTEN happens in the equities markets, out of the depths of decline comes a new beginning. And the cause can often be one or more catalysts that had previously been ignored. In the case of the Nasdaq, one of those catalysts was the nerd kings and their fledgling computer tech companies. They promised to radically change the face of business: The paperless office would allow companies to operate faster, cheaper, and better. Companies hoping to remain competitive would have no choice but to plant a personal computer on every worker's desk.

Meanwhile, stocks on the Big Board and on the Nasdaq's NNM received a major boost from big money, specifically overseas money that mostly sought out powerhouse U.S. firms. Roughly $198 billion in overseas money circulated in the U.S. capital markets in 1980. By decade's end, that amount was nearly $4.2 trillion.[11] Much of it came from Japan, where an economic bubble of near biblical proportions was in progress. Real estate values in Tokyo reached such preposterous levels that the few acres of land within the royal palace for a time exceeded the value of every building on every street in Manhattan, and the total value of real estate in Tokyo exceeded the value of all the property in the United States. The U.S. stock markets offered a relatively safe way for the Japanese to leverage that value.

Big Board stocks got another boost from the takeover barons who put companies on Dickensian regimens in order to squeeze more value out of their share prices. Speculators like Ivan Boesky bought shares of companies that seemed ripe for a corporate raid, boosting their share prices, while a tangent industry led by Michael Milken dreamed up imaginative ways to finance those raids.

The result was a speculative buying frenzy based on very little that was substantive. The money flowing into U.S. markets from overseas did bolster stock prices. But it did not make companies necessarily more productive. Likewise, the share price boost reaped from a hostile takeover often had more to do with increased speculative demand for those shares than with any improvement the raiders hoped to make in the company they had snatched. Nevertheless, overseas investors and the raiders at home succeeded in pumping up the volume on the exchanges. And not just on the NYSE. Trading on the Nasdaq at the time was near 150 million shares per day, less than one-tenth of its present level, but within striking distance of the 189 million shares traded daily on the Big Board.[12] Share prices in the United States rose to post–World War II highs between 1983 and 1987.

Something had to snap. The signs were clear. Volatility increased, as it always does during the crazed weeks before a crash. On Black Monday, the Dow dropped more than 500 points, hastily dispatching almost $1 trillion in aggregate market capitalization to "money heaven." The Nasdaq, meanwhile, lost roughly 100 points.

And panic reigned. People waited on the phone for hours to get through to their mutual fund managers or brokers. A popular joke following the crash asked how to get a broker down from a tree. The answer: Cut the rope.

Markets and Metamarkets

SO, BEYOND THE fact that markets were being pumped higher by speculators and overseas investors, why did stocks fall so suddenly? Some said that investors feared a renewed rise in interest rates. Others blamed the huge Reagan budget deficits as well as America's growing trade deficit with Japan. Still others cited rumblings in Congress to limit future takeovers, thus putting an end to the rallies they had sparked.

If those were the root causes, a catalyst of some kind was still needed. That catalyst, according to many, was provided by the enormous, nearly-out-of-control derivatives markets. As *Time* magazine correspondent John Greenwald described it, a hidden universe of futures and options investments by the market's big players had emerged. Valued at a breathtaking $14 trillion, it amounted to more than three times the aggregate value of NYSE stocks traded in an entire month. "Much of the smart money is really riding on computer-generated hyperso-phisticated financial instruments that use the public's massive bet on securities to create a parallel universe of side bets and speculative mutations," Greenwald wrote.[13]

By the 1980s, this parallel universe of derivative invest-ments had become global in scale, and it closely linked curren-cies with the world's stock and debt markets. Corporations were among the heaviest users of derivatives—since futures and options allowed a company to hedge the cost of raw materials, their own stock price, as well as the non-dollar-denominated value of their assets worldwide. Institutional investors, hedge funds, and securities firms also turned to the derivatives market for both hedging and speculating, drawing the linkages be-tween markets into an ever tightening knot. There are "inter-locking commitments of trillions of dollars," remarked famed investment banker Felix Rohatyn. The world economy would likely remain safe from catastrophe so long as the markets and the relationships they encompassed functioned smoothly.

But expect the world financial system to go into arrhythmia if these commitments ever broke down, he mused.[14] Tightening the knot even further were the new light-speed trading net-works and globe-spanning exchange-linkages. What happened in the U.S. markets seamlessly carried over to trading in Tokyo and then to Europe the instant those exchanges opened for business. In addition, changes in stock values were reflected in-stantly in the prices of their derivative products—at least that was how it was supposed to happen. At times, minute differ-ences existed between the value of derivatives and stocks. On Black Monday, those differences widened into chasms.

Countdown to Meltdown

ON OCTOBER 15, 1987, the House Ways and Means Com-mittee approved a bill that would have disallowed interest deductions on debt used to pay for a corporate takeover.[15] That may well have provided the initial spark. Whatever the case, when markets opened the following Monday, the computer programs that had been devised by the rocket scientists triggered sell orders. Momentum grew as mutual fund shareholders called their brokers to cash out. This meant that the mutual fund managers needed to liquidate shares in order to pay defecting shareholders in cash. The problem was that by this time, the cascade of orders was deluging both the NYSE and the Nasdaq.

Indeed, some market makers on the Nasdaq did as their counterparts had done decades earlier. They simply refused to answer the phone. Lacking buyers other than the market makers themselves, some stocks ceased trading altogether. Trading in option contracts of the affected stocks at the Chicago Board Options Exchange (CBOE) was likewise halted. The result, in the minds of many analysts who have looked at the 1987 crash, was a dangerous disconnect between the derivatives markets and the equities markets. In other words, the prices of equities were no longer predictive of the prices of derivatives and vice versa. Stock index futures began selling at a large discount and even ceased trading for a time. In the back offices of the financial powerhouses, there was real reason to panic. Rumors circulated that banks were refusing to extend loans to brokers to bail them out. The system appeared on the brink of collapse.

Some claimed that luck was the only reason the world financial system avoided disaster. But prompt action by the government also played a role. No one was about to repeat President Herbert Hoover's mistake during the crash of 1929 and keep silent. Thus, both the White House and the Treasury Department made coordinated announcements aimed at calming public fears. Hasty phone meetings took place between officials at the U.S. Treasury and their counterparts in London, Tokyo, and elsewhere. All agreed to pump liquidity into the markets. Still, by noon on October 20, the market continued to drop. Rumors and misinformation continued to spread up and down the Street, including one rumor that several major market participants, among them a major clearinghouse, were about to fail. Meanwhile, brokerage firms, swamped with customer orders, pressured the NYSE and the National Association of Securities Dealers (NASD) to close their markets down. The markets might well have closed. But in the darkest hour, the first tentative signs of a turnaround emerged. A faint all-clear signal came from the derivatives markets that had sparked the downfall in the first place. Stock index futures contracts began ticking upward. By Friday, calm had been mostly restored. As a General Accounting Office study of the crash later put it dryly, "The market break was extraordinary in terms of the speed and extent of falling prices and skyrocketing trading volume. This crisis showed that the size and potential impact of increased linkages between the equities markets and futures markets could change the character of a financial crisis."[16]

Mandatory Executions

IF THAT WAS the case, how could the stock markets repair the damage and restore public confidence? Officials at the Nasdaq swiftly imposed a solution of their own, one that would soon prove highly unpopular with market makers.

Previously, a market maker who could not be reached by phone could receive a trade via SOES (small-order execution system), the Nasdaq's automated order-routing system. The problem was that during the crash of 1987, participation in SOES was voluntary, meaning that a market maker who received a SOES order was not obligated to make the trade. And on Black Monday, many dealers had in fact refused to accept SOES orders. After investigating reasons behind the crash, NASD officials, with prompting from the Securities and Exchange Commission (SEC),[17] decided that SOES needed to be mandatory. And in June 1988, the NASD received SEC approval for its new plan that would require any market maker posting the inside quote for an NNM stock to accept the trade of up to 1,000 shares (depending on the stock) at the price they advertised.

For the individual investor, the rule marked an important milestone. If you sent a market order to be executed at the prevailing best price, there would be a buyer of last resort. In a rapidly falling market, you might not like the price you received, but you could always exit a trade.

Trading As War

AS OFTEN HAPPENS, an innovation designed to solve one problem ends up creating still another. For market makers, this is exactly what happened. When SOES became mandatory, a new species of trader, the SOES bandit, quickly devised ways to use the system to their benefit. SOES bandits were in fact the original day traders—people who earned a living by trading their own accounts. They congregated in specialized brokerages that offered direct access to the Nasdaq's SOES system, forerunners of the many day-trading firms that would arise less than a decade later. Nasdaq requirements allowed brokerage firms to use SOES only for their own customer orders, which was an offhanded way of saying that the firms could not use SOES to trade on their own behalf.[18] Instead, the idea behind this Nasdaq ruling was to give brokerage customers guaranteed access to the market, albeit through the medium of a broker. That broker might receive a call from a customer and then use SOES to automatically execute the customer's trade—a painfully slow process during a market meltdown perhaps. But it was still better than the customer's not receiving an execution at all.

What Nasdaq planners apparently failed to realize following the crash of 1987 was that SOES brokerages would make access to the market directly available to their customers. That is, they would allow their customers to route their orders by themselves. And that is exactly what a few SOES brokerages set themselves up to do. They offered self-service trading. What SOES traders received at these brokerages was a fast computer terminal, armed with trading software and hardwired to the Nasdaq via a dedicated network connection (this in the pre-Internet era). As stock quotes fielded by Nasdaq market makers changed in something close to real time, the SOES bandits hovered over them like raptors. Usually, market makers priced their shares in tandem with one lead dealer, known as the ax, for a particular stock. When the ax raised the offer price, for example, the other market makers would follow suit. Bid prices usually adjusted accordingly, maintaining the spread. But sometimes there were time lags. Market makers would not rescind or adjust their quotes fast enough, or, in some cases, their systems did not transmit those quotes fast enough. So once again, if the ax moved a stock's offering price higher, another dealer might unintentionally sale price his shares because a SOES order was already traveling at light speed to execute the trade against him.

Thus, a SOES bandit could buy at the sale price from that market maker and quickly sell those shares to another market maker, again using SOES's mandatory execution feature. Trading the 1,000-share maximum allowable on SOES, the pennies made by SOES bandits quickly added up. A lightning-fast, 5-cent profit would total $50. And SOES traders could squeeze out 10 such profitable trades per day. Many did. By 1995, more than 80 percent of the share volume on SOES originated from SOES day-trading firms.[19]

Over the years, a war of words broke out between SOES bandits and Nasdaq market makers. SOES bandits claimed that they were providing increased liquidity to the market, thus making it more efficient. In addition, they claimed that they were keeping Nasdaq dealers on their toes by forcing them to keep their quotes current. Market makers, for their part, charged that SOES bandits were really professional traders, not the kind of retail customers whom SOES had been designed to serve. Moreover, the dealers said, they were forcing market makers to maintain wider spreads in self-defense. And this in turn was costing retail customers dearly. The SOES bandits were likely wounding market makers, too. According to a NASD study, deluges of SOES orders were the reason that some market makers reduced the number of stocks they covered.[20]

In truth, SOES bandits did enjoy a clear trading advantage over market makers. SOES traders could send an order out for immediate execution via SOES, whereas market makers had to enter their orders manually. And sometimes they had to negotiate them electronically via a parallel Nasdaq-run network called SelectNet, which market makers used when trading with each other. Nasdaq rules at the time forbade market makers from entering SOES orders on behalf of their customers for stocks in which they made a market. And they could not use the SOES's mandatory execution feature for trades they made on their own behalf.

More important, the trading software used by SOES bandits clearly outgunned anything the market makers had available at the time. SOES traders could create entire queues of orders and cancel them at any time, often with a single keystroke. The software was even designed to spot and exploit market-maker quotes that were "stale."[21]

No surprise that Nasdaq market makers quickly complained that SOES bandits were ruining them. And the NASD quickly devised some innovative remedies. In August 1988, just two months after SOES executions became mandatory, a NASD rule change forbade SOES users from splitting larger orders—of, say, 5,000 shares—into 1,000-share pieces, a practice known as order splitting. Then, in December, the NASD prohibited SOES orders to be placed through so-called professional trading accounts (PTAs). "A PTA was defined to include any account in which five or more day trades had been executed through SOES during any trading day or where a professional trading pattern in SOES was demonstrated."[22] Other NASD rule changes took effect in the 1990s. These included limiting the size of SOES trades to 500 shares and limiting a market maker's maximum exposure to SOES orders during the trading day.

The SEC granted the rule changes, clearly siding with market makers. This was in part because the SEC itself had helped foist mandatory SOES executions on the Nasdaq's dealers. Regardless, the effect was to curtail SOES banditry as a viable trading strategy.

But the SOES bandits themselves did not give up without a fight. And they had a vocal leader in Harvey Houtkin, who was chairman and chief executive officer of All-Tech Investment Group, a day-trading brokerage. In his book *Secrets of the SOES Bandit,* Houtkin says that he never really liked the term, which he claims was invented by market makers to give these original day traders a bad rap.[23] Houtkin painted the SOES market-maker controversy in clear David-and-Goliath terms. Thanks to SOES, powerful Nasdaq market makers found themselves facing a new kind of competition, and their natural response was to try to quash it.

SOES bandit proponents brought this basic argument to court when they successfully challenged the idea of PTAs. In 1993, the U.S. Court of Appeals for the District of Columbia Circuit decided that the definition of PTA was unconstitutional. It also sent the case to the SEC, asking for evidence "of its assertions that failure to restrict professional traders from SOES would cause market makers to cease making markets or widen spreads."[24] The NASD subsequently withdrew the PTA provision.

SOES bandits cheered their victory. Within months of the court decision, SEC sentiment would turn starkly against market makers. That was thanks to an obscure paper published by two finance professors that grew into a scandal that would rock the Nasdaq for several years. While the SOES bandits were making off with their profits at the expense of market makers, the market makers themselves would soon be accused of schemes to siphon off far larger profits from the markets at the expense of their customers.

CHAPTER 7

THE SCANDAL YEARS

ENTER THE 1990S, when, despite a mild recession at the decade's beginning, the outlook for the America economy and the financial markets would never be more bullish. Little wonder. The era marked a kind of unheralded victory celebration. The Soviet Union would soon be nothing more than a bad memory. Meanwhile, millions of people in nations that had scarcely been heard from since before World War II were suddenly free. Their economies, which had been stifled by decades of Communism, were now opened wide to Western businesses. The result, many predicted, would be vast new markets for U.S. exports.

Elsewhere, Western Europe's constantly bickering states were putting the final touches on their planned union. For the first time since the Roman era, a single currency shortly would be accepted across the Continent. And that, too, many in the United States believed, would help create a vast unified market for American companies. Here in the United States, the quick Persian Gulf War victory had greatly boosted the nation's confidence. Business and political leaders now held high hopes for something called the peace dividend. No longer would U.S. taxpayers be saddled with the burden of paying for the missiles and aircraft carriers needed to hold the Soviet Union in check. Finally, that money could be put to more productive uses. For the first time since perhaps the 1920s the United States could focus all its considerable energies on what it had always done best: creating vast wealth through private enterprise.

While much has been made of the consumer boom that followed World War II, little thought has gone into the link between the Cold War victory and the 1990s boom that followed. It had been American technology that had forced the Soviet economy into bankruptcy and ultimately won the Cold War. Redirected with amazing speed, that technology would now bring about an unprecedented prosperity.

Stock markets inevitably factor into their prices the prevailing outlook for the future. And during the 1990s, this was especially true of the tech-driven Nasdaq. Between 1990 and the start of 1999, the Nasdaq composite rose sevenfold, from 500 to over 3,500 points, soundly outperforming the New York Stock Exchange (NYSE) composite, which failed to even double during the same period. On Wall Street, the center of the market swell, those employed by the financial industry were raking in fortunes faster than economic analysts could tally them. And these newly minted millionaires were transforming New York in the process. Young couples were overheard at restaurants alternately discussed hiring British nannies and on-line investing while drinking Cote Rotie at $150 per bottle.[1]

Fortune magazine, reviling the market's excesses, asked the question on its cover, "HAS THIS MARKET GONE TO THE PIGS?"[2]

But the Nasdaq's rise also captured the imaginations of average Americans. Stories of fortunes made on fledgling new companies like Snapple, Netscape, and Blockbuster Video were regular conversation topics at office water coolers. One clear sign of just how cozy average Americans had gotten with the financial markets during the 1990s was attendance at the many investing expos held around the country. Among the most popular of these events—perhaps because admission was free—was "The Money Show," held in cities like Boston, Las Vegas, and Orlando. Thousands thronged the mammoth exhibition halls, parading past row after row of booths where vendors hawked everything from financial planning services to mutual funds to the newest investing Web sites. In adjacent rooms, guest speakers included stock gurus like Michael Murphy or Louis Rukeyser, who gave their solemn take on the market's direction.

It was in one of these adjacent rooms at the Orlando Money Show that Alfred R. Berkeley III, then the recently appointed president of the Nasdaq Stock Market,[3] found himself standing before a lunchtime crowd in March 1997. Facing the audience, Berkeley extolled the Nasdaq's phenomenal successes of the late 1980s and 1990s. One of his favorite stories, he said, "is the retired school teacher from the Seattle area who told us she bought 100 shares of Microsoft, at the time a small hometown start-up. She got in on the initial public offering back in 1986—and never sold." Berkeley then explained that the 100 shares purchased by the retired schoolteacher for about $21 each had since split several times, and they were now worth something like $342,000.[4]

No doubt, the Nasdaq had been responsible for many thousands of similar success stories. However, Berkeley's speech was not aimed at simply hyping the Nasdaq. Rather, he was part of a highly organized campaign of damage control. "Responding to concerns you might have with respect to the market," he told the audience, "is why we're at this conference." During the mid-1990s, the National Association of Securities Dealers (NASD) was forced to launch its damage-control efforts following a series of investigations by the Securities and Exchange Commission (SEC) and the Justice Department over price fixing and other alleged abuses by some NASD member firms. These investigations and the resulting charges and lawsuits led to cries of foul play in the business press. And they would severely tarnish the group's reputation for several years. At a time when evidence of America's astounding new wealth could be found in any supermarket parking lot filled with high-priced SUVs, here was a sign that Wall Street insiders who were already sweeping millions from the market had succumbed to rampant greed. Now it appeared as if they were stealing billions directly from investors' pockets. As a consequence, the Nasdaq and its member firms were being forced to pay out hundreds of millions of dollars.

However, in the ensuing years a different view has emerged. It is now clear—as the next two chapters will discuss—that few outside Wall Street circles really understood the full scope of what went on, including some who were involved with the investigations. Indeed, it is possible that the abuses were less pervasive than what was alleged. Some even maintain that little wrongdoing may have occurred at all.

But best to start at the beginning.

The Big Deal over Odd-Eighths Quotes

WHAT WOULD BECOME known as the Nasdaq marketmaker scandal began obscurely enough. Two professors, William Christie of Vanderbilt University and Paul Schultz of Ohio State University, announced that they had studied a sampling of 100 of the most actively traded Nasdaq stocks during 1991. In particular, they wanted to learn how market makers quoted the prices of those stocks to investors.[5] What they discovered was that market makers appeared to consistently avoid quoting bid or ask prices in odd eighths.[6] For example, suppose that a market maker were quoting shares of XYZ stock at $30^1/4$ bid. Wishing to increase his inventory, for whatever reason, he might raise the price he was willing to pay. But rather than raising it to $30^3/8$, he would jump it to $30^1/2$, thus avoiding the odd-eighths quote. Market makers do more than post prices at which they are willing to buy shares. They post sell prices as well. And when posting sell, or "ask," prices, Christie and Schultz observed that market makers likewise avoided odd-eighths quotes.

On the surface, it appears as if the market maker is actually cheating himself out of one-eighth point per share. That is, he is paying one-eighth more by posting a bid at $30^1/2$ than he would at $30^3/8$. True enough. But Christie and Schultz's research implied that by avoiding odd-eighths quotes, the market makers were creating artificially wide spreads—the spread being the difference between the bid and ask price that each market maker quotes. As a rule, market makers profit from a stock's spread and not the actual price for which they buy and sell the stock. This is because, over the course of the trading day, the prices of individual stocks routinely fluctuate. The spread follows these fluctuations. If you were to buy a stock and then immediately sell it back, in addition to commission costs, you would lose an amount equivalent to the spread.

The money would be pocketed by the market maker. And under normal circumstances, this would be deemed fair payment for holding the stock in inventory and assuming the risk of ownership. Nevertheless, for market makers wider spreads meant bigger profits. But these profits could only be had, Nasdaq's critics charged, if everyone went along and did their part to keep spreads wide. By doing so, an individual market maker might lose out on the profit potential from a single trade, but like a loyal union member who refuses to break the strike line, the market maker in the long run hoped to benefit from the wide spreads tacitly enforced by everyone through the hundreds of trades he or she made daily. Traders who broke ranks with their cohorts and narrowed spreads found this out when they reportedly received irate phone calls from other market makers.[7]

Christie and Schultz noted studies that showed that spreads on the Nasdaq were an average of 15 to 18 cents wider than NYSE-traded stocks of comparably sized companies. This negated the potential argument that Nasdaq spreads were wider than average because of the large number of small-cap, lightly traded issues listed there and the relatively higher risks associated with trading those stocks. If Christie and Schultz's finding was true, it meant that investors were being cheated.

This was the exact opposite of how many believed the Nasdaq market was supposed to function. Recall that on the NYSE, a single specialist more or less monopolized trading on the exchange, whereas on the Nasdaq various dealers or market makers stood ready not only to buy stocks but to sell them as well. In theory, because many dealers were competing with one another on the Nasdaq, spreads should be narrower. For this reason, Nasdaq specialists had not been subjected to many of the stringent regulations that their specialist counterparts on the NYSE had been. Competition should have kept them honest, unless they somehow colluded to keep spreads wide. As the authors wrote:

> We believe that this surprising result reflects an implicit agreement among market makers to avoid using odd-eighths in quoting bid and ask prices and that a large number of market makers per stock is not necessarily synonymous with competition.[8]

The authors acknowledged that there might be some other cause for the odd-eighths quotes. They went on to discuss how differences in the structure of the NYSE and the Nasdaq might lead to differing practices. Like the technical details that surface when resolving an international trade dispute or antitrust case, these differences between markets patterned after the NYSE and the Nasdaq appear arcane to many. And they might even be dismissed, were it not that billions of dollars were perhaps involved. Essentially, the differences had to do with the way limit orders were treated on both markets. Limit orders are orders to buy or sell stocks where the investor specifies the price at which he is willing to trade. They differ from the more common market orders that are executed at whatever the prevailing price happens to be. And that is true whether the limit order is sent to the NYSE or to the Nasdaq.

However, at the time it could be said that the NYSE treated customer limit orders with more respect than the Nasdaq. On the NYSE, the price that appears for a stock may be the price that a specialist happens to be bidding for its shares at that moment. However, it may also be the price that a small investor advertises he or she will pay for the same shares via a limit order. If the limit order price is superior to the price that the specialist is advertising at that moment, the specialist is obligated to post that price for other investors to see, even if this means placing the customer's limit order price ahead of his own. The customer limit order, in this case, becomes the best available price for the stock at that moment. And that order will execute the next time a market order arrives at the specialist's post.

Put another way, on the NYSE, limit orders at the time gave market participants a more accurate, transparent picture of the prevailing price of a stock. Talk about empowerment. If XYZ happens to be selling for $40.65 and you would like to buy it for $40.70, you simply enter a limit order for the higher amount. The specialist trading XYZ will put your order ahead of his own. If a seller takes the other side of your trade, the $40.70 limit order you entered will represent the market capitalization of the company at that instant in time. You could raise the market capitalization of XYZ by tens of millions of dollars—at least for that moment—simply by entering a limit order.

On the Nasdaq, nothing remotely like this took place during the time of the Christie and Schultz study. Instead, numerous dealers quoted prices that they were willing to buy and sell shares for. In addition to fielding different bid and ask prices, each market maker might also maintain a different spread between his bid and ask price. The resulting melee of prices is difficult to follow, as anyone who has watched the action on a Level II screen can attest. But here is the significant difference: When customers at that time entered limit orders, they were normally sent first to their brokers, who in turn might route them to a particular market maker. However, the market maker, unlike the NYSE specialist, was under no obligation to display your limit order, even if it reflected a better price than he was offering at the time. Thus, customer limit orders did not alter the price of the bid and ask. For this reason the Nasdaq was sometimes referred to as a quote driven market, since market makers display quotes that form the basis for price negotiation. By contrast, the NYSE was said to be an order-driven market, since actual limit orders fielded by the specialist or a customer determined the price at that instant. On the Nasdaq, the only time you could detect the presence of a limit order is if it was executed. In that case, it might show up as the execution price of the last trade. The bottom line was that, simply by glancing at the bid and ask prices broadcast by market makers as part of their Level II quote display, it was impossible to know how many people had posted limit orders inside those prevailing spreads. Only the market makers knew how many, and that gave them a big advantage.

Flak Attacks

CHRISTIE AND SCHULTZ planned to publish their results in the December issue of the *Journal of Finance*. However, word of their research reached the press in late May. The result, predictably, was a public relations nightmare—one that the NASD and its members at first badly mishandled. A panicked meeting was held at the office of Bear Sterns headquarters on Tuesday, May 24. The NASD brought along its heavy guns. The NASD's chief executive officer, chief operating officer, and president, Richard Ketchum, stood with William Broka, senior vice president of trading and market services, and John Wall, executive vice president of marketing and market operations. The three addressed a group of more than 100 market makers representing all the NASD member firms. NASD officials reportedly told those gathered to narrow spreads so that they would be in line with those of other exchanges.[9]

Some of the market makers present blamed the SOES (small-order execution system) bandits (see chapter 6) for the wider spreads, saying that the flood of orders they sent forced market makers to keep spreads wide as a protective measure. But the NASD officials reportedly argued back that SOES bandits were no longer a credible excuse for the wide spreads, thanks to rule changes in December 1993 that reduced the exposure to SOES orders that market makers were obligated to trade. Spreads had remained wide despite the rule changes.[10] If they did not narrow quickly, Nasdaq officials reportedly stressed, the result would be heavy-handed regulation by the NASD. More ominously, it would permit the SEC to meddle in the NASD's own turf.[11]

The message at the Bear Sterns meeting was received perhaps too well. By the end of the week, the spreads on stocks such as Amgen, Cisco, and Microsoft miraculously narrowed by 50 percent. And market makers began quoting prices in these stocks in odd eighths. By then, the *Wall Street Journal,* the *Los Angeles Times,* and other newspapers had picked up the story. As Christie and Schultz wrote, "The results for Apple and Microsoft indicate that the switch to quoting odd eighths occur almost simultaneously for all dealers."[12]

What better evidence could there be that price fixing had in fact occurred? As one money manager noted, "The ultimate weirdness is that they [the spreads] changed after the study was released."[13]

The Nasdaq submitted a study of its own rebutting Christie and Schultz's results to the *Journal of Finance*. But this tactic also backfired. After all, the journal had published the works of Nobel laureates such as William Sharpe and Harry Markowitz. Clearly, it had its standards. The editors accepted just over 6 percent of papers submitted. Nor was the journal a stranger to scandal. A 1992 paper that it published by two professors from the University of Chicago had caused a firestorm of controversy for attacking the beta, the classic measure of market volatility. The Nasdaq rebuttal was soundly rejected by the journal's peer review committee. When the Nasdaq appealed to the editors, they too rejected it. Later, lawyers suing Nasdaq market makers reportedly pointed to the rejection as further evidence of Nasdaq wrongdoing: "A lame industry rebuttal has been rejected twice by the *Journal of Finance*," they wrote in one of their briefs.[14]

Alas, the NASD's problems were just beginning. By July, civil lawsuits alleging collusion had been filed against "33 major dealers." The Justice Department began looking into possible antitrust violations in October.[15] Meanwhile, the NASD's critics charged that the practice of quoting in odd eighths had been common knowledge within the financial industry for years. Worse, not only did the NASD know about it, but NASD officials were accused of covering up any attempts to make it known. By doing so, the NASD had shirked its responsibilities as a self-regulatory organization, they charged. Critics also claimed that the SEC was aware of the practice. And it too had failed to take action. The latter charges more or less forced the SEC's hand. In November 1994, the SEC launched an investigation of the NASD's conduct as a self-regulatory organization.[16] In the course of the investigation, the commission interviewed hundreds of financial industry officials and listened in on hours of taped conversations between market makers. The results were published in a 56-page report called the "Report Pursuant to Section 21(a) of the Securities Exchange Act of

1934 Regarding the NASD and the Nasdaq Market," which later became known simply as the 21(a) Report. It was full of bad news for the Nasdaq.

A Chinese Market

FOR STARTERS, THE SEC accused Nasdaq market makers of systematically indoctrinating new colleagues on the how they were expected to quote shares to one another. Failure to follow the rules was thought to be "unprofessional," as the following official transcript illustrates:

> Q: And through the period December '93 through December of '94, do you observe the market makers entered relatively few odd-eighths? And by that I mean, with perhaps one or two exceptions *under 10 percent of their quotes were odd eighths* in McCormick [a stock].
>
> A: Yes, ma'am.
>
> Q: *And again, is that, in your professional opinion, because those market makers had three-quarter-point dealer spreads and did not want to enter what were termed "unprofessional markets"?*
>
> A: *Yes, ma'am.*
>
> Q: How is it that all of the market makers knew that entering an odd-eighth quote could be unprofessional?
>
> A: *Young traders were trained over the years not to put in unprofessional markets, "Chinese markets." . . . This was part of the . . . traditional and ethical on-the-job training that all of us got, and it encompasses not only that you don't put in unprofessional-looking "Chinese markets," it . . . grew out of a self-imposed industry standard of ethics and conduct.* So that's my answer as to why everybody seems to be doing this, because most of the people were trained the same way. [Italics in the original.][17]

But that was only the beginning. Nasdaq market makers traded with each other via telephone. And for purposes of verification, these conversations were routinely recorded. The resulting evidence proved damning. If a market maker appeared to follow the odd-eighths pricing convention, his colleagues at other firms were not averse to picking up the phone and complaining about it. The SEC investigation labeled such calls harassment. Here's one example:

> Trader 1: *Who trades CMCAF in your place* without yelling it out?
> Trader 2: . . . Sammy.
> Trader 1: Sammy who?
> Trader 2: It may be the foreign department . . .
> Trader 1: What?
> Trader 2: The foreign didn't realize they had to trade it.
> Trader 1: Well, he's trading it in an eighth and he's embarrassing . . .
> Trader 2: . . . foreign department.
> Trader 1: *He's trading it in eighths and he's embarrassing your firm.*
> Trader 2: *I understand.*
> Trader 1: You know. *I would tell him to straighten up his* [expletive deleted] *act and stop being a moron.* [Italics in the original.][18]

Traders testified that when firms continued to violate the pricing convention, they were punished in other ways, including the refusal of other market makers to execute deals. Coercion of this kind reportedly formed only one component of a little-understood system of incentives that rewarded those who went along with the quoting convention. For example, while many market makers technically competed with each other for retail order flow for a particular stock, one market maker or market-making firm would often emerge as that stock's dominant dealer called the "name." And as a *Forbes* magazine investigation[19] revealed, the less dominant dealers would mimic the name's spread. Some even programmed their trading workstations so they would automatically mimic the name's bid and ask. The rewards to market making firms were considerable. The NASD estimates that the 1992 gross profits generated by the firms making a market in its stocks at about $2.76 billion— an increase of 50 percent from four years earlier, *Forbes* reported. Operating margins in at least one case were as high as 25 percent. Little wonder, the number of market making firms reportedly rose from 407 in 1986 to 472 ten years later.

Some market-making operations were a division of a larger firm that dealt directly with retail customers. In such cases, profits from the wider spreads amounted to a two-fold commission. This commission could in turn be passed down to the firm's brokers. The *Forbes* study revealed that while firms paid their brokers "33 percent of gross commissions" on NYSE listed stocks, commissions on Nasdaq stocks reached 40 percent. The added commission, of course represented a powerful incentive for brokers to recommend Nasdaq stocks over those of exchange-listed shares. And this was a reason many firms may have stayed with the Nasdaq, since the aggressive sales of their stock would bolster the price.

Rigging Trades

IN SHORT, FIRMS could make higher profits trading OTC stocks, whether hawking shares to customers or acting as middlemen in trades. This had been the case back in the earliest days of the OTC market. The Nasdaq network was launched to bring order to the pricing process. Now some dealers had devised a way to use the Nasdaq to collude on spreads. It turned out that price fixing was the least of the abuses uncovered by SEC investigators. According to the 21(a) Report, in numerous cases market makers worked together to coordinate their price quotations, their transactions in securities, and their trade reports. Investigators discovered that some market makers deliberately misquoted the prices that they were willing to trade stocks for. In some cases, their motive was to assist other market makers by creating artificial increases or decreases in the stocks' prices. In other cases, several market makers acted in concert to systematically raise or lower a stock's price, in effect trading the shares back and forth among one another or stalling before they reported an executed trade. All such actions were at the expense of their clients, to whom the market makers owned a regulatory responsibility to provide a quality and honest execution.[20]

The report also accused some market makers of sharing information about the size of customer orders, even the identity of their customers, when this knowledge might telegraph a short-term price move. This, too, amounted to a betrayal of their clients' trust, and a costly one, if the client engaged in block trades. For example, if a large institution was buying up shares of XYZ stock, this presented an opportunity for other market makers as a group to buy up and then profit by selling them—a cozy arrangement.

In the end, the SEC's charges boiled down to four areas: tape painting, front running, refusing to honor posted quotes, and delaying reported trades.[21]

Tape painting refers to the practice of broadcasting phony quotes in order to deceive investors about the direction the market is taking. The term originated in the days when quotes were disseminated via ticker tape. In 1994, quotes appeared on computer screens. But the effect was the same: Investors are compelled to pay more or sell at a lower price than they might have ordinarily.

In such cases, a market maker might call on other market makers to assist in misquoting stocks. As the SEC study noted, their motives for this might include having a sizable customer order or an inventory imbalance they wished to correct. The following taped transcript illustrates this:

On June 17, 1994, a market maker (Market Maker 1) in the common stock of AES Corp. (AESC) had an order to buy a quantity of AESC stock. Market Maker 1 entered a bid of $18¼, a quarter point above the other bids in the market, to attract sellers. Another market maker (Market Maker 2) had an order to sell AESC stock. Market Maker 2 called and asked Market Maker 1 to lower its bid because Market Maker 2 wanted to pay less for the stock it was buying (as the counter party to the order to sell that it had received).

MM 2: I've just seen you go ¼ bid. Without like going through a whole bunch of, you know, ——— I know I got a bunch of these for sale at the opening. I would rather buy them at 18, if you know what I'm saying. If there's a ticket to write, I will write it with you [meaning I will sell some AESC stock to you if you are looking to buy some].

MM 1: There absolutely is a ticket to write.

MM 2: OK.

MM 1: I can make a sale at the opening myself.

MM 2: You can?

MM 1: Yes.

MM 2: OK, so.

MM 1: As long as it's [name withheld] I can go down.

Trading records indicate that Market Maker 1 dropped its bid price to $18. Market Maker 2 proceeded to purchase 8,000 shares of AESC stock at $18. In the meantime, Market Maker 1 sold 16,700 shares at $18½ to its customer, of which 7,500 shares were sold short.

Market Maker 2 subsequently sold 6,500 shares to Market Maker 1 at $18¼. Market Maker 2 injured the interests of the seller by asking Market Maker 1 to lower its bid price so that Market Maker 2 could pay $18 per share, rather than $18¼ (a difference of $2,000 for the entire trade). Market Maker 1 was also a participant, since it changed its bid at Market Maker 2's request, to create a deceptive appearance to the market, and made it harder for the seller to observe the true level of buying interest.[22]

A variation on this arrangement, called front running, could prove even more lucrative for a market maker. Front running relies heavily on information that only the market maker is normally privy to. Here is how it works: Suppose that you are a market maker and receive a customer buy order for 10,000 shares of XYZ stock. You are well aware that such a large order will inevitably move the price higher since it will sop up any shares for sale that may be available at that moment. Thus, rather than simply fielding the 10,000-share offer, you first buy 1,000 shares yourself, hold them in inventory, and then field your 10,000-share order. When XYZ's price rises, you can sell the shares you bought for a quick profit. Front running is particularly harmful to large institutional traders. Because they parlay thousands of shares at a time, they routinely run into something called market impact, that is, the extra cost they must pay because their large order adversely affects supply. Estimates vary, but market impact can add from 1 to 4 percent or more to the cost of a trade depending on the trading volume of the stock involved. Some say it is the reason index funds often outperform managed funds. Front running, if it occurs, only exacerbates this problem.

The market makers' third deadly sin was refusing to execute orders at their own posted quotes. This is more a defensive mechanism than one designed to skim excess profits from a trade. Market makers back away from honoring their own quotes when they believe that the other trader knows something they do not. Once again, suppose that you are a market maker quoting the price on XYZ, the stock of a large computer manufacturer, as it drifts within a narrow range. Suddenly, a large sell order hits your bid price. You know that the order originates from a highly regarded institutional trader who specializes in the computer sector. And so you have to ask yourself, Is there news out there that will send this stock tumbling in a minute or two? If so, should you too be a seller? By refusing to honor quotes, market makers may create a self-fulfilling prophecy. That is, they may widen a stock's actual spread, causing its price to drop as a result. Other market makers, seeing what you are doing, might follow suit. And they likely would be joined by day traders. The end result might be a sudden drop in the stock's price and in the absence of news. The effect is a little like a school of fish scattering in shallow water when a cloud causes a shadow on the sandy bottom.

Perhaps the clearest case of collusion among market makers was in the fourth category of the SEC's complaint: late trade reporting. Delayed trade reporting can help market makers secure profits without their customers' or regulators' knowledge. By trading among themselves, they can run up the price of the stock, each profiting along the way. The SEC cites an example of delayed trade reporting that went awry:

> Three market makers arranged for a sequence of four trades in the common stock of PXRE Corp., in which shares sold by Market Maker 1's customer would ultimately be bought by Market Maker 3's customer. Market Maker 3 did not want its customer to see the true sequence of trades and obtained Market Maker 2's promise to hold its trade report and asked Market Maker 2 to secure Market Maker 1's agreement to hold its trade reports. Market Maker 1 agreed to hold its trade reports for ten minutes. Market Maker 2 told Market Maker 3 that Market Maker 1 would hold his trade reports but omitted to say for ten minutes only. The trades occurred as follows:
>
> 1. MM1 bought 20,000 shares at $24^{1}/_{2}$ from its customer at approximately 12:15 P.M. (Trade A).
>
> 2. MM1 sold 20,000 shares at $24^{9}/_{16}$ to MM2 at approximately 12:18 P.M. (Trade B).
>
> 3. MM2 sold 20,000 shares at $24^{19}/_{32}$ to MM3 at approximately 12:23 P.M. (Trade C).
>
> 4. MM3 sold 20,000 shares at $24^{11}/_{16}$ to its customer at approximately 12:24 P.M. (Trade D).
>
> These trades were reported, however, in the following sequence:

1. MM3 reported its sale of 20,000 shares at $24^{11}/_{16}$ to its customer at 12:24:51 P.M. (Trade D).

2. MM1 reported its purchase of 20,000 shares at $24^1/_2$ from its customer at 12:25:01 P.M. (Trade A).

3. MM1 reported its sale of 20,000 shares at $24^9/_{16}$ to MM2 at 12:28:00 P.M. (Trade B).

4. MM2 reported its sale of 20,000 shares at $24^{19}/_{32}$ to MM3 1:26:12 P.M. (Trade C).

None of the last three trades was reported with an ".SLD" modifier, which would have identified it as a late trade report. Because Market Maker 1 reported its lower priced trades immediately after Market Maker 3 reported its trade with its customer, Market Maker 3, in an angry frame of mind, spoke to Market Maker 2:

MM3: So now I got ———, okay. . . . I hope I don't have to cancel the trade, but I might have to because as soon as the ——— guy [MM3's customer] sees it, you know, the ——— guy is going to start jumping up and down, okay.

MM2: Were you able to sell it?

MM3: I sold 'em. I mean the guy didn't get the ——— report yet, you know what I mean?[23]

A perfect example of collusion? Note how, according to this SEC example, the market makers collectively pocketed several thousand dollars as a result of this trade—at the expense of the customer. Practices like this show the difficulties regulators face when analyzing trade reports to detect abuses. And they helped foster the belief that the markets were rigged by insiders. If large investors such as the client in this example could fall victim to collusion, what chance did ordinary investors have?

So why did so many traders apparently go along with such practices? Peer pressure was a chief reason, according to one trader who admitted that he had made calls questioning other market makers' "unprofessional quotations." According to his testimony, "No man or woman who is a trader wants to have people think you are a fool, at least not when you are working for a reputable firm, you have institutional clients out there. . . . And that's the kind of pressure I'm talking about."[24]

Whatever the reasons, the resulting damage would be horrendous. The Nasdaq would spend an enormous sum placating the SEC and its other critics, as you will see in the next chapter. And after a great deal of stumbling, it would undergo a massive restructuring. Sadly, recouping from the market-maker scandal would occupy the Nasdaq at a time when the tech-heavy market continued its long march skyward. However, unforeseen by anyone, the restructuring would also be the catalyst that radically transformed securities markets around the world. And it would help bring investors to the playing tables in numbers never seen before.

CHAPTER 8

THE EVIDENCE GETS UGLIER

OFFICIAL OUTRAGE IN Washington, D.C., where the National Association of Securities Dealers (NASD) maintained
its offices, continued to mount as more details of the spread-
fixing scandal surfaced. When the news first broke, the evidence had merely pointed to those market makers involved.
However, as the investigations proceeded, blame began to
fall increasingly on the NASD as well. The NASD's critics
charged that the association had known full well about the
abuses by its members. But it had done nothing. As a result,
the NASD faced a barrage of attacks during the waning
months of 1994—and from three fronts. Lawyers launched

class-action suits against the Nasdaq's major market-making firms in July. The Justice Department began its investigation in October. By November, the Securities and Exchange Commission (SEC) was moved to act.

The SEC investigation would continue well into 1998[1] and would ultimately prove the most damaging. The taped transcripts of market makers colluding or enforcing the odd-eighths quote edict (see chapter 7) were bad enough. But the SEC had also caught the NASD itself red-handed. According to the SEC, officials at the NASD had been aware of the odd-eighths quote scandal since 1990.[2] As proof, the SEC cited a letter sent in August 1989 by the New York Stock Exchange (NYSE) to a Nasdaq-listed company. The letter brought up the fact that Nasdaq spreads were wider than the spreads for comparable NYSE stocks. And for that reason, it urged the company to jump ship and list with the NYSE. A copy of the letter eventually reached the NASD high command, where it caused enough of a row that the NASD Trading Committee met to talk about it the following June. Most of those in attendance also worked for NASD-member market-making firms.[3] While keeping the identities of those at the meeting confidential, the SEC was able to report in detail about what went on. At least one person in attendance urged his colleagues to narrow the spreads, or else risk further defections to the NYSE. Someone else reportedly countered that the pricing convention represented an "ethic" or "internal matter." In the end, the committee took no definitive action, deciding that the odd-eighths quote convention was not something they should legislate against. Instead, it was viewed as a "commercial issue." If anyone should look into the matter, those at the meeting concluded, it was an industry trade group, such as the Security Traders Association of New York.

The issue of wide spreads surfaced again at a March 1992 meeting of the NASD's Quality of Markets Committee. Topics at the meeting mirrored those that would later surface in the

SEC's own investigation. The alleged intimidation of market makers who failed to adhere to the quoting convention was discussed, as were other ways market makers allegedly enforced the convention. The results of the meeting and other findings were summarized in an internal NASD report that became known as the June 1992 Memo. Among other things, the memo urged the NASD to stand behind those who broke the odd-eighths convention. "We need to support those market makers who attempt to compete through the price improvement process and also make it clear that tampering or using coercion in influencing other's [sic] pricing decision is a violation of fair trade practices."[4] In fact, the June 1992 Memo described how spreads had actually increased by 63 percent between the first quarter of 1989 and May 1992. The memo was reviewed by some of NASD's executive management.[5]

Remedial Reforms

THE NASDAQ'S RESPONSE to the June 1992 Memo was to make narrowing spreads a corporate goal during the course of that year. Various suggestions were put forth, including revamping SOES (small-order execution system) order handling rules to limit market maker exposure and placing a cap on the acceptable width of spreads. These suggestions notably came after NASD planners had devised a revamped electronic order-execution system called N*Prove. This was intended to replace SOES, which provided a direct link between retail customers and market makers. The NASD's market-making firms had long cited SOES trading as a key reason that they were forced to maintain wide spreads. Under the SOES system, smaller customer orders were routed by wire directly to market makers, where they were automatically executed. However, particularly in fast markets, the market makers were often unable to update their quotes quickly enough to reflect the current market price. Thus, a skilled retail trader using SOES and a powerful trading software package could buy stocks at a price lower than the prevailing price in the market and then quickly sell them elsewhere at the higher current price. (See chapter 6 for a more complete discussion of SOES trading tactics.)

Responding to the alleged threat of SOES traders, called SOES bandits, the NASD had already modified its SOES. N*Prove took these changes further still. It gave market makers 15 seconds to decline incoming small orders. But it also allowed customer limit orders to be displayed in a kind of customer-based Level II display. N*Prove was formally submitted to the SEC in 1994. But because of concerns voiced by the SEC, the proposal was withdrawn before the SEC formally acted on it.[6]

The SEC report on its investigation cited a third instance where the NASD had failed to act on evidence of spread fixing. In late 1993, NASD officials received a draft of the Christie and Schultz study, with its seemingly damning evidence.[7] But, as noted in the previous chapter, the NASD's response at the time was to try to refute its results. All in all, the SEC charged that knowledge of violations was widespread during the early 1990s. And by ignoring the evidence, the NASD had shirked its responsibilities as a self-regulating organization.

But the SEC must have known full well that it had ignored the evidence, too. On December 8, 1992, it had received a letter from the American Stock Exchange alleging that "Nasdaq quoted spreads almost never vary, and that dealers do not narrow spreads because of concern that other market makers will not 'play ball' with them and help them lay off position risk."[8] Also, on August 16 of the following year, in full view of the financial community, *Forbes* magazine reported that "Nasdaq market makers were reluctant to narrow the spreads and made complaining telephone calls to market makers who did."[9] Neither incident had sparked an SEC investigation.

The Rudman Report

ROUGHLY SIX MONTHS after news of the market-making scandal first broke, the NASD did take a stab at real reform on its own. In November 1994, right at the time the SEC was launching its own probe, the NASD Board of Governors created a kind of internal affairs investigative panel called the NASD Select Committee on Structure and Governance. It was chaired by former U.S. Senator Warren Rudman, who would later manage Senator John McCain's 2000 presidential run. The group[10] included several former SEC regulators,[11] and it soon became known as the Rudman Committee. The Rudman Committee's mandate was "to review the NASD's governance structures and the NASD's oversight of the Nasdaq market"[12]

As it looked for where to lay blame, the Rudman Committee deconstructed the NASD's entire regulatory and disciplinary processes as well as its organizational structure. Tellingly, it found that the NASD was ruled over by "a host of committees" and that each committee had the ability and the authority to look out for its own interests. One committee in particular, the Trading Committee, had "significant influence over the Nasdaq market and trading systems."[13] The Trading Committee functioned as the NASD board's eyes and ears when it came to the Nasdaq market. It recommended rules. Yet all the while, it guarded the interests of Nasdaq market-making firms. "It is quite literally a traders' committee," the Rudman Committee noted, "and more importantly, a dealer's committee."[14] That is, it was a committee headed by market makers for market makers.

Rudman's investigators also looked at other Nasdaq standing committees, including the Market Surveillance Committee and the SOES Users Committee, noting that market makers dominated the decision making there as well. To prevent another spread-fixing scandal from occurring, the NASD's committee structure needed reforming, the Rudman group said.

There had to be some separation of church and state. Accordingly, in the report it submitted to the NASD on September 15, 1995, the Rudman Committee recommended that the NASD be transformed into a kind of holding company with two separate divisions under its wings. The first division would oversee operations of the Nasdaq stock market, while a separate division, called NASD Regulation, Inc., would handle regulatory and disciplinary issues.

To keep the interests of market makers at bay, the Rudman Committee also recommended that the majority of NASD board members come from outside the ranks of NASD member firms. That is, they should not be employed by trading firms. At the time, the NASD board had 20 percent public representation, while one-third of the Nasdaq board was composed of outsiders.[15]

Reforming NASD's board struck at the heart of what the SEC and others had often viewed as a basic flow in the association's organizational structure. According to this view, the NASD as a self-regulatory organization was constantly at cross-purposes with itself. On the one hand, it was mandated to provide an honest and open playing field to the public. Yet at the same time, it was a membership organization, governed by those who naturally wanted to champion their own interests. Thus, in retrospect it seemed inevitable that the NASD's governing committees had allowed their colleagues to stray.

Summarizing its findings, Rudman described NASD's disciplinary process as basically sound. Problems arose because the NASD had grown too large to pursue all potential wrongdoers. "The inescapable fact is that the NASD's structure was tailored to the relatively insignificant OTC markets of an earlier era, not the second largest securities market in the United States."[16]

Taking its cue from that conclusion, a September 19, 1995, press release announcing the NASD's acceptance of the Rudman Committee results pointed out that NASD at the time oversaw 5,400 securities firms, with a total of 57,000 branch offices, and an estimated 500,000 "representatives doing business with investors, making it by far the largest self-regulatory organization in the securities industry." The statement also noted that trading volume on the Nasdaq had doubled to 74.3 billion shares between 1990 and 1994."[17] Keeping tabs on all that was indeed a tall order.

Nevertheless, many charged that the Rudman report merely stated the obvious. Further, they said that its recommendations did not go nearly far enough. In a March 1996 editorial, *Chief Financial Officer* magazine found fault with two of the report's recommendations. First, the NASD reorganization would be too cumbersome to work, the writer claimed. "The parent board plus two subsidiary boards would number about 50 members in all, and thus be particularly susceptible to politicization and indecision." Second, the NASD would still control Nasdaq, and so the fundamental conflict of interest would persist. Interestingly, the writer noted that, given Nasdaq's structure, dealers had little interest in measures that would benefit the market as a whole. Since Nasdaq was a non-profit organization they had nothing to gain financially if the market itself became more profitable. However, if those dealers were to become shareholders of a privatized Nasdaq, then they could reap the rewards as the market grew.[18]

The solution put forth by the writer and others was that the Nasdaq become a publicly held company, to be regulated by the federal government. The precedent for this could be found in public utilities and with the Federal Home Loan Mortgage Corporation (Freddie Mac). That recommendation would be taken to heart by the NASD at the start of the new millennium.

Its critics notwithstanding, SEC officials reportedly faced strong pressure from financial firms to rubber-stamp the Rudman Committee's recommendations. Yet they were reportedly angry about the report, charging that the Rudman Committee proposals were only cosmetic and that they would fail to keep market makers in line.[19] Knowing that they faced an uphill battle to get SEC approval, NASD officials nevertheless accepted the Rudman Committee's recommendations just four days after they were submitted.[20]

The Justice Department Investigation

ROUGHLY 10 MONTHS after the Rudman Committee released its results, the Justice Department weighed in with the results of its own investigation. On July 17, 1996, the department charged 24 major Nasdaq securities firms with "fixing transaction costs."[21] The firms named were some of the Street's largest and best known at the time, including Merrill Lynch, Goldman Sachs & Co., Dean Witter Reynolds, and J. P. Morgan Securities.

All the firms named could breathe a sigh of relief, however, since the Justice Department statement had not cited collusion or called for criminal penalties or fines.[22] What the department did call for was improved compliance procedures. Trading firms were required to install taping systems to monitor and record 3.5 percent of all trader telephone conversations at their over-the-counter desk. Any evidence of wrongdoing had to be turned over to the Justice Department within 10 business days. Moreover, Justice Department officials could show up at a firm's office, unannounced, and listen in on trader conversations themselves if they desired.[23]

Like the Rudman Committee report, the Justice Department actions faced public criticism. Lawyers in the class-action suits against Nasdaq firms tried to halt the department-invoked settlement by going to court. The lawyers suing brokerage firms were reportedly upset with a provision that disallowed the use of the tapes in any future legal actions. However, the judge in the case maintained the provision.[24] Other critiques of the Justice Department decision wondered why no fines were levied and no criminal action was taken. The most vocal criticism came from investor advocate groups and smaller Nasdaq-member broker-ages[25] that had long felt underrepresented by the NASD.

The SEC Investigation

THE SEC FOLLOWED the Justice Department action with the results of its own investigation on August 7, 1996. Like the Rudman Committee, the SEC focused attention on the Nasdaq's inner workings and how these had led it to alleged wrongdoing. The report noted that the influence of market makers permeated deep within the NASD's decision-making process and that market makers strongly influenced the discipline of offending member firms. Like the Rudman Committee, the SEC also looked for endemic flaws in the NASD's structure:

> Much of the market makers' influence over the disciplinary process came from their participation in the District Business Conduct Committees ("DBCCs"). The DBCCs have had a "grand jury" function, in which the NASD staff must seek DBCC authorization to initiate a disciplinary action. The DBCCs also serve as adjudicative bodies, which decide the outcome of litigated enforcement proceedings and approve settlements. The grand jury function provides the NASD's industry members with the ability to veto NASD staff enforcement recommendations and allows them to prosecute those cases they, sitting as members of the DBCC, deem appropriate. The adjudicatory role of the DBCC provides NASD members with a powerful and central role in the self-regulatory process.[26]

In other words, by acting as a grand jury, the DBCCs were able to decide for themselves whether the evidence warranted further action. "Meaningful self-regulation does not require that industry representatives also perform a grand jury function in the disciplinary process," the SEC said. "The objectivity and impartiality of the disciplinary process will be advanced by re-moving the DBCCs from the grand jury function and the po-tential for abuse that such a role entails."

The SEC also chastised the NASD's Market Surveillance Department for lax enforcement. For example, the report said that if a customer did not receive an execution at the quoted price as required, he or she had to file a written complaint with the Market Surveillance Department before the disciplinary process could even begin. Cases "could take months to re-solve," the SEC noted. Discipline often amounted to "letters of caution" or small fines. And even then, the complainant was not granted an executed trade. "Thus, backing away com-plaints were effectively discouraged," the SEC noted, "both by an ineffective procedure for enforcing the rule and by the ab-sence of adequate sanctions for demonstrated misconduct."[27]

While the SEC claimed that the NASD was reluctant to dis-cipline its own members' wrongdoings, it charged that the NASD zealously pursued outsiders who were at odds with its member firms. SOES trading firms in particular were singled out for NASD scrutiny, according to the SEC. Market makers had long complained about being deluged with SOES orders—enough to affect their ability to maintain an orderly trading environment.

This "precipitated a concerted effort by the NASD staff to bring disciplinary actions against SOES firms," the SEC said. "Substantial resources" from the NASD's New York office and the Market Surveillance Department were involved in the crackdown on SOES firms.[28] Those SOES firms singled out by market-maker complaints were "subjected to special SOES 'sweep' examinations, which in some cases resulted in discipli-nary actions." The NASD directory even contained a special telephone number to report violations, according to the SEC.

In its conclusion, the SEC stated simply, "The Commission has determined that the NASD's conduct . . . demonstrates a fail-ure to comply with its statutory obligations" as a self-regulatory organization.[29] The conclusion gave the SEC the right to impose sanctions. As you will see in the next chapter, these had already been worked out with the NASD by the time the results of the SEC investigation were released. As SEC Chairman Levitt later told a *Business Week* reporter, the problems at Nasdaq "should have been resolved a long time ago."[30]

Foes and Friends

IN THE WAKE of the SEC findings, the business press lambasted the NASD. The *Wall Street Journal,* for example, charged that the NASD "resembled a private club as much as the overseer of a professional market."[31] Echoing that view, *Business Week* charged that NASD officials saw the scandal as a public relations problem and that a short list of member firms "whose self interest was the status quo" influenced decision making at the top of the organization. Merrill Lynch, Smith Barney, and Dean Witter were specifically named.

The *Business Week* editorial also claimed that the NASD had fought the SEC investigation at every turn.[32] For example, accounts surfaced that the amount of Ketchum's bonus in 1995 was contingent on whether the SEC actually initiated disciplinary action against the NASD. When Levitt reportedly complained, the NASD withdrew the provision.[33] Ketchum later told the *Washington Post* that the bonus was intended to allow the NASD to devise a settlement without official action. He also said that he would have resigned if he had thought otherwise. Then in yet another case of mishandled public relations, it was revealed that when the NASD commissioned its own economist to study spread-fixing accusations, the economist's contract had reportedly contained a provision that if the NASD did not like the results, it would pay an extra $1,000 to silence the report.[34]

By late October of 1996, perhaps as part of the fallout from the investigations, the number of companies defecting to the

NYSE reached a record 69. During the entire previous year, 62 companies fled to the Big Board, up from 41 in 1994. A spokesperson for the NASD claimed that the defections had very little to do with the bad press. Rather, they were to be expected since the total number of Nasdaq-listed companies had grown from 4,094 to 5,437 from 1991 to 1996. More listings simply meant higher turnover.[35]

Yet, throughout its ordeal, the NASD was not entirely without allies. In July 1995, about 14 months after the scandal broke, the Financial Economists Roundtable (FER), a group of senior economists who regularly comment on macroeconomic issues, released a report aimed at casting doubt on the spread-fixing findings by the SEC and others. According to the group's statement:

> The Financial Economists Roundtable is skeptical that an effective and sustainable collusive arrangement is possible among Nasdaq dealers. Both economic theory and history provide substantial support for the belief that effective collusive arrangements generally require that two conditions be met: (1) there are a small number of firms, and (2) there exist significant barriers to entry. Neither of these conditions is met in the Nasdaq.[36]

True enough, over the years there had been perhaps tens of thousands of market makers plying their trades day after day. Getting such a large group to go against their individual interests and adhere to the quoting convention would seem difficult at best. Even so, the FER conclusion would still seem incredible in light of the intercepted taped conversations by the SEC and the Justice Department. Offending market makers were harassed.

Nevertheless, the FER cited other explanations for the wide spreads that were at least plausible to those familiar with the nuances of how the Nasdaq worked. For one thing, the FER noted, the Nasdaq trading system at the time was unlike the Big Board in an important respect: It did not display customer limit orders that arrived by wire. Thus, the spread broadcast by a market maker might appear wider than might actually be the case. The following example should illustrate this: A market maker trading XYZ stock might advertise a bid price of 10.75 and an ask price of 11. If a limit order arrived at 10.85, it would be invisible to anyone watching the trading screen, because no rule at the time required the market maker to display the limit order price. The market maker always had the option of executing the trade. Alternately, he might ignore it. If the trade were executed, it would be broadcast as the last sale. Other market makers might then choose to adjust their quotes accordingly. When market makers did execute a limit order in this way, it was known as price improvement. And indeed, price improvement was a common practice among Nasdaq market makers. Some might provide preferential pricing to valued customers when those orders were received through their own firm. Or the market maker's goal might be to acquire or sell shares. In either case, however, they would be reluctant to share this information with other dealers.

The FER's other explanation as to why spreads were wider on the Nasdaq had to do with a practice called preferencing. To understand preferencing, think again of the Level II screen that traders watch during the course of their day. Each bid and ask quote from a market maker is listed on the screen in order of price. As a trader, you might choose to single out a particular market maker and send an order directly to him, that is, preference that market maker. You might do this because you want to pick up as many shares as you can within a given price range, for example, because you expect the price to rise at any moment. In addition, you might use preferencing because you think that a particular market maker is a heavy buyer or seller at that moment and might give you the price you want.

In practice, preferencing is not unique to the Nasdaq. It exists with Big Board stocks to an extent. But for the most part, all NYSE orders theoretically pass through the specialist where they are either executed or else displayed for other investors to see. By contrast, Nasdaq market makers often want to avoid being deluged with orders, especially if they have reason to suspect that those on the other side of the trade may have more information than they about a stock's near-term direction. By widening their spreads, they can protect themselves while still executing limit orders in secret if they wish. As the FER noted, "Preferencing . . . may reduce the incentive for a dealer to improve bids or offers."[37]

At the time, one of the most common forms of preferencing was something called payment for order flow. Payment for order flow occurs when market makers in essence pay a kickback to retail brokers in exchange for orders from their retail customers. These orders—provided that they are market orders—are executed at the market's best prevailing price, as required. Market makers love to receive retail orders because they are said to be uninformed. That is, a retail customer is unlikely to know that the stock he or she is trading is about to make a significant price move. Therefore, they can be executed without fear. Market makers compete for retail orders by offering ever larger kickbacks. And this kickback is in lieu of a narrower spread. (The advent of decimalized quotes and the resulting narrowed spreads has since greatly reduced the practice of payment for order flow.)

Like Picking Produce

ODDLY ENOUGH, THE Congressional Budget Office also released an analysis of Nasdaq spread fixing. The report, titled "Price Fixing at Nasdaq? A Reconsideration of the Evidence," was written by Susan Woodward, who would later serve as chairman of the stock research firm Sand Hill Econometrics. Her analysis echoed many of the points raised by the FER. "I conclude that there is scant evidence of price fixing on Nasdaq," she wrote, though she hastened to add that "None of my analysis should be taken to imply that the SEC's other complaints are not serious."[38]

For starters, Woodward noted that "neither the SEC nor the NASD had rules against the use of any particular increments for quoting prices." Rather, she said, the SEC preferred to let the market dictate both spreads and prices. Moreover, she said that the important thing to focus on was not so much the spreads but the actual prices of the stocks themselves. In other words, who cares whether you are paying 25 cents as opposed to 15 cents more for a stock as a result of the spread if you still manage to buy that stock at $1 below what it might cost if traded through some other market. Do you begrudge Wal-Mart its markup if it is the cheapest place in town to buy groceries? That fact, Woodward claimed, was something that the SEC and other investigations failed to even address. But it is especially relevant to the Nasdaq. With thousands of smaller, lightly traded companies among its listings, the Nasdaq must have a way to ensure that there would always be a buyer and a seller for those stocks. And the way to do that was to fairly compensate those who were doing the buying and selling: the market makers. Wider spreads were thus a necessary evil.

Woodward then set about building her case on several fronts. For one thing, she noted that market makers, as everyone agreed, make their money on the spread and not on the level of prices. The more orders they receive, the more profit potential. Thus, while they might maintain wide spreads, they would have an incentive to charge competitive prices in order to attract more order flow. Conversely, "if dealers succeed in keeping spreads too wide, this will depress stock prices generally. Assets that are cheaper to trade, other things equal, are worth more," she claimed.[39]

Woodward also weighed in on the practice of preferencing, explaining that it naturally led to higher prices—again in the form of wider spreads. Preferencing, she explained, was akin to selecting oranges individually from a basket in a supermarket or buying them in bulk:

> The per pound price of the loose fruit is always higher, even if the loose fruit is exactly the same fruit emptied from the bags. This is because the customers who choose the loose fruit choose it adversely to the interests of the grocer. They choose the better, less blemished specimens, and leave the worse.[40]

No one, she said, accuses grocers of price fixing. Instead, we acknowledge their right to charge a higher price since it reduces our risk of getting blemished fruit.

Hidden Markets

TO GET A true picture of spreads on the Nasdaq, many financial experts believed, you needed to look at Instinet. A private trading network that allowed Nasdaq dealers to trade directly among themselves, Instinet accounted for anywhere from 15 to 25 percent of volume on the Nasdaq.[41] Instinet at the time was the more or less exclusive domain of skilled, institutional traders who bought and sold stocks for pension funds and mutual funds. For this reason, the traders knew how to negotiate with one another by fielding differing prices. The actual negotiation took the form of fielding and then retracting offers at varying price increments. And it had the effect of narrowing spreads. In fact, spreads on Instinet likely represented what spreads on the Nasdaq would be if limit orders were displayed and a comparable amount of informed price negotiation took place.

The same phenomenon that occurred on Instinet also occurred on a second private trading network, called SelectNet. According to the FER:

Alternative interdealer markets for Nasdaq listed stocks may reduce the incentive for dealers to post quotes that will narrow the displayed spread. An example is SelectNet, which is an interdealer trading system that allows dealers to trade among themselves at prices different from those available to the general public. Such parallel markets permit dealers to adjust their inventory without the need to offer better quotes over Nasdaq.[42]

If nothing else, these arguments siding with the Nasdaq reveal that trading is a lot more complicated than even those who performed the SEC study may have surmised. The findings also offer the possibility that the irate phone calls and other documented cases of harassment were indeed an attempt to enforce a convention that no one viewed as necessarily sinister—just as market makers had insisted all along. Nevertheless, much of the trading occurring on the Nasdaq had been done in secret. And secrecy inevitably breeds suspicion. Accordingly, as you will see in the next chapter, when the SEC searched for ways to reform the Nasdaq trading, its focus was on making it more transparent.

CHAPTER 9

THE RULES CHANGE

IT TOOK THE Securities and Exchange Commission (SEC) more than two years from the start of its investigation to lay down its actual punishment against the National Association of Securities Dealers (NASD) and its member market-making firms. That punishment took the form of the new order-handling rules enacted on January 20, 1997. Those rules required market makers "for the first time to show investors the size and prices for certain orders. The SEC also directs the market to open previously exclusive electronic systems, including Instinet and SelectNet."[1] The edict, though seemingly simple and spelled out in plain language, likely went over the heads of most investors. Only experienced traders could infer the radical changes that would result from the SEC's decision. And even top officials at the Nasdaq didn't foresee the far-reaching changes the new order-handling rules would bring.

The term "order handling" refers to the steps market makers are required to take when they receive buy and sell orders from customers. The changes announced in January 1997 would be the most sweeping since the earliest days of the over-the-counter market. Trading on the Nasdaq would now more closely resemble trading on the New York Stock Exchange (NYSE). As a consequence, market-making firms would need to spend millions in order to make their computer systems compliant. In addition, since the new rules were designed to narrow spreads on Nasdaq stocks, those same market makers would likely lose out on untold millions more as they watched the trading profits on each transaction grow smaller and smaller.

Those millions in losses would now theoretically go into the pockets of individual investors. Finally, as will be discussed more fully in chapter 11, by directing "the [Nasdaq] market to open previously exclusive electronic systems, including Instinet and SelectNet," the rules gave those individual investors access to an entirely new trading medium: the so-called ECNs (electronic communications networks). ECNs directly matched orders from buyers and sellers. If you bid $10.50 for XYZ stock, for instance, and someone else posted an ask price for the same amount, the match would take place automatically by computer. No market maker would intervene.

At the time, Nasdaq operated its own ECN called SelectNet, which mainly handled orders between dealers. Because it was a direct matching system, dealers could post and withdraw bids and offers as a form of negotiation and price discovery. Instinet, a privately owned trading network functioned much the same way. Nasdaq customers did have access to another Nasdaq-administered network called SOES (small order execution system). However, trades executed through SOES were normally routed to a market making firm. Perhaps because such direct matching systems would have cut into dealer profits, SelectNet and the other ECNs that existed at the time were available invariably to professional traders. But thanks to the SEC's new order-handling rules, anyone with a home PC would soon be able to patch into the market directly, using this same powerful tool. As chapter 12 will detail, the revolution in day trading and online investing was the result.

More Transparency

BESIDES OPENING UP trading on ECNs, what else did the order-handling rules require? Principally, they forced market makers to display their customers' limit orders. Before 1997, market makers who received limit orders from clients were under no obligation to broadcast them over the Nasdaq's Level II quote display. Thus, a trader watching the display might see that the price of XYZ stock was $10.25 bid and $10.50 ask. If that trader was bent on buying the stock, she would have no idea that someone had sent a market maker a limit order to sell at $10.40 since that order was hidden. If she sent in a market buy order, it would be executed at $10.50, and she would thus likely lose out on that 10 cents per share.

The SEC claimed that hiding limit orders from view gave market makers an unfair advantage. Obviously, it deprived traders of executions at more favorable prices. But maybe just as important, it prevented all traders from seeing the best prices available in the market and also the number of shares that were being offered to trade at those prices. Both pieces of information are crucial in determining short-term market direction. And with volatile Nasdaq stocks, short-term moves might amount to shifts of 10 percent or more in a stock's value. Thus, market makers in possession of limit order information had a clear advantage—an advantage that resulted in excess profits. As the SEC explained:

> [A] market maker that holds a customer limit order has, in effect, a private "option" to execute the order as principal. The longer this "option" remains open, the more time the market maker has to determine whether it can profit from executing the order as principal. This private market maker "option," however, is potentially detrimental to the execution opportunities for the limit order. The Display Rule will limit this "option" and expose the order to market-wide trading interest.[2]

Bottom line: Hiding orders was now verboten. And for good reason. Instead, the SEC's new rules gave Nasdaq market makers four choices when they received a limit order that bested their own prices: (1) They could substitute the limit order's price and size for their own quote, so that all market participants could now see the new quote on their Level II displays. (2) They could execute the limit order. In this case, the market might see the limit order price and size when it was broadcast as the last sale. (3) They could route the order to an ECN, provided that the ECN was accessible to all traders. (4) They could send it to another market maker, who would be subject to the same options as the first.[3] Whatever option was chosen, the end result was bound to be a far more transparent and more liquid market, according to the SEC.

Yet all this still begs the question, why did the SEC focus on limit orders as a means to reign in the kind of market-maker abuses that had prompted its investigation? After all, many traders never even use limit orders. So-called market orders that automatically execute at the prevailing best price are preferable if you want to buy or sell a stock quickly. In addition, most retail brokers have traditionally defaulted to a market order when their customers called in their trades; unless they specified otherwise.

However, skilled traders realize that in many instances it is preferable to allow a stock's price to reach a desired short-term price level before trading it. For that reason, limit orders could be said to originate from more sophisticated investors since they represented a form of price negotiation. And as such, they were considered a more valuable means of determining short-term price. Now that this price was being broadcast to anyone who subscribed to a Level II quote display, market makers would be forced to compete against each other if they wanted order flow that would enable them to profit from the spread. They would also need to compete with the limit orders of their own customers. Both actions would tend to narrow spreads, the SEC said.

In addition, thanks to the order-handling changes, savvy traders who placed limit orders via their computers might actually be able to see them broadcast if the orders represented the best bid or ask price at that moment. And if these retail traders subscribed to Level II quote displays, they might be able to see their order displayed by a particular market maker. Rather than passively accepting trades, retail traders could now actively participate in determining a stock's price. By competing against market makers, they could become the market.

The SEC made plain what it believed the net effect would be: "The Commission believes that this result will reduce the possibility of certain trading behavior on Nasdaq that was recently the subject of a Commission investigation."[4]

Even though they were forced to change their ways, market makers still retained a strong house advantage. Namely, they could view the orders queued up in their own systems that were just off the best prices they were quoting. This knowledge is particularly useful at the market open. When the market is closed, orders from retail traders and others often collect overnight. By analyzing the number of buy and sell orders present in their systems, market members are able to get a sense of whether a stock will jump up or down in price when the new day's trading begins. The information lets them set their own opening price for the stock. Significantly, this opening price jump—in technical terms the gap—from the previous day's close is often the biggest price change a stock will make during the trading day. And so it represents the biggest opportunity for profit. Individual traders, on the other hand, can only guess at what the number of backed-up buy and sell orders might be at the open. Thus, any bets they make would be against dealers who possess better information. And although traders might guess correctly now and again, in the long run the dealers always hold the advantage.

The new order-handling rules likewise did not change another potent advantage that market makers possess: the ability to short stocks without waiting for an uptick. Short selling is selling borrowed shares. When they are repurchased at a lower price, the trader is able to profit. An uptick occurs when a stock trades above the price of its previous sale. When markets are rapidly trending downward, upticks may become rare events, however. When upticks do occur, retail traders who wish to sell short rush in to exploit them. The available buyers are quickly taken out by the short sellers, so only traders who are fastest on the draw are able to exploit this strategy when it is applied to the short term. Being exempt from the uptick rule allows market makers to sell short whenever they choose. Theoretically, this is so that they can always be in a position to meet buyer demand. But in a fast-downtrending market, it also affords them considerable opportunity for profit.

Fear and Loathing on the Street

EVEN THOUGH MARKET makers retained powerful advantages under the new order-handling rules, many in their ranks still greeted the rules with suspicion and fear. Partly for that reason, it took the SEC months to actually implement its new order-handling rules, although it had not taken the SEC long to actually devise them. On September 29, 1995, just days after the Rudman Committee results were announced (see chapter 8), the SEC issued the rules for comment. Elements of the new rules had previously surfaced in the SEC's Market 2000 Study, which was aimed at smoothing the transition to automated markets. In addition, the NASD itself over the years had proposed various schemes for the display of some limit orders. Nevertheless, the SEC's call for comment generated more than 150 responding letters from investors, trade associations, and academics as well as the NASD. Although many were supportive, some voiced a laundry list of gripes.

A major fear was that the rules would transform the Nasdaq into an auction market much like the NYSE. In an auction market, a specialist acts as the buyer and seller of last resort. But the specialist will otherwise work to match orders between buyers and sellers without adding or subtracting from his own inventory. The effect of limit orders involuntarily replacing market makers' own bid and ask quotes would be somewhat the same. Day traders themselves could compete for spreadlike profits with the market makers. And under the new rules, market makers were now required to allow this competition and even to facilitate the matches to a degree.

These same critics believed that the Nasdaq market worked well because it allowed competing dealers, not limit orders, to set the price for a stock. Just as competing sides in a court proceeding lead to a kind of synthesis, the prices fielded by the dealers would determine the stock's true price. At least two dealers theoretically vie with each other for each stock listed on the Nasdaq. With heavily traded stocks, many more market makers were in the fray. No other traders were as knowledgeable about how that particular stock traded. Thus, according to this argument, the price that resulted from this dealer competition was superior to the information conveyed by a limit order.

This was particularly true in the case of the small, less liquid stocks that made up the bulk of listings on the Nasdaq. Limit orders might even be used to manipulate the prices of illiquid stocks. If you want to raise the price of XYZ, a small-cap stock, just bid $1 more than the stock's prevailing price. Your bid will be instantly executed, and it will cause a momentary blip in the stock's intraday chart. But it is unlikely that other traders will follow on. Your bid would be an anomaly. However, if someone illegally colluding with you met your bid, a new short-term support level might be achieved. Progressive sales might bid the price higher still. Finally, as other buyers were lured in, the colluding traders could sell and allow the price to fall. As you will see in chapter 11, stock manipulation schemes like this occurred frequently during the late 1990s. Significantly, limit orders proved especially easy to use to manipulate stocks during after-hours trading. That is, after the market closed and market makers themselves ceased trading. Until the market reopened the following morning, the market consisted solely of limit orders fielded by individual traders.

Critics of the new order-handling rules also voiced fears that higher commissions might wreck havoc with the market. The reason for their concerns requires some explanation. At the time, online brokers were already charging rock-bottom commissions for market orders. But with market orders, brokers also receive a hidden commission in the form of payment for order flow, which is paid to them by market makers. Payment for order flow might amount to pennies per share, and on larger transactions it might easily exceed the amount a customer pays in commission. Brokers did not receive payment for order flow for the customer limit orders they sent to market makers. Thus, to compensate for that lost revenue, limit orders typically carried a higher price. Therefore, according to this argument, more limit orders would result in less payment for order flow, and so brokers would be forced to recoup this revenue by charging higher commissions.

This actually happened, at least to an extent. At the turn of the century, as trading volume plummeted following the crash and spreads narrowed as a result of decimalization, payment for order flow slowed to a trickle. Brokers found themselves losing money. And so they increased fees and looked for other ways to recoup the lost revenue. However, during the height of the market boom, trading volume continued to soar. More and more brokers rushed in to offer online trading. And the fierce competition among these online brokers resulted in steadily declining commissions for both market and limit orders. Popular online brokerages, such as Datek, charged just $10 for limit orders, down from the hundreds of dollars that full-service brokers might charge for similar sized orders. At least one online broker that catered to experienced traders lowered its commissions to just $1.

Perhaps the thing that concerned critics of the order-handling rules most were the costs of upgrading their computer systems so that customer limit orders could be automatically displayed. Estimates put that cost in the millions of dollars for each firm. At the same time, market makers were sure to see their profits shrink as a result of the narrowed spreads. The double whammy would force many market makers to quit the business. If the number of market makers is reduced, liquidity in the market likewise suffers. And this would especially hurt trading of micro-cap companies. It might even inhibit future companies from raising money in the markets, or so the argument went.

Again, this rather dire prediction did come true, at least in part. Research sponsored by the NASD found that while spreads of heavily traded stocks did decline as a result of the rules, the spreads of thinly traded stocks were not significantly affected.[5] This may have been because fewer market-making firms now maintained markets in small-cap stocks. Indeed, full-service firms, like Salomon, Morgan Stanley, and others, reportedly cut back on the number of Nasdaq stocks they traded. Merrill Lynch reportedly reduced the number of stocks for which it made a market from 850 to 500.[6]

Yet at the same time, profits continued to accrue to market makers as volume on the Nasdaq rose steadily, somewhat offsetting the losses resulting from the narrowed spreads.

A Captive Market

PERHAPS THE WORST criticism of the SEC action came from outgoing NASD Chairman Joseph Hardiman. Just days before he left his post, Hardiman complained publicly about the SEC's "micromanagement." And he warned of the consequences if outsiders who lacked a real-world understanding of how the Nasdaq worked were given a free hand to meddle.

Although this may have seemed like the complaints of a person who felt victimized by the scandal at the time, Hardiman had a point. The SEC may not have fully understood the implications of the order-handling rule changes. Citing a lengthy chain of cause and effect, one group of analysts from First Security Van Kasper (now Wells Fargo Securities) noted that limit order rules, having cut back on the profits of market makers, also had at least one unintended result: Market makers were compelled to ignore fundamentals in the course of their trading. "Today's order-driven market has for the most part become a numbers game in which only a few dealers still consider fundamentals," the analysts said.

Put another way, the market makers had no choice but to adopt minute-to-minute, hair-trigger tactics because they now competed with day traders who used the same tactics. Trading had become a kind of guerilla war. And quotes based to a degree on the stock's fundamentals had become the first casualty. Such quotes simply would not hold up in the face of legions of day traders who progressively bid a stock's price up or down. The end result has been increased volatility. Indeed, volatility on the Nasdaq increased every year since 1995, according to the Van Kasper analysts. During the first half of 2000, the year the tech bubble burst, prices on the Nasdaq moved by 1 percent or more on 79 percent of trading days.[7]

The End of the Affair

ALMOST A YEAR after the SEC handed down its new order-handling rules, the final shoe dropped on the NASD and its member firms. On December 27, 1997, some 30 NASD securities firms settled a class-action suit over the alleged price fixing, reportedly paying $910 million in damages. At the time, it was the largest civil antitrust settlement in history. Six other firms had reached settlements on their own, paying out a reported $98 million.[8] Not one firm named admitted to any wrongdoing. The settlement, while huge, was small in comparison to profits earned by the market-making firms involved. For example, some analysts believed that trading Nasdaq stocks earned Merrill Lynch an estimated $300 million in 1995.[9]

Now that all the disciplinary actions had been meted out, was there to be a lasting stain on the Nasdaq? In all likelihood, the answer is no. Despite all the blustering by the business press and the government over spread fixing and despite the huge fines, the scandal remained far off the radar screens of average investors. Most did not understand the nature of the charges. And even if they did, it was hard to comprehend why anyone should worry about odd-eighths quotes—tiny fractions of a point—when hot technology stocks were regularly wracking up $3, $10, and $20 gains in a single day's trading.

Ironically, Nasdaq market makers likely benefited more than they suffered as a result of the scandal. Had Christie and Schultz not launched their investigation, it is likely that the NYSE increasingly would have cited the issue of spreads in its efforts to lure companies away from the Nasdaq. One analyst who consults with companies on the listing of their shares told *USA Today* that some companies did not want to be seen as permitting their shareholders to pay more for their stocks than they should, and so they had defected to the NYSE.[10]

Economic history might also have been written differently if Christie and Schultz had not broken the spread-fixing scandal. If the NYSE had managed to lure the flock of upstart tech firms that were to launch in the next couple of years, the coming bubble market might well have been tempered because their trading would have been less volatile on the Big Board.

As it turned out, the NYSE did not lure trading away from the Nasdaq. But another potentially more powerful competitor did. Within a short time, thanks to the SEC's order-handling rules, ECNs would steal an estimated one-third of trading volume away from Nasdaq's market makers. The flight of order flow to ECNs would become one of the chief challenges facing the new team taking over the Nasdaq in the wake of the scandal. Central to the policies of this new team would be ways to maintain the Nasdaq as the single conduit for stock trading. If they could succeed in doing that, they could clone the Nasdaq in countries around the world.

CHAPTER 10

THE PLAYERS CHANGE

MARCH 1997: IT had been three weeks since Frank Zarb moved into his office at the headquarters of the National Association of Securities Dealers (NASD) on Washington's K Street. And still the room was in disarray. Photos he planned to hang on the wall lay scattered about on the floor, including one showing the former energy czar as a younger man, inspecting oil pipelines in the frozen wastes of Alaska.[1] But as the NASD's newly appointed chairman, Zarb had more important matters to focus on than hanging up old mementos. In the course of the year, some 91 companies would leave the Nasdaq for the New York Stock Exchange (NYSE).

Fast-growing computer maker Gateway was perhaps the most prominent defector—and maybe the most painful. A high-tech firm headquartered on the plains of South Dakota, Gateway epitomized what the Nasdaq was supposed to be all about: a market for spry, upstart technology firms. More painful still, the Gateway defection followed the flight of two comparable high-profile tech firms: Bay Networks and America Online.[2] Some in the business press openly wondered, If "the stock market for the next 100 years" could not hold onto its brightest stars, what was its future?

But this was only one of the problems Zarb faced as he began his new job. Even as firms fled to the NYSE, the NASD still found itself in the crosshairs of the Securities and Exchange Commission (SEC). In the wake of the market-maker scandal, the SEC itself faced accusations that it had not acted swiftly enough to punish the NASD. "Nor has the SEC emerged unscathed," the SEC's chairman, Arthur Levitt, admitted to reporters during a press conference: "To the extent these practices [by Nasdaq market makers] took place on our watch, we should have acted sooner," he said.[3] Now the SEC's own reputation depended on how quickly the NASD could adopt the reforms agreed to that previous August. If the NASD could not steer clear of trouble, still more blame would fall on the SEC.[4]

For that reason, Levitt realized that the NASD needed a strong board of directors who could direct its reforms. And so he had reportedly placed Zarb on his short list of recommendations to succeed Joseph R. Hardiman, the NASD's retiring chairman. Officially, Levitt denied any direct involvement in the choice of Hardiman's successor. "The NASD nominating committee said, 'Can you help us to get good people?'" he told the press.[5] Whatever his involvement, Levitt was notably pleased with Zarb's appointment. "I've known Zarb for more than 25 years and seen him operate in many situations," he said. "I can think of nobody better suited to dealing with the problems of the NASD and the Nasdaq market."[6]

In fact, Levitt and Zarb's relationship harked back to 1969, when Zarb went to work as back-office operations manager for Cogan, Berlind, Weill & Levitt (CBW&L), the brokerage firm where Levitt served as partner. Back-office operations typically occupy the bottom rung on Wall Street's status ladder. Workers there plodded away at a firm's boring but necessary tasks like internal auditing and the clearing of trades as well as compliance with federal regulations. Meanwhile in the front office, successful brokers, money managers, and analysts command huge salaries and are worshiped as gods. "The front office guys were all Ivy League characters who truthfully sold stocks and bonds to daddy's friends," recalls Zarb.[7] He himself had earned a B.S. and M.B.A. from New York's Hofstra University. His father, he says had worked his whole life for a company and never owned a single share of stock.

Nevertheless, the job was an opportunity to show that he could focus on the nitty-gritty details. Notably, this was a time when fierce competition was forcing brokerage firms to automate their back-office operations. Thus, Zarb was fond of saying that the job put him on the front lines at the very start of the automated trading revolution. Lessons learned there would prove invaluable almost three decades later. When Zarb joined CBW&L, the firm was relatively unknown outside Wall Street's old-boy network.[8] Later, following a series of acquisitions, CBW&L would morph into Shearson Lehman Hutton.[9] But by this time, Zarb had left Wall Street for Washington.

In 1971, Zarb served as assistant secretary of labor under President Nixon. Then, from 1974 to 1978, he served as President Ford's energy czar, where his task would be far more complicated. The energy crisis hit right at the time of Watergate, an economic downturn, and the U.S. retreat from Vietnam. The nation was in its deepest malaise since the Great Depression. And government was widely blamed for its ills. Zarb's task was to coordinate the efforts of many government agencies in order to keep the wheels of the nation moving. Though he would continue to serve in some capacity during the later administrations of Reagan, Bush, and Clinton, Zarb left Washington and returned to Wall Street in 1978. He had been tapped as a senior partner at the investment banking firm Lazard Freres & Co., where he oversaw international and domestic finance deals as well as mergers and acquisitions. In 1988, he left Lazard Freres & Co. to become chairman and chief executive officer of the brokerage firm Smith Barney, then a division of The Travelers Inc. Once again, Zarb proved himself an adept administrator. Smith Barney recorded a $100 million pretax loss when Zarb took the helm. Much of that loss stemmed from failed risk-arbitrage trades in the aftermath of Black Monday in October 1987. To quell the losses, Zarb cut costs, and he focused the firm on retail trading.[10] By 1993, when Zarb left Smith Barney to take on broader responsibilities with The Travelers Inc., the brokerage reported an after-tax profit of $200 million.[11]

Little wonder, then, that Zarb was Levitt's choice to run the beleaguered NASD. Here was a man with friends on both sides of the aisle in Washington and a man who also understood well the intricacies of how markets worked. In an interview, Zarb said one of the reasons Levitt and others at the SEC favored his appointment was his turn-around experience at Smith Barney. "Levitt said something that I'll never forget," Zarb recalls. "'All the things you've done in your life up till now qualify you to do this. This market needs to be fixed.'"

Some saw Zarb's new role as chairman as similar to that of a court-appointed trustee at a company that had filed for bankruptcy. The SEC and the business press would be watching his every move. Zarb, however, says he saw it differently. Well off and in his early 60s now, Zarb made it known that he was not taking up the job to build up his résumé. This would be the culmination of his career.[12] Moreover, Zarb says that to him, the NASD was the "soul of the industry. For that reason alone it deserved to be saved. He had no illusions about the difficulties ahead, however. At the NASD helm he'd be charged with pushing through reforms that might be to the industry's long-term benefit. Problem was, he says, sometimes the "industry doesn't appreciate having integrity driven into its soul. The NASD had the hard job, but the job nevertheless of challenging the industry to change a lot of its practices. And it didn't do that. So it failed itself and it failed the industry."

At the same time, Zarb recognized that powerful and fundamental forces were at work

"It was clear, he says, "that the world was moving toward a more democratized model of equity ownership." As evidence of that, he pointed to the growing popularity of company profit sharing plans. In the 1990s profit sharing took on an unprecedented new meaning as stock options in fast-growing tech firms created thousands of new millionaires. Zarb explains:

> We had an enlightened generation of boomers who were computer literate and had a keen interest in sharing in some of the wealth that they helped to design. And we had companies that saw participation as a way of keeping key employees. The Microsofts, the Intels, and the Starbucks were the companies of the people. And the pipeline was beginning to look fuller.

To Zarb and his new colleagues at the NASD, it became increasingly clear that Nasdaq had a critical role to play in this new economy where the prospect of wealth through stock options was luring the best and the brightest from throughout the world. If workplaces were becoming in a sense more democratized through profit-sharing and stock options, the market where those options eventually ended up must likewise be democratized. "It was no question that democratizing the market was a key objective," Zarb says. But in order for that to happen, people needed to have confidence in the market. "Confidence only comes with a sense of integrity." The public needed to know that the Nasdaq was being adequately policed.

Mending Fences

THE REFORMS MANDATED by the SEC were in addition to the new order-handling rules that market makers had been ordered to follow. To an extent, they paralleled the recommendations made by the Rudman Commission. And they were implemented more through lengthy negotiations than by feat. When Zarb took command, NASD officials had already undertaken the task of splitting up the association to include the Nasdaq stock market and a separate regulatory arm called NASD Regulation, Inc. (NASDR). In addition, NASD officials had agreed to spend $100 million over five years to beef up the NASD's enforcement proceedings. The SEC explained that this amount was in lieu of a fine.[13] Part of that $100 million would go toward maintaining an independent internal auditing staff charged with making sure that procedures were followed to the letter. The NASD was also told to create an audit trail so that it would be able to trace back and document questionable stock trades and other practices. Likewise, for the first time all Nasdaq member firms were required to execute trades on the same time clock. This would allow orders to be tracked each step of the way when necessary. This reform was intended to prevent market makers from rigging trades by shifting stocks back and forth among themselves. The clock would build a bulletproof paper trail.

Finally, to ensure that the NASD's internal decision making did not reflect only the objectives of member firms, the NASD had already acted to open its important governing boards to "at least 50 percent independent public and non-industry membership." The SEC specifically named the National Nominating Committee, the Trading/Quality of Markets Committee, the Arbitration Committee, the Market Surveillance Committee, the National Business Conduct Committee, and the Management Compensation Committee.[14]

The effect of the SEC reforms would be to transport the Nasdaq eons beyond its laissez-faire origins. The Nasdaq by this time was the second-largest stock market in the world. New systems and new discipline were required. However, to many NASD member firms the SEC action represented a bitter humiliation. Some market makers believed that the SEC's charges were overblown and unfair. And they resented the fact that they now faced falling profits as well as the huge costs of complying with the SEC's new order-handling rules.[15] Adding insult to injury, the NASD announced that it would fine at least one brokerage, J. P. Morgan Securities, Inc., $200,000 in part for failing to comply with the new order display rules.[16]

For these reasons, Zarb no doubt knew that he would likely face strong resistance from member firms—just as he knew that he must perform a delicate balancing act between their interests and those of the SEC. On the one hand, he would need the cooperation of NASD member firms if the Nasdaq were to remain viable in the public's mind and also to prevent the NYSE from picking away at its most prized listed companies. In the case of the latter, Zarb would especially need the millions in fees that members paid the NASD each year to keep operations running smoothly.[17] But the incoming NASD chairman also knew that he needed to hang tough in the face of member complaints or else face the wrath of the SEC. In one interview, Zarb told a reporter that he would not tolerate attempts to block his reforms.[18]

Here again, Levitt would prove an indispensable ally. "It's inevitable that some will complain that we're hurting the market by reducing profitability," Levitt told reporters. "That's the perennial refrain uttered at every turning point in the industry, from registering the stock in the 1930s to unfixing commissions in the 1970s. It's a phony argument."[19]

Also backing Zarb's reform efforts were legions of so-called buy-side traders. These were the people who bought stocks, often in blocks of thousands, for institutions and mutual funds.

They had been perhaps the biggest victims of the spread-fixing scandal. "On the buy-side you are facing wider spreads than you would expect to see," William Christie, the man who broke the market-maker scandal, told a group of colleagues at a conference on market reform. Buy-side traders "worry about execution costs, and quotes do matter if you cannot get inside the spread. If you are forced to pay those quotes, they matter a lot!"[20]

Building a Team

WHILE JUGGLING THE interests of member firms and regulators, Zarb also faced challenges from his own staff. Low morale reportedly plagued the NASD's 570 employees. Many were leaving for other jobs.[21] Among Zarb's first orders of business was reassuring those staffers who remained that the bad times would pass. "All institutions have difficult times," he said. When the Nasdaq reformed, it would become a stronger, happier place.

In order to enact his reforms, Zarb first needed to streamline the NASD's cumbersome decision-making process. Too many board members on too many committees had contributed to the lax enforcement in the past. Thus, in June, just months after he took office, Zarb announced a major proposed restructuring. "We're part of an industry that moves with great speed," he explained. The NASD must be reorganized so that it could keep up. A total of 48 board members had previously looked over the shoulders of the NASDR and the Nasdaq stock market. Meetings of subsidiary boards might be held in one month while the decisions they reached were not acted on by the parent board until weeks later. Zarb cut the number of board members to 27 while slashing the number of meetings by more than half, coordinating the schedules of subsidiary board meetings with the parent board so that matters of business could move up the line faster. With the changes, the Nasdaq board and NASD Regulation's board both functioned more or less like committees of the parent, NASD board. Each member of the Nasdaq board, for example, also had a seat on the NASD board.[22]

Perhaps looking toward the day when the Nasdaq might indeed be spun off as a separate company, Zarb proposed especially deep cuts in its board membership, from 16 to between five and eight members. That board would have broad authority to make rules for the market.

Zarb's restructuring proposals were no doubt designed to take the NASD away from the overweighted rule-making model used by associations and universities and substitute a corporate model that could react faster. Zarb also needed a strong on-the-ground team to manage day-to-day operations. Fortunately, that team was already largely in place. Chief among them were three key players: Alfred R. Berkeley III, Richard G. Ketchum, and Mary L. Schapiro.

The Technician

ALFRED BERKELEY WAS appointed president of the Nasdaq by outgoing NASD Chairman Joseph Hardiman.[23] He also enjoyed the firm backing of powerful Nasdaq board members, such as Richard M. DeMartini, president and chief operating officer of Dean Witter Capital, and Michael W. Brown, chief financial officer of Microsoft.[24] Brown and Berkeley had known each other since the days when Microsoft first became a public company. And Berkeley would call on that company's technical expertise to transport the Nasdaq onto the Internet.

Both Brown and DeMartini liked Berkeley because he possessed a thorough knowledge of how markets operate and a deep familiarity with new trading technologies. A former Air Force captain, Berkeley served 24 years at Alex Brown and

Sons. While there, he, like Zarb, gained extensive experience in back-office operations. At the time, the firm was dependent on mainframe computers dating back to the 1960s. Berkeley worked diligently to update everything, from order processing to teleconferencing.[25] Later he put that knowledge to work as a senior banker with Alex Brown's corporate finance department, where he arranged financing for computer software and electronic commerce companies. And he had been advising the Nasdaq on implementing new technology since 1991.[26]

Among Berkeley's first jobs in the Zarb NASD was to upgrade the Nasdaq's operating software so that it could process the SEC's new order-handling rules. This turned out to be a huge task, since it required not only that Nasdaq's systems be fault tolerant in their compliance, they must seamlessly integrate with each of the market's member firms. In an interview, Berkeley estimates that some 450 people were involved in the work, many located at the Nasdaq's computer centers in Trumbull, Connecticut, and Rockville, Maryland. Programmers worked 16-hour shifts, returning home for an hour or two of sleep. And they kept up this pace for seven days a week and for weeks on end. "They basically locked themselves down and delivered," says Berkeley. The market had to continue functioning without a hitch throughout the work. "It was a huge, high-risk, high-pay-off strategy. The public has no idea how hard it was and how hard these guys worked."

His other task was mending fences with Nasdaq-listed firms. Here, in particular, his mild-mannered personality would come in handy allaying their growing concerns over the Nasdaq's future. It was a critical effort. Despite the fact that thousands of companies traded on the Nasdaq, the market remained dominated by a very short list of behemoths, chief among them Intel, Microsoft, and Cisco. The top 1 percent of Nasdaq companies accounted for 13 percent of its market cap. The top 20 percent accounted for 83 percent. Thus, a single defection would prove to be a stunning blow.

In addition to keeping listed companies firmly in the fold, Berkeley was charged with expanding the Nasdaq's market share. Here, his experiences at Alex Brown would help. But the effort still required spending a good deal of time traveling the world on the Nasdaq's behalf, talking with the management of bright, young companies. He was laying the groundwork for Zarb's vision of a marketplace for fast-growing firms throughout the world. And it was not simply an altruistic goal. The Nasdaq's long-term survival depended on its establishing a strong global presence, where much of the market's growth would ultimately be found. In that regard, it competed fiercely with the NYSE for new listings. At the start of 1998, only 8 percent of companies listed on the Nasdaq came from outside the United States.[27]

Berkeley also helped formulate the Nasdaq's broader strategy. For help, he turned to the consulting firm McKinsey & Company. As he explains:

> I hired McKinsey to find out who our customer was. And it turned out not to be an easy question. And the reason is that we receive money from our [listed] companies and from market makers and from data vendors. But it turns out our real customer is the investor from whom we receive nothing directly. A market needs to understand that even though it receives no money from its investors it needs to put its investors first.

The way Berkeley saw it, a market that didn't serve its end users would fall short at serving its other constituents. If investors didn't come to the Nasdaq table, listing companies would look for them in some other market. To win over these end users, Berkeley spent much of the time on the road speaking to investment groups. Here his task was pure public relations. As rising markets increasingly commanded the attention of Americans, few understood how the Nasdaq market operated, and fewer still understood how the SEC-mandated changes would be of benefit to everyday investors who traded Nasdaq shares. As Berkeley told audiences, the narrowing spreads were saving investors an estimated $2 million per day.[28]

As part of that public relations effort, Berkeley helped spearhead development of the Nasdaq's own Web site. The goal was to create a kind of financial information portal for Nasdaq-listed companies. Visitors need only enter a stock's ticker symbol for a lengthy report on the stock to emerge. Much of this information had until recently been kept only in libraries, brokerage offices, and government bureaus. Compiling it into a coherent report that an investor could act on normally took days. Now this institutional-quality information was online and accessible within seconds. Berkeley liked to say that the Web had led to a Jeffersonian revolution in investing. No longer was information held fast by a ruling elite. Instead, the Internet had created a level playing field where everyone could gain access to the same information. In reality, market makers, institutional traders, and hedge fund managers still had access to better information, and they could get at it faster than any day trader sitting at a home computer. Nevertheless, the Nasdaq Web site, reportedly one of the largest online addresses built by Microsoft, was an impressive effort. The site rose to the 24th-most-visited Internet portal by mid-1998—and that despite strong competition from literally hundreds of financial portals, such as Finance Yahoo and Quicken.com, that were springing up at the time.

Berkeley said that in designing the Nasdaq Web site, his guiding philosophy was to "embrace the technology, use the technology to move the organization ahead." In this case, it was to use Nasdaq's Web presence to develop ever stronger relationships with customers and suppliers. If that required changing the business model "to take advantage of what the technology can do," then so be it.

At the time, thousands of companies throughout the world were likewise taking their businesses online and revamping their strategic thinking accordingly. But the Nasdaq, which was at heart a networked information provider to begin with, had better success than most at using the net to cement customer relationships. An example of this was another Berkeley-led effort, in this case to develop a private extranet called Nasdaq Online. It was aimed at listing companies. And it was accessible only to their board members and their highest-level executives. Nasdaq Online pulled together Nasdaq data feeds and additional information from third party vendors to give listing company heads a window seat to the Nasdaq that might otherwise cost thousands per month, or alternately take hours to ferret out. But Nasdaq Online packaged the information so that it could be accessed by any Internet-linked PC. And unlike sophisticated terminals used by traders that resembled fighter jet cockpit displays, Nasdaq Online organized its critical data so that it could be readily accessed by busy executives. The result likely endeared them to the Nasdaq market. If company CEOs saw that their stock price was dropping, for example, they could reportedly look up what institutional traders were selling off huge blocks of shares. Likewise, they could instantly track analyst actions and news stories affecting their company. The site was designed by a New York-based company called Micro Modeling Associates (now called Plural Inc.), which also reportedly put together the familiar "wall" of quote displays at the Nasdaq's Times Square MarketSite.[29]

The Tactician

WITH BERKELEY HARD at work on cementing customer relationships and on upgrading technology at the Nasdaq, Zarb also needed someone intimately familiar with how the NASD worked—both internally and with its regulatory overseers. For that, he turned to Richard Ketchum, who had been president of the NASD. Ketchum had served a similar function under

Hardiman. According to media accounts some believed that Ketchum had not acted aggressively enough when faced with evidence of dealer collusion. However, Ketchum emerged from the SEC investigation as a rising star, assuming the post of president of the Nasdaq in 2000. While Berkeley reported to an independent board as well as Zarb, Ketchum was given far more autonomy. He reported to Zarb.[30] Ketchum was likewise given a broad array of additional responsibilities. He ruled over everything from the office of corporate counsel to finance, strategic planning, public relations, and human resources. In addition, he supervised the NASD groups that dealt with state and federal governments.[31]

All this was for good reason. To Wall Street insiders, Ketchum was the man who made "the trains run on time." He was the man best able to keep the big picture clearly in mind. In particular, he could work closely with the SEC on the minute details of implementing the reforms.[32] That is what he had done during the course of the SEC investigations, and he would continue to play that role.

Indeed, it was a logical role for someone who had once been on the adjunct faculty of Georgetown's School of Law. Ketchum served with the New York law firm Milbank, Tweed, Hadley and McCloy briefly before joining the SEC in 1977. He eventually rose to the position of director of the Division of Market Regulation at the SEC. The job gave him oversight authority over both the Nasdaq and the NYSE. In addition, during his tenure with the SEC, he had worked to develop the so-called national market system that enabled anyone with access to a networked computer to discover the best current price for a security. That experience would later prove crucial during Ketchum's career at the Nasdaq as strategists there worked to create a central order book.

With Ketchum at the helm, the NASD and its subsidiaries launched an aggressive outreach program aimed at educating individual investors. By their own admission, they had their work cut out for them. "Sixty-three percent of Americans can tell a halfback from a quarterback, but only 14 percent can tell a growth stock from an income stock," a series of NASD-produced public service announcements lamented. In a further bid to mend fences, the announcements also encouraged viewers to check out the backgrounds of brokerage firms and individual brokers to see whether they had run into regulatory problems in the past. "We can't tell you there haven't been occasional problems in our industry, but we can tell you who they are," the announcements said.[33]

The media effort was tied to an ambitious educational Web site called Individual Investor's Services. The site would eventually feature online video lectures as well as articles on investing basics. One application designed for experienced investors was a simulator that allowed anyone to play the role of a Nasdaq dealer, buying and selling shares in fast markets.

These online efforts represented further recognition on the part of the Nasdaq that the future of investing was indeed on the Web. Online brokerages and privately funded financial portals were likewise springing up all over the Internet. And the Nasdaq was forced to play catch-up. Nevertheless, the Nasdaq had a particular advantage in name recognition, and this was especially true outside the United States. Nearly 30 percent of visitors to the NASD Web sites came from overseas.

While Berkeley helped spearhead the design of the next-generation Nasdaq electronic marketplace and Ketchum kept a tight reign on operations, the Nasdaq still needed someone who could demonstrate that the "market for the next 100 years" was resolute in keeping its players honest.

The Top Cop

THAT JOB WENT to the third key player in the Zarb administration, Mary Schapiro, who had headed the NASDR since

1996. In some sense, Schapiro had the most difficult task of all. Roughly 5,500 brokerage firms with 670,000 registered representatives now plied their trade on the Nasdaq. She was charged with watchdogging all of them. A lawyer by training, Schapiro, like Berkeley and Ketchum, had extensive experience overseeing the securities markets. Thanks to appointments by both President Reagan and President Bush, she had also served 10 years as an SEC commissioner. Just two years before being tapped to run the NASDR, she had been appointed by President Clinton to chair the Commodity Futures Trading Commission. There she oversaw the regulation of all the nation's futures markets. Some thought her presence an open affront to the male-dominated world of futures trading—an affront that was aggravated further by her campaign to reform the commission's enforcement operations. One futures exchange member reportedly made it known that he would not take orders from "a five-foot, two-inch blond."[34] The smart money on Wall Street speculated that if Schapiro were successful at mopping up the NASD's remaining errant members, her eventual reward would be chairmanship of the SEC.

With the support of Zarb and other key players, Schapiro mounted a sweeping campaign to clean up the NASD's bad rep and quash remaining foul play among Nasdaq dealers. In August 1997, she helped reorganize the NASD's disciplinary procedures that had drawn so much criticism from the SEC. Previously, 11 district committees and the Market Regulation Committee authorized the investigation of complaints. Now when an investor came to the NASD with a complaint about an unfair trade, he or she would not have to face a review board made up of securities industry insiders who might be inclined to side with their colleagues. Instead, under a code of procedure approved by the SEC, professional hearing officers would handle disciplinary hearings and head up the three-member hearing panels. Each panel member had one vote. Thus, the balance still might be tilted in favor of the defendants. But it was a step in the right direction. The new rules resulted directly from the NASD's settlement with the SEC.[35]

Schapiro likewise moved to punish member firms whose wrongdoing had until then managed to avoid NASD censure. In July 1997, for example, the NASDR fined 20 brokers for allegedly paying an imposter to take the qualifying exam for them. The crackdown was part of an investigation that had been ongoing since 1996. In all, some 41 registered representatives were singled out as culprits. In addition to fines of $25,000 or more each, they were made to forfeit any commissions they had earned. Schapiro was adamant that the punishments were justified. "Entrance exams are a cornerstone of NASD Regulation's investor-protection framework," she said.[36]

Old Habits Die Hard

A FURTHER SERIES of investigations and subsequent actions by the NASDR revealed that some market makers persisted in the very abuses that had rained condemnation on the Nasdaq after Christie and Schultz broke the market-maker scandal. In November 1998, for example, the NASDR fined a trader with Olde Discount Corporation, $15,000 for allegedly harassing a market maker who had narrowed the spread of a Nasdaq-listed stock.[37]

Other stiffer fines—some totaling hundreds of thousands of dollars—would likewise be levied against traders and firms that veered from the rules. The effect, no doubt, was to convince the SEC and the public that the new team at the Nasdaq was serious about mending the market's errant ways. "Once it became clear to the SEC that the leadership in place was going to do what needed to be done to make it right," says Zarb, "they [the SEC] became supporters and no longer adversaries."

But NASD's dealer firms may well have seen these actions as nothing less than a purge, made worse when NASDR's own enforcement people became zealous in their jobs. As Zarb notes:

> Often times the people in the field were right [in taking the action they did]. But they had a poor bedside manner. There's a sense that you're young and you've been training and you . . . may tend to get cocky and sometimes arrogant. And that was unacceptable. Because if we were going to be good, smart, tough regulators you can do that at the same time and also be courteous and polite. So we actually had courses in bedside manner. We started an institute with Wharton [the University of Pennsylvania's Wharton School of Business] to train not only our own people but people in compliance [departments] at the firms so that they could be better schooled in regulations.

Still, some on Zarb's team openly worried that in the aftermath of the whole market maker scandal, the market makers themselves were being shoved into too tight a corner. "Have we moved the pendulum so far over in favor of the investors that we have damaged the attractiveness for the market maker?"[38] Alfred Berkeley asked.

He had a point. Heavily traded stocks, like Dell, Cisco, and Microsoft, that had made the Nasdaq world famous might trade just fine in the absence of market makers. But liquidity might quickly disappear for the thousands of lightly traded stocks of emerging companies—the future Dells and Ciscos—unless there were buyers willing to take shares from retail investors and also sell those investors shares on demand. Bottom line: The Nasdaq needed its market makers. And it would only prosper if they did, too.

In fact, as you will see in the next chapter, the NASD would strongly rally on the side of its member dealer firms as ECNs (electronic communications networks) quickly cut deep into their profits. The Nasdaq's strategy was to try to collar all the ECNs beneath the giant umbrella of the Nasdaq. "The key

question Nasdaq has to answer is: Are we going to let technological change happen outside of our market or are we going to
embrace change, wrestle with its implications and have some
influence on its outcome," Berkeley told a group of technology
leaders.[39] Many at the Nasdaq saw ECNs as leading to a fragmented market that might be devoid of liquidity. If that happened, if liquidity dried up, Nasdaq's smaller stocks would be
subject to the same kind of manipulation and huge spreads
found on lightly traded Third World stock markets. The result
would be unprecedented volatility. And many companies that
were able to qualify would simply transfer their listings to the
NYSE. The Nasdaq's former chief operating officer, Patrick
Campbell, described the problem succinctly along with the
NASD's initial strategy for dealing with it:

> Fragmentation is not good. Fragmentation hurts liquidity. Recog-
> nizing that alternative trading systems are going to continue to
> grow we want to make sure that the Nasdaq stock market is the
> primary stock market where all this comes together. [We want an]
> open inclusive model in business as well as technology. [Our goal
> is to] create the critical mass that will enhance liquidity. Nasdaq
> is best positioned to do this in one central place.[40]

There in a nutshell was a chief reason Campbell's boss,
Frank Zarb, was fortunate in putting the problems of the market-maker scandal behind the NASD. A far worse threat
loomed. Fast, nimble, and unencumbered by many of the regulations the Nasdaq itself faced, ECNs would shortly prove to
be a formidable foe. As Zarb relayed in an interview:

> We didn't see the ECNs coming, and we should've. When that
> happens you ask yourself why. But it was a good wake-up call . . .
> that we have to provide a check on the market and provide the
> market with what it needs. If you don't it's going to get that with-
> out you.

CHAPTER 11

THE RISE OF THE ECNS

LATE AT NIGHT on January 6, 2000, something peculiar was happening in the after-hours markets. Someone—or more likely a group of people—was "fluffing" the stock of restaurant chain Atomic Burrito (ATOM). At the time, some 24,000 shares of ATOM might trade on an average day. But that night's volume hit 240,000. ATOM's price shot up from 88 cents to $3. The next day shares dropped to $1.28.[1] (Two years later, ATOM shares were quoted at 4 cents apiece.)

ATOM's rise had all the markings of a typical fluff-up or pump-and-dump scam, where—unbeknownst to a company's management—con artists talk up a stock on the Internet by flooding financial chat threads with positive news, true or not, in the hopes of pushing the stock's price higher. Then, once they have whipped up a buying frenzy, the scammers sell into the hordes of naive investors, causing the stock's price to plummet as a result. In a variation on this scheme, investors who short the stock might mount a similar illicit e-mail attack on financial chat threads, spreading vile rumors about a company in the hopes of driving its stock price down.

Indeed, by the turn of the century, many stock scammers prowled financial Web sites after the close of regular trading. Because the regular exchanges had shut down for the night, such scamsters performed their frenetic buying and selling on ECNs (electronic communications networks) that remain open to handle orders after hours.

ECNs proved an ideal venue for after-hours pump-and-dump scamsters, mainly because the market's daytime overseers had gone home at the close of regular trading. Thus, company officials and financial reporters might not even be aware that a stock was being attacked until it was over, and legitimate after-hours traders, conned by the scam, had already lost a bundle. But most important, the market makers that keep the Nasdaq running smoothly during the day would have long since left their posts. As a result, traders were forced to deal directly with one another in the dead of night. This reduces volume sharply. On October 12, 2001, for example, a paltry 52.5 million Nasdaq-listed shares[2] changed hands overnight—at a time when the Nasdaq frequently experiences two-billion-share days. Cut volume back to a trickle, and the opportunity for abuse rises in tandem.

After-hours trading was just one of the many changes wrought by ECNs. Although developers hardly imagined that they would be a medium for scams. ECNs are private, totally automated trading networks that directly link buyers and sellers. During the day most trades go through market makers, who buy shares from sellers and sell them to buyers at a slightly higher price, thus profiting from the spread. ECNs were different. For example, instead of dealing with a market maker a trader wishing to buy stocks using an ECN would have to exactly match the price offered by the seller. (More on this later.) Since the late 1990s, anyone with the right online brokerage account was able to trade stocks on ECNs. However, trading on ECNs has actually been around for decades. The practice began as a way for institutional investors and market makers to trade large blocks of shares both during and after the market close. Having a private trading network suited them just fine because ECNs enabled them to cloak their buying and selling from the market as a whole. While Nasdaq Level II quotes posted the name of the market-making firm right alongside the bid and ask prices, they displayed, ECNs simply listed those prices, giving participants total anonymity. As a rule, the trades did not even register on the Nasdaq network. Thus they were invisible to the public eye. In fact, few retail investors even knew that this vast behind-the-scenes trading arena existed. Like politicians making backroom deals away from the public eye, the anonymity afforded by ECNs helped professional traders move stocks among themselves without causing short-term price fluctuations that cut into profits.

All this changed when the Securities and Exchange Commission (SEC) implemented its new order-handling rules in January 1997. Recall from chapter 9 that those rules, resulting from the spread-fixing scandal, required market makers to act on a limit order they received themselves, display the order as their own, or send it to an ECN that all traders could access. In the latter case, the source behind the order would still remain anonymous. However, the new SEC rules also gave all investors access to ECN trading. Private trading networks with odd-sounding names like BRUT, REDI, Archipelago, and Island suddenly entered the average investor's vocabulary. And just as quickly the number of participants posting bids and offers over the Nasdaq expanded exponentially. Instead of a dozen or so market makers showing the prices they were willing to trade a stock for, the Nasdaq Level II display was now open to everyone. An industry—indeed a revolution in trading—had sprung up virtually overnight.

The ABCs of ECNs

EXACTLY HOW DID this new industry affect everyday investors? In order to understand that, it is helpful to look more closely at what typically happens to the trades you make that do not go through ECNs. As it turns out, any number of things may happen, especially in the case of market orders for Nasdaq stocks.

As a first possibility, your online brokerage might route your order to its own trading desk (although not all brokers maintain trading desks). Once the order arrives, it is the job of traders there to take the opposite side of customers' trades. If they do so, they are required to match the market's current best price. When your broker takes the trade, it earns the spread, just as market makers on the Nasdaq do. However, brokers will buy and sell shares using the firm's account only if they like the prevailing price. If they do not like the price, they may route your order to a particular market-making firm with whom they have a relationship. That firm, too, would profit from the spread. These days decimalization has narrowed spreads to as little as a penny with some heavily traded stocks. However, prior to decimalization, if you bought 100 shares of a stock that was heavily traded, you might in effect pay 12 cents per share because you were buying at the top end of the spread. On a 100-share order, that 12 cents would amount to $12. Add another $12 when you decide to sell the stock and take your profits. All told, the cost of owning the stock for a short time could be $24, plus commissions. Your stock would have to move up that much just for you to break even.

Now imagine that you are a professional trader hired by a mutual fund to unload 10,000 shares of a stock. Suddenly, that $12 cost of the spread jumps to $1,200. But with many stocks, particularly those of smaller, lightly traded companies, the cost would be far higher because such a large order would temporarily flood the market and bring the stock's price down. Insiders call this toll "market impact."

Needless to say, professional traders have long known that to trade profitably they needed to find a price that is somewhere between that bid-ask spread. The easiest way to do that is through a limit order as opposed to a market order. Limit orders allow you to specify the price you are willing to accept. If you enter a limit order on a Nasdaq stock, it may still go to a market maker, just like a market order. However, there is no guarantee the trade will occur because the market maker may simply display the order or, as required by the SEC's order-handling rules, send it to an ECN. Meanwhile, you are still waiting for an execution. And during that time, the market might well move in the opposite direction, in which case your order would never get filled.

Therein lies the reason that professional traders migrated to private networks. They needed to execute their orders quickly. Instead of waiting for the market to match the limit order's price, professional traders often prefer to ferret out buyers and sellers themselves. ECNs helped them do just that. Say that you are a professional trader wanting to dump 50,000 shares of XYZ stock for an average price of around $17 per share. Gazing at your Level II display, you attempt to feed the order out little by little by hitting a list of bids. That is, each time you spot a buyer on your screen, you can select, or "preference," that buyer. The transaction occurs instantly at the price each bidder specifies. The buyer might be a market maker whose name appears alongside his bid and ask on the Level II quote display. Alternately, the buyer might be someone displaying an anonymous bid on an ECN. Market conditions may force you to sell some shares fractionally below your $17 target price. Conversely, you may get lucky and sell shares at a slightly higher price. Thus, by varying your price a fraction up here, a fraction down there, you could gradually "piece out" a large order of stock at an acceptable average price.

They Put the Direct in Direct Access

EVEN AFTER THE change in order-handling rules, retail traders did not have ready access to ECNs. A limit order fielded by a retail customer might find its way to an ECN. In addition, most brokerages by the late 1990s allowed customers access to a single ECN for after-hours trading. But to easily use ECNs during the regular market hours, you needed to sign up with a special kind of broker, called a direct access broker. So, along with the dozen or so ECNs that eventually competed with one another in the wake of the SEC's rule changes, literally dozens of direct access brokers emerged to let their day-trading customers patch into ECN trading. Among the best known were CyBerCorp.com, Tradecast.com, Tradescape.com, and Terra-Nova Trading.

Direct access brokers themselves prompted a revolution in trading. Instead of routing orders for their customers in the laborious old method of sending them first to their own trading desks and then, perhaps, to a market maker of their own choosing, direct access brokers let their customers decide for themselves where they wanted their trades to go: perhaps to an ECN called Island or to Merrill Lynch's market maker or to Instinet. In other words, they gave their customers direct access to the market. Customers could single out a particular market maker whose bid they liked and, zap, the trade would take place. If you saw a bid on Island or REDI that you liked, you could hit that bid, and once again, in a flash, the trade took place. Suddenly, thousands of active, individual traders were using the same tools that institutional traders had long used, and their quotes were appearing in competition with Nasdaq's veteran dealers.

Getting inside the spread could save you a few cents per share every time you traded. Day traders, making thousands of such trades in the course of a year, earned their living this way. And the stocks day traders used to earn a living were invariably Nasdaq stocks. That is because the trading software offered by direct access brokers couldn't display New York Stock Exchange (NYSE) stocks with anything like the granularity made possible by the Nasdaq Level II screen. Trading of NYSE shares occurred on the NYSE itself and on regional exchanges and within certain trading firms as well as Instinet (see below). However, no commonly available trading platform showed quotes from all these sources in a single display. Therefore active trader strategies like preferencing and negotiation were far more difficult with NYSE stocks. Thanks to ECNs and the involvement of numerous dealer firms the Nasdaq Level II display revealed a market where numerous participants vied for trades simultaneously, thus making possible a multitude of highly complex trading strategies (see chapter 12). The result was that hordes of day traders began buying and selling Nasdaq stocks, almost exclusively, which in turn shifted the OTC market into a yet higher gear. The consequences of this were both good and bad. Volume rose, as did prices. But as you'll see in the next chapter, so did volatility.

Origins of an Invisible Market

PRIOR TO THE change in order-handling rules, the great majority of professional traders that used ECNs went to one in particular, Instinet, which was built way back in 1969 by a former broker named Jerome Pustilnik. Pustilnik's idea was to create a trading venue centered on high-volume NYSE stocks, not

OTC (over the counter) issues. He devised Instinet as an alternative to the Big Board specialists who held a virtual monopoly on the trading of individual stocks there. The network would function much like proprietary trading firms, such as Weeden & Co., that attempted to capture order flow from NYSE specialists. The difference was that whereas Weeden employed flesh-and-blood traders, Instinet would be totally automated. Trading on it would thus resemble trading on the Nasdaq. And in that sense, Instinet pre-dated the Nasdaq system by more than a year. Using Instinet, any trading firm that rented a dedicated video display terminal could theoretically patch into a global network.

At the time, however, most professional traders were more comfortable working the phones than using computer keyboards. So Instinet's volume remained sluggish for over a decade. It was not until the early 1980s that it started to catch on in any significant way. That was when Wall Street's rocket scientists (see chapter 6) began experimenting with it. They already used computer programs to generate buy and sell signals. Thus, they likely felt comfortable doing their actual trading over a computerized network. Instinet's all electronic network gave them the superhuman speed they needed to capture tiny per-share profits from such things as index arbitrage trades.

Like Instinet, the nation's regional exchanges had also long competed for order flow with the NYSE. It was one former specialist at the Pacific Stock Exchange named William Lupien who realized that Instinet was ignoring the vast universe of OTC stocks. Soon after joining Instinet around 1983, Lupien was named its chief executive officer.

Still the network plodded along with only a few hundred users. The big change came in 1987, when British media giant Reuters bought out the network for a reported $110 million.[3] (By some accounts Nasdaq had also been a potential buyer.) For Reuters it was a timely investment. The market crash later that year revealed the critical shortcomings of the Nasdaq's market-maker system. During Black Monday, volatility exploded after market makers allegedly ignored the phone calls that signaled orders from panicked investors. Thus, in the wake of the meltdown, professional traders realized that they needed an alternative means of unloading shares in a hurry.

Having built up Instinet's volume to respectable levels, Lupien exited in 1988. However, he would resurface roughly a decade later with a radical new vision of what an ECN should be. Meanwhile, Instinet continued to prosper. By the mid-1990s, more than 5,000 brokers subscribing to the system were paying Reuters handsome fees to rent dedicated terminals and proprietary software. The network itself was handling a staggering 20 percent of Nasdaq's daily volume. Revenue in 1996 was a reported $588 million. By this time, not only was Instinet handling trading on the Nasdaq, but links tied it to 15 other stock markets around the world.[4] While it grew as a portal to the world's stock markets and amassed growing legions of loyal users, Instinet remained, technically speaking, a brokerage. As a brokerage it created links to international exchanges by purchasing seats on them, just as any brokerage might. (Other ECNs would likewise set themselves up as broker dealers, which is the category under which they were regulated by the SEC.)

During the time that Instinet was expanding internationally, the company's research-and-development department concocted ever more elaborate tweaks to the ECN's trading software, giving its traders advanced analytical tools to evaluate short-term trends and a plethora of ways to field their bids and offers. A trader, for example, could show an offer for 5,000 shares while holding back thousands more in the event a crowd of buyers surfaced. Traders often used these advanced tools to test bids and offers in an effort to "discover" a stock's prevailing price. Since it was largely professionals trading with one another on Instinet, the prices at which trades occurred reflected the prevailing price consensus even more so than trades on the Nasdaq as a whole. Prices on the Nasdaq might represent panic selling on the part of less savvy retail investors, whereas trades on Instinet originated from level-headed professionals.

The industry term for these complex online negotiations that professional traders engaged in is "price discovery." And price discovery proved especially important during periods of international turmoil. At such times, dealers needed to follow a stock's price in the long hours between the close of one day's trading and the start of the next—as well as look for ceilings and floors during volatile periods when the market opened.

Needless to say, as a 24-hour trading arena linked to exchanges around the world, Instinet served as living proof that Nasdaq Chairman Frank Zarb's vision of a global stock exchange might indeed work. And in the years ahead, as you'll see in chapter 17, it would see itself as a rival to the Nasdaq. Nevertheless, even following the order-handling rule changes, Instinet's global reach existed primarily to serve professional traders.

The Open-Source Trading Network

RATHER THAN FOCUSING on institutional traders, a new generation of ECNs that emerged following the SEC's order-handling rule changes targeted the growing number of online day traders—and for good reason. An ECN needed liquidity if it was to survive. And day traders in particular might wrack up volume comparable to professional dealers. Many day traders routinely traded 1,000-share blocks. Some might make 50 or more roundtrip trades per day. Thus, a single trader might account for 100,000 shares of trading volume.

One of the most successful ECNs catering to active traders was Island. And in personality, it could hardly be more different than Instinet. Whereas Instinet, with its British ties, came off as an exclusive country club for traders from patrician financial firms, Island began as a rebellious upstart, which neatly mirrored the attitudes of the freewheeling day traders it served. Even Island's offices on lower Manhattan's Broad Street, practically at the NYSE's doorstep, were a seeming affront to Wall Street conventions. Computer cables created a tangled web on the office floor. And while legions of Wall Street's minions padded through the financial district in suits, Island's founder, Joshua Levine, is said to have prowled Island's offices dressed in jeans and socks. And he reportedly kept a pet lizard in his cluttered office.

Like some of its ECN competitors, Island was an outgrowth of a brokerage that catered to active traders. In Island's case, the brokerage was called Datek. (They are now separate companies.) Datek's founders had developed a trading platform, similar to the kind used by professional traders, that allowed customers to route orders directly to the Nasdaq market. But while Bloomberg and Instinet's trading platform required a dedicated terminal, the Datek platform could run on an ordinary PC. In addition, instead of requiring a private network, it could transmit and receive orders via the Internet. Both innovations cut costs dramatically for traders and made it possible for virtually anyone to trade actively.[5]

Island, launched in February 1996, began by matching orders for Datek's own customers. Months later, when the SEC announced its new order-handling rules, Island suddenly was uniquely positioned to take advantage of the changes. The new order-handling rules allowed Island quotes to be displayed on Nasdaq's Level II screen, right alongside those of dealers. As time passed, Island also made it relatively easy for the growing number of day-trading firms to route orders through its system. Volume on Island grew steadily in tandem with the late 1990s bull market. By the start of 1999, the ECN was handling roughly 10 percent of the Nasdaq's daily volume—but with a staff of only 19 whose average age was 25.[6]

Like Instinet and the Nasdaq itself, Island's management team devised grandiose plans for growth. In 1999, Island launched into the difficult and lengthy process of becoming a stock exchange. The move would put it on par, at least from a regulatory standpoint, with the NYSE. More important, it would enable Island to trade NYSE stocks without relying on network connections provided by the Nasdaq. Later, Island also forged ties with the ECN Access Europe to give investors there direct access to the U.S. market.

In November of 2001, Island edged past Instinet as the highest volume trading network for Nasdaq securities. [7] And it has done so in large part by garnering a huge, loyal following among active traders. Part of that loyalty no doubt stems from the fact that Island provides free of charge the sort of market data that the Nasdaq continues to charge fees for. For all intents and purposes, Island's Java-based order book (the list of bid and ask prices for a particular stock) looks just like a Nasdaq Level II quote display. But unlike a Level II quote display, you did not have to sign with a broker to view it. And you did not have to pay $10 per month in exchange fees or $300 per month in software rental fees. Anyone could view it just by going to the Island Web site. Providing an order book for free set a tone of openness that other ECNs would quickly mimic.

Island's order book, when viewed in isolation, possessed one serious drawback, however. Quotes on Island show prices of trades only on that ECN. At the same time, trading was proceeding fast and furious on other ECNs. Nasdaq market makers were fielding their own offers and jousting with an exploding number of day traders. If you were one of those day traders, you needed to see the big picture. To meet that need, several ECNs have built something called "smart order routing software" into their systems. The software first scans the order book within its particular ECN to find the best price. Failing that, it sends its orders to the market at large. The software effectively linked together all subscribing ECNs as well as the market as a whole. And in some cases it enabled users to custom configure the path their orders might take as well as the priority they wished to give their orders.

The prospect of linked ECNs would eventually pose an even bigger challenge to the Nasdaq itself. It's counteracting strategy was to become the central conduit through which all trades passed. Yet as a membership organization, it could hardly innovate as quickly as the nimble private companies that managed ECNs. And so, for many months as it readied new software platforms designed to compete with ECNs, the Nasdaq could only watch as this new generation of ECNs clawed away at its market share. The consequence for its dealer firms was lost revenue. Instead of paying dealers the spread, active traders were paying ECNs access fees.

A Chain of Islands

ARCHIPELAGO WAS PRECISELY that next-generation ECN. Like Island, Archipelago had close ties to a popular day-trading software provider, Townsend Analytics, the same company that designed the Real Tick day-trading software platform used by scores of brokerages catering to active traders. Also like Island, Archipelago maintains a Java-based order book that anyone can view for free on the Web. However, the Archipelago order book includes quotes from other ECNs, and so its prices in theory more closely follow the prices listed on the Nasdaq Level II book.

In late 1999, CNBC bought 12.4 percent of Archipelago. The ECN's other partners include financial firms Goldman Sachs, J.P. Morgan, and American Century Investors.[8] The involvement of these financial powerhouses reveals how they are hedging their bets in the rapidly changing equity market environment, even as they possess a stake in Nasdaq's long-term success. If their own traders continue to lose out on trades, the lost revenues might be made up by the fees charged by an ECN.

Some criticized CNBC for stepping beyond the bounds of traditional journalism when it bought a de facto stake in the very market it was reporting on. But the network was really only following in the footsteps of two other financial media giants. Bloomberg, publisher of magazines, books, radio shows, and television programming, also owned an ECN widely used by institutions called Bloomberg Trade Book, while British media giant Reuters owned Instinet.

And indeed, Instinet has also made an investment in Archipelago. Then in a move that further typifies the byzantine relationships that now exist among ECNs, media companies, and financial firms, in late November 2001, Archipelago announced plans to merge with another fast-growing ECN, REDIbook. Like Archipelago, REDIbook enjoyed the backing of some of the nation's largest financial firms, including Schwab and Fidelity. According to an Archipelago statement, the two ECNs would handle an average daily volume of some 460 million shares, both from the Nasdaq and the NYSE.[9] A month earlier, Archipelago had announced an even more ambitious merger, this time with the Pacific Exchange. The SEC approved the deal—which had been in the works for over a year—on October 25, 2001.[10] The new Archipelago Exchange would trade not only Nasdaq stocks, but also shares listed on the NYSE and the Amex.

Too Much Information

NOT ALL ECNS were successful. Some set themselves on the bleeding edge of innovation and fizzled as a result. One of the surprising failures was a radical new trading network called OptiMark, launched by former Instinet Chief Executive Officer Bill Lupien. Lupien tried to create a turbocharged Instinet for institutional traders. His start-up company operated out of a storefront office in Durango, Colorado. And Lupien saw the placid location as proof that new trading systems were rapidly transforming global financial markets. "Prior to the Internet we thought in terms of point-to-point communication. Now things bounce around all over the place," he said.[11]

Nevertheless, Lupien had plenty of help from the nation's financial epicenters. OptiMark's backers included Goldman Sachs & Co. and other investment banks, plus 15 percent owner Dow Jones & Co. Also, thanks to the high regard Lupien enjoyed in the industry, OptiMark quickly achieved direct patches into the Pacific Exchange and the Nasdaq. All OptiMark needed to succeed were enough professional traders to pump its volume up to a few million shares per day.

OptiMark was designed to eliminate the need for market makers and specialists while still providing sufficient liquidity. Lupien's ingenious solution was to aggregate everyone's orders together, using sophisticated artificial intelligence (AI) software. If you wanted to buy 100 shares of Ford, your order got lumped together with Vanguard's order for 500,000 shares, with Merrill and Fidelity's order, and so on. Because orders were aggregated by price, the system offered even more anonymity than a typical ECN book, where individual quotes appeared by themselves. Aggregating orders forced traders to react strictly to buy- and sell-side volume, without clueing them in as to who the participants might be. In other words, none of the users would buy or sell from specific individuals or firms. Instead they simply dipped into a common pool of liquidity. (Later, as described in chapter 17, this idea of a common pool of liquidity would be applied to the aggregated quotes that formed part of Nasdaq's SuperMontage trading platform).

Here in a nutshell is how the system was supposed to work. OptiMark's AI algorithm, developed in conjunction with IBM, enabled institutional traders to piece out orders automatically, something they previously had to do with exquisite care by hand, while their attention was focused unwaveringly on each tick of the market. However, before any automated trading actually began, traders created something called an anonymous profile. A profile might specify the number of shares a trader was willing to buy or sell at a predetermined series of prices. The algorithm scanned a trader's profile along with the many other profiles in the system for a particular stock. Then it executed the trades where matches occurred, subtracting its commission.

Lupien believed that OptiMark's computerized matching system would arrive at prices light-years faster than traders using computer terminals, pumping up volume on the exchanges as a result and enhancing liquidity. Moreover, he claimed that the actual prices arrived at would be more indicative of a stock's actual worth. "To the extent that we can reduce the risk of an institution trying to buy or sell a large block [of shares], we're going to free up their ability to trade that block," he said. Trade after trade, liquidity would snowball. "The institution that quickly sells 5 million shares will also want to quickly turn around and buy 5 million shares."

In the end, however, traders appeared reluctant to learn OptiMark's seemingly complex programming. And their reaction hit at the core of the debate over whether electronic matching systems like OptiMark could really outwit human traders and their gut-based strategies. "Institutional traders are going to continue believing that they can beat the system," explained James Angel, a professor of finance at Georgetown University, "especially the guys on the trading floor whose job it is to work the orders. Their value added is they sit there and decide how to break up the order and feed it out into the market."[12] Indeed, Angel believes that traders revel in such poker strategies. "With trading everyone wants to know what everyone else is doing, but no one wants to reveal their information. There's always the concern somebody knows more than you do."

But that is not to say that similar systems might catch on in a big way with investors in the future. If the complex process of creating a profile on OptiMark could be automated and made invisible. Investors could field orders through a variety of networks and via a variety of complex means, with all the necessary processing taking place in the background.

Who Let the Dogs Out?

THAT WAS THE promise of the future. In the here and now, the Nasdaq still had much to fear from ECNs. With Island and Archipelago, for example, seeking to become exchanges, the Nasdaq faced competition from the NYSE as before but also from three powerful electronic rivals that together were responsible for more than one third of its volume. Each was able to provide customers with niche advantages that the Nasdaq could not since regulations forced the Nasdaq to cater to all customers. Thus, Instinet, with offices in New York, London, Paris, Frankfurt, Zurich, Tokyo, Hong Kong, and Toronto and with links to numerous foreign stock markets, could already provide the kind of turnkey global network that Zarb envisioned for the Nasdaq. Likewise Island, in addition to providing a U.S. conduit for European traders, was the user-friendly alternative at home.

Finally, Archipelago might in the end prove the most formidable competition to the Nasdaq. Thanks to its ties to Townsend Analytics, Archipelago can draw on a vast in-house technical knowledge base, which may make it faster on its feet and more innovative than the Nasdaq. In addition, by aggregating orders from other ECNs within its order book, it has supplanted a huge share of Nasdaq volume already. Then there is Archipelago's West Coast location, in the heart of Silicon Valley, enabling it perhaps to attract listings and become the trading venue of choice for start-ups based there. Other smaller ECNs discovered ways to differentiate themselves as well. MarketXT launched in order to focus mainly on after-hours trading. Then it broadened its strategy by trying to cater to institutional traders. NexTrade, another ECN, promoted its 24-hour trading environment.

With ECNs storming the palace gates, Nasdaq officials at first warned that they were siphoning off liquidity and that they might well fragment the market. As a result, investors would find it impossible to know whether they were getting the right price. "Fragmentation is not good. Fragmentation hurts liquidity," said one former Nasdaq official.

If ECNs operated in total isolation, then fragmentation would indeed be a risk, akin to running from one auction room to another in order to ensure you were getting the best price. But ECNs were able to link together, as Archipelago had done, to eliminate this problem. In addition, the argument fails to take into account the fact that institutional traders had been trading billions of shares over ECNs for years despite the low volume and lack of liquidity. Had they adversely impacted the market? The truth is that ECNs never threatened to seriously fragment trading during the day. After all, the best quotes on any given ECN got displayed right alongside the best quotes by market makers on everyone's Nasdaq Level II screens.

By the end of the 1990s, officials at both the Nasdaq and the NYSE realized that they too needed to beat the ECNs at their own game or else risk losing still more market share. Their solution was to create ECN-like networks of their own. The NYSE, for example, moved forward with what it calls NYSE Direct+. It would allow customer orders to be matched directly. Other refinements at the NYSE included an order book depicting far more information than the NYSE specialists previously allowed investors to see. The NYSE had good reason to move quickly. NYSE Direct+ debuted roughly a year after ECNs gained the ability to trade NYSE stocks. And so far, those ECNs have managed to steal something like 10 percent of the NYSE's share volume.

The Nasdaq's plans went a step further, and they formed a focal point of its strategy through the early part of 2000 and

2001. Seeing the imminent rise in trading volume, Zarb announced that he was doubling the capacity of Nasdaq's computer system only three weeks after he assumed the chairman's post. "We have one of the world's largest private communication systems," a top Nasdaq official boasted.[13] The network, built by MCI WorldCom, was able to handle eight billion shares daily. Then there was the Nasdaq's SuperMontage strategy to link competing ECNs together under the Nasdaq's umbrella by aggregating quotes of the same price from the entire market—ECNs included—within a single display.

To fend off ECN competition, the Nasdaq also revamped its own ECN-like order-routing networks, beginning with SOES (small-order execution system) and SelectNet (which had been set up to handle larger transactions). SOES and SelectNet were combined to form something called SuperSOES. Like the old SOES and SelectNet, the new SuperSOES will mainly serve as a conduit (a kind of backbone network), routing orders from brokers, market makers, and ECNs.

Nasdaq officials harbored far more ambitious plans for SuperMontage, scheduled for launch in 2002 (see chapter 17). SuperMontage will resemble Level II, displaying a list of best bid and offers from ECNs and market makers. Another window will aggregate five levels of similar-priced orders from the entire market. Liquidity would come from member dealer firms and ECNs if they chose to subscribe, and from foreign investors. The end result, Nasdaq planners hoped would be the deepest common pool of liquidity available anywhere. "The Nasdaq is the only market that has the technology to create the critical mass that will enhance liquidity and link to different kinds of systems," a former official said. Like ECNs, Nasdaq's SuperMontage would charge fees when transactions occurred. Significantly, Nasdaq's plans were closely tied with it becoming a for-profit exchange. Then like ECNs, it too could react quickly to whatever new sweeping changes in trading technology came along.

Some predict that SuperMontage will put ECNs out of business or alternately transform the Nasdaq into the largest of several ECNs. Others disagree. And they point to the technical difficulties and political fights that the Nasdaq has so far encountered as it struggles to push SuperMontage forward. The NASD efforts to separate the Nasdaq market from the regulatory body and the move to make the Nasdaq a publicly traded company in its own right also are in part motivated by the need to quell market-maker descent. With the Nasdaq functioning as a public company, market-making firms' shrinking profits could be offset by generous ownership stakes in SuperMontage.

12

DAWN OF THE DAY TRADER

DURING A HOT summer afternoon in 2000, Brendan De-Lamielleure sat in the spare room of his apartment, staring at his computer screen, getting madder by the second over the erratic way the market was moving. "Everything I get out of runs. Everything I stay in just comes right back where I bought it," complained the then 28-year-old former professional trader from St. Louis. What DeLamielleure meant was that every time he bought a stock thinking it would rise, the stock hovered at its current price or, worse, retreated slightly. But if he sold the stock to cut his losses, then soon after it would typically move up in price. In other words, he was second-guessing the market and getting it wrong more often than he would have liked.

Like a lot of traders at the turn of the century, DeLamielleure was finding that the market was becoming less and less forgiving, less and less predictable. This was a total turnaround from prior years, when the market wracked up new highs practically on a daily basis. Thanks to those heady times, DeLamielleure had decided to quit his brokerage job and take up day trading. It was a smart move, as it turned out. Working out of his home, glued to his PC, DeLamielleure took about $1 million in profits from the market.

During the late 1990s' tech boom, thousands of neophyte day traders regularly jousted toe to toe with large institutional traders and market makers. Their perpetual wars were in a sense the ultimate online game. True, untold thousands of Web addicts spent their spare time playing Internet games like *Doom*. But that hardly compared to the exploits of the day-trading subculture. Here were ordinary people who often let their entire life savings ride on wildly volatile Nasdaq stocks—day after day. Collectively, they congregated within a tight network of ECNs (electronic communications networks), online brokerages, and financial Web sites, the likes of which had never been seen before. During the late 1920s' market boom, when over-the-counter trading as we know it today became wildly popular, active investors gathered in brokerage houses across the country to read the latest stock prices that emerged from the ticker tape machine. Now, the communication was entirely online. Skilled day traders could monitor what people were saying about a stock in a chat room, then e-mail friends for their opinions. In addition, they could explore the company's Web site, read real-time news, and purchase the latest analyst reports, all without leaving their computers. Hours, perhaps even days of data collecting and analysis could be accomplished in mere moments.

At the heart of this fathomless financial information network was the Nasdaq itself, which was proving itself the ideal arena for their blood sport. Indeed, as the Nasdaq soared ever higher, day trading emerged as one of the Internet's killer applications. Day trading depended on fast communications and access to vast amounts of information—things unavailable before the Internet's arrival. Day traders also took advantage of the Internet's unique ability to cut out whole layers of brokers and other middlemen. They could buy and sell shares instantly from any number of sources. This was a quantum leap from how stock trading had existed just a few years before, when a customer called in an order to his broker and waited to receive confirmation in the mail or perhaps via a phone call later. Online brokers reduced that waiting time to minutes, while the specialized brokers used by day traders cut it down to milliseconds.

Day traders needed this speed to extract gains of a penny or so per share. Such gains were often at the expense of less-savvy everyday investors. But just as likely, day traders fought against one another. And their ongoing wars caused stocks to move up and down in price. Day-trading coach Oliver Velez described these wars succinctly. Every day in the market, he says, "is nothing more than a tug of war between two groups: the buyers and the sellers. The objective of the trader should be to find the specific point where the balance of power has shifted."[1]

Thus, the market as a whole became a kind of huge virtual casino, while each stock that traded there was like a table at that casino. And day traders were able to choose literally from thousands of tables. But where casinos were based largely on luck, success at trading meant being faster, smarter, and gutsier than your foes. Beyond that, you could play the day-trading game however you liked.

And wherever you liked. Therein lay day trading's other powerful appeal: You could earn a living at it, maybe even get rich. But unlike most other businesses, there was no need to hire employees, rent office space, or deal with burdensome government regulations. And you did not have to master salesmanship or office politics. If you were a victim of corporate downsizing midway through your career, day trading was an alluring alternative. You could start the moment your check cleared at your brokerage.

A Business Like Any Other

SMALL-BUSINESS OWNERS, already used to operating freely, were particularly attracted to day trading. One West Coast day trader described how he got his start after he grew tired of the photography business. "Photography is a kind of feast or famine business," he recalls. "You make good money when you're busy. But then when it slows down you go crazy." That trader, incidentally, went on to make hundreds of thousands in the market—more than he could probably hope to earn as a photographer.[2]

Yet on another level, there are interesting similarities between photography and day trading. Both are male-dominated professions. Both professions also tend to attract free-spirited, creative types. In addition, both professions require a similar amount of start-up capital. A professional photographer would likely need $30,000 to $50,000 in start-up capital to purchase lenses, lights, and other studio equipment. Day traders often began with a similar amount. Assuming that a photographer billed his time at $1,000 or more per working day, it was relatively easy to see a 300 to 400 percent annual return on that investment. Day traders hoped for similar returns.

Many in the financial community questioned whether such returns were possible, however, even in a raging bull market. A study by the National Association of Securities Dealers (NASD), for example, found that 77 percent of day traders lost money. Those who did not earned just $22,000 over an eight-month period. To reach its findings, researchers examined the records of 124 traders and found only two cases where earnings reached $100,000 or more.[3] Because of findings like these, the Securities and Exchange Commission (SEC) mounted a campaign of its own on its Web site, warning newcomers about the dangers of day trading. "Day traders typically suffer severe financial losses in their first months of trading, and many never graduate to profit-making status," the warnings read. "Day trading is an extremely stressful and expensive full-time job."[4] These assertions, however, ignored the fact that day trading was a relatively new phenomenon. Nearly all new businesses of any kind lose money at the start. And the great majority ultimately fail. In addition, thousands of professional traders regularly wracked up profits for themselves and their firms using the same tactics and tools used by day traders.

The Hard and Not So Hard Core

WARNINGS BY THE financial establishment did little to squelch the ranks of day traders. Instead, as the number of day traders grew, a collateral industry consisting of schools, online brokerages, and financial Web sites sprang up overnight to support them. This industry included discussion Web sites, such as Silicon Investor and Raging Bull; news sites, such as CBS Market Watch and TheStreet.com; two magazines, *Active Trader* and *Online Investor;* plus at least three financial television networks: CNNfn, CNBC, and Bloomberg TV. Add to this group an estimated 5,000[5] specialized financial Web sites. Many of these sites sprang up to reach the 10 million people who traded through online accounts. But the content of most seemed clearly geared to active traders. Some subscription sites featured real-time online commentary from expert traders in chat rooms packed with novice traders eager to learn their moves. Still other financial Web sites used sophisticated computer modeling software—previously available only to institutions—to thoroughly analyze a stock. One site, Validea.com (as in "valid idea"), devised automated investment programs that mimicked popular investment styles: contrarian investing, for example, or growth or value investing. Another site, called VectorVest.com, let subscribers enter a stock symbol and receive a detailed report on the stock's prospects. The result was a deluge of financial information available to the public the likes of which had not been seen since the late 1920s market boom. A few years before, an avid investor might subscribe to *Barron's,* the *Wall Street Journal,* and perhaps *Investor's Business Daily* or *Value-Line.* And a relatively small group subscribed to specialized investment newsletters that cost hundreds of dollars annually. Now financial information deluged the Internet from thousands of sources. There were real-time business news feeds from Reuters and Dow Jones, JagNotes and others. Other sites, such as Zacks .com, published consensus earnings estimates from thousands of companies, information that typically moves a stock's price. But many companies deliberately understated their forthcoming earnings so as not to disappoint the Street once the official announcement was made. As a result, some Web sites, such as WhisperNumbers.com, attempted to relay these whispered earnings numbers. A few critics called the proliferation of financial Web sites investment pornography. With so many sources of information to choose from, the most difficult task facing a trader was often how to isolate what was useful.

Amateurs Go Pro

ACCURATE ESTIMATES OF the number of day traders remain hard to come by. Some put the number of hard-core day traders at just 5,000 to 8,000.[6] This group consisted of the most hyperactive traders, those who traded much like regular Nasdaq dealers. Hyperactive traders might make 50 or more trades per day. Often they profited from the tiniest moves in a stock's price, buying 1,000 shares of a stock, for example, then waiting a few minutes before selling at perhaps 12 cents per share higher, giving them a $120 profit before commissions. To make money, they needed to repeat this winning round-trip trade perhaps eight or nine times a day. With commissions at the time running about $20, day traders might easily spend $300 or more per day, or $100,000 or more per year. At the end of the day, this breed of day trader cashed in their chips. That is, they sold all their stock—the better to sleep at night and start fresh when the market reopened. Many of these traders worked in brokerage-provided trading rooms where they were furnished with computers, trading software, and fast Internet connections.

For every hard-core day trader, there were dozens if not hundreds of traders who still hung on the market's every tick day after day. One financial editor, put the number of active traders at about 100,000 before the crash of 2000. Others said it was much higher. "Over a million active investors are surfing the Web each day," estimated the cofounder of a popular financial chat site. Some believed that this vast group accounted for more than half the total trades on the Nasdaq each day and that the number of active traders might grow to five million in the coming years.

Survivors, Programmers, and Risk Takers

WHATEVER THEIR NUMBERS, active traders tended to come from all walks of life. David Gordon, who runs the popular on-line trading Web site TrenchRat.com, was a former swimming pool salesman. He took up trading while he was recovering from a serious bout with cancer. "When you're laying on your back, there's not too many ways to make money. So it was like a trade I had to learn, like an electrician." Another Midwest-based trader, named Bob Martin, managed to make roughly a million dollars in the market while working full time as a lawyer. Scott McCormick tapped into his knowledge of artificial intelligence software that he learned working on Defense Department and NASA projects to design trading programs that he says boosted his portfolio by at least 50 percent annually.

Tim Bourquin's experiences with day trading are likewise unique. [7] A former police officer in the Los Angeles area, for a time Bourquin was assigned to the department's Career Criminal Unit. Working in plain clothes, Bourquin and fellow officers hunted down car-jackers, violent robbers, and other confirmed bad guys. Once a camera crew from the reality TV show *LAPD* followed Bourquin and his cohorts in the course of their work. "The good thing about being a police officer was that my schedule can change to whatever hours I need it to," Bourquin recalled. By working nights as a cop, he was free to day trade during regular market hours.

Bourquin came to law enforcement and then day trading after serving as a broker for several years, a job he says he did not like. "It's more stressful handling other people's money. With myself, if I trade and I lose money I consider it tuition, and I go on."

Buying and selling stocks on behalf of his clients, Bourquin also traded on his own and found that he was losing too much:

> The buy-and-hold strategy just didn't make a whole lot of sense for me. I'd see a 30 percent profit and then have it wiped out the next week. And I thought, "This is ridiculous. Why don't I take advantage of these fluctuations and try and sell it at the top, wait for it to come back down, and then buy again?"

His results improved once he took up day trading. Early on Cisco became one of his favorite trading stocks. "It tended to move in a similar way each day, depending on what kind of news it had," he recalls. "If it had good news or no news it tended to jump up right at the beginning. After the first 30 minutes it almost always came back down to where it started to trade again." And it continued to roll in a predictable way following lunch. Bourquin used sophisticated charting software that closely tracked a stock's price and volume in an effort to analyze and then predict these rolls.

"I usually throw up a tick-by-tick chart during the day and watch the charts develop and really try to find those bottoms and the tops of each of those rolls." By watching such short term charts, he says:

> You really get a good feeling for how much volume is coming through or how much is being offered at a certain price. If I can make a sixteenth and eighth on each of those ups and downs during the day, if I can do that four or five times during the day, then I'm doing pretty well.

As the months progressed, Bourquin further refined his strategy. He steered toward stocks in the $50 to $75 price range. "I would have about four or five stocks that I would watch continuously all day. So I would be real familiar with them and get to know their behavior almost in the sense of being able to predict their behavior on an intraday basis."

His earnings from trading gradually began to equal his policeman's salary, while day trading increasingly became part of his normal routine. Arriving home from work at around 11 P.M., while his wife was sleeping, he would leap into studying his charts and map out the strategies he'd use when the markets opened the following morning.

> There are often times where I have no idea what the company does. I just know the symbol. Or I'll know just a tiny bit from what I see on the Dow Jones News Service. They're in some sort of semiconductor business or some sort of waste disposal. But that's the extent of it. I have no idea what their price earnings are, I have no idea what their sales were for last year or if they're making money or losing money because when I'm watching that intraday chart, I really could care less about any of that.

On some days he would make thousands from his deft moves. But on other days he might lose as much or more.

> It's those days when you really second-guess yourself and you wonder, "Is this really something I can do full time?" Just when you think you're a little bit smarter than the market, something will just blow you away, and you realize that this thing is a lot bigger than you will ever be.

To help alleviate some of the stress of trading as well as to share strategies with others, Bourquin started Day Traders of Orange County. Day Traders of Orange County eventually transformed into Day Traders USA, a nationwide group. Bourquin, one of the original and more visible day traders, then moved on to cofound the Online Trading Expo, which unites traders from all over the country at conventions in major cities.

Why Day Traders Love the Nasdaq

LIKE BOURQUIN WITH his noontime rolling stocks, every trader perfects a trading strategy that succeeds for him or her. Brendan DeLamielleure developed his strategy while working for a professional trading firm. It worked something like this: First he identified a heavily traded, household-name tech stock. In the late 1990s, the Internet incubator company CMGI nicely fit the bill. When the stock moved up on some good news, De-Lamielleure quickly bought stock of a similar though smaller company, a second-tier stock, as he described it, the theory being that the second-tier stock also would experience a short-lived pop.

DeLamielleure's system appears simple on the surface. But he, like Bourquin, backed it up with complex chart analysis. DeLamielleure's charts divided the market into neat five-minute segments. And he watched the action via his computer with several monitors, powered by a professional-grade trading program and a fast Internet connection to his online broker. Thanks to this setup, which cost thousands, the moment DeLamielleure spotted an opportunity, he could let his order fly to any Nasdaq market maker or ECN he chose and receive an execution almost instantaneously.

Therein lies the reason that many day traders preferred the Nasdaq to the NYSE. With its hardwired connections to numerous dealer firms and ECNs the Nasdaq was built for speed. And speed was precisely what day traders like DeLamielleure needed if they were to successfully enter and exit dozens of trades per day. The hyperactive trading patterns of day traders in a sense mimicked what the Nasdaq's professional dealers were doing: scalping quick profits from the spread. With day traders and market makers competing against each other, the Nasdaq became awash with liquidity. "Pretty much the Nasdaq floats itself," DeLamielleure says:

> No one supplies liquidity to the Nasdaq anymore. That's in the past. Now it's just complete peer trading. If something gets out of whack with New York [the NYSE], the specialists step in. But now on the Nasdaq, if something gets out of whack, it's the day traders and the market makers who correct it.

Market makers were not ecstatic about having to compete with day traders. With day traders snapping up their order flow, spreads narrowed further, cutting into their profits. Yet market makers also benefited from the liquidity that day traders brought to the market, DeLamielleure insists:

> A lot of times market makers use day traders to help take them out of positions or help them move their institutional [orders] for them. A lot of times, I don't know how they would get out of these stocks if it weren't for day traders providing more liquidity in the market. Some of these things just never traded before.

In other words, if a market maker wanted to buy or sell a large quantity of stock, he, like day traders, benefited because there was a greater number of buyers and sellers waiting in the wings.

Anatomy of a Momentum Trade

WITH MARKET MAKERS and day traders constantly jousting for control of the Nasdaq, the patterns of trading often resembled high-stakes poker games. "No one shows any size anymore," DeLamielleure said. "If someone does show size, you have to treat it as quite suspect. If all of a sudden you're looking at the screen and someone shows 10,000 shares at half above the market, there's a good chance that somebody's short. And they're just trying to lean on it."

DeLamielleure says he succeeds when he is able to outwit other traders or when he does not fall into their traps. As he explains:

> Let's say someone's sitting on the bid, a market maker, selling stock at 25 and prints 10,000 shares, and he keeps printing and keeps printing. Then he disappears, and then all of a sudden there's Instinet an eighth higher. People start buying on Instinet, and it's printing 10,000 shares, 20,000 shares. And Instinet might disappear, and then he might reappear, buying back the same shares you just bought from him. But he's paying a lower price. He's just playing games with you.

Ironically, one result of these perpetual poker games was increased volatility—ironic because added liquidity is supposed to suppress volatility. But groups of day traders acting independently could cause a stock's price to swing wildly. This sort of volatility resulted from one trading strategy in particular: momentum trading. When day traders sensed a move occurring in a stock, they rushed as a group to buy it. Here, the structure of the Nasdaq proved helpful since it made it particularly easy to acquire shares in a hurry. Each market maker and ECN was a prospective sales outlet. As each seller was taken out, the stock's price would tick up since it was replaced by the next seller's slightly higher price. This phenomenon helps explain why certain stocks during the period experienced price rises of $10 to $30 or more in the course a day. At some point, day traders would sense that a plateau had been reached in the stock's price. And they would run for the exits with their profits. Here again, the Nasdaq made exits easy, simply because it encompassed buyers from a multitude of dealing firms and ECNs.

Because they had multiple buying and selling outlets at their disposal, day traders were able to devise innumerable strategies as to where and how to direct their orders. "My best days are when I never have contact with a market maker, when I am completely buying on Island, selling on Island. And then if I have to use another ECN, I go through SelectNET," says De-Lamielleure.[8] That is, he could buy on Island and sell on Island moments later, as if the ECN were the only trading arena open for business an island by any other name.

Bells and Whistles

DIRECTING ORDERS TO specific ECNs like Island required special trading software. This software was available only from so-called direct-access brokers. And it was eons removed from the browser-based trading programs familiar to most Americans with online brokerage accounts. To understand the differences, it is helpful to see first how a browser-based trading program executes a trade. When you request a price quote from a browser-based broker, you are basically sending an e-mail from your own computer to the broker's server. The server then locates the quote data that you requested. Then it constructs a customized Web page containing this information and sends it back to your computer. Building this Web page can take time because other customers might be requesting information along with you, taxing the server. Delays can also occur due to heavy traffic on the Internet.

Day traders could not hope to compete with professional dealers if they were forced to use a slow browser-based broker. Instead, most signed on with direct-access or day-trading brokerages, such as CyberCorp.com or Tradecast.com, or one of their dozens of competitors. Direct-access brokerages gave day traders advanced ultrafast execution platforms. With those platforms came real-time charts and quotes. These were created directly on the user's PC rather than on the broker's server. That was because direct-access trading software itself resided on your desktop PC and not on a broker's server. A desktop PC could display updated information much faster than a broker's server because, unlike the server, it did not have to compete with the hundreds of other requests for server time from the brokerage's other customers. With a direct-access broker, the only information that traveled from that broker's server to your desktop was streaming quote data.

Newer day trading software makes use of Java applications to build functionality directly on users desktops. And, day-trading software suppliers continue adding increasingly sophisticated features to their software. You could send orders off with a single keystroke, for example. Analytical programs scanned the market looking for stocks that showed signs of making a move. The software could be programmed to send out an alert when a stock traded within certain parameters— for example, or when it rose in price by more than 50 cents on higher-than-normal volume. Traders could also arrange charts and blinking market quotes as they wished on their home computers. Those computers might have as many as eight monitors.

The Pursuit of Order Flow

MANY DIRECT-ACCESS brokerages charged rental fees upward of $300 per month for their software. But these fees were waived if a trader made a minimum number of trades per month. Eventually, competition among direct-access brokers prompted some to give their software away. Still other direct-access brokers also began charging commissions of just a penny or so per share. Meanwhile, Schwab, E*Trade, and Fidelity all announced stripped-down active-trader software in a bid to keep their day-trading customers from defecting. Hedging its bets, Schwab bought popular direct-access broker CyBerCorp.com. The $488 million price paid amounted to $195,000 each for the firm's 2,500 customers. And it astounded many. However, some of the broker's customers, because of their heavy trading, paid commissions equal to that amount each year. In fact, CyBer-Corp.com's 2,500 customers trade an astounding 20 million shares per day, ranking the firm among the nation's top nine online brokers.

Day-trading brokers continued to be successful at recruiting new traders for as long as the market maintained its meteoric rise. Active trading created a kind of firestorm within the Nasdaq. As volume and liquidity rose, so did stock prices—a natural consequence since people will always pay more for something if they know that they can quickly sell it for about the same price. Meanwhile, the popularity of day trading grew as broadband Internet connections reached more and more areas of the country, giving people there the necessary fast access to the markets.

And this created a firestorm of another sort. Day trading could not have existed were it not for the Internet providing an inexpensive professional-quality connection to the market. (Before the Internet arrived, active traders were forced to use expensive private-network connections to the market.) Likewise, the money that this growing group of day traders poured into the market actively sought stocks in Internet companies, which were the best-performing stocks at the time. Thus, day traders had a direct hand in fueling the Internet's growth. But, as you'll see in the next chapter, another, perhaps more important symbiotic relationship between day traders and Internet companies was also at play. And that had to do with day traders' love affair with volatility.

13

THE BIG BALLOON

INFOSYS TECHNOLOGIES LIMITED was precisely the kind of company that Frank Zarb had in mind when he outlined his dream of a 24/7 global stock market. Based in Karnatka, India, Infosys does contract Internet development work, mainly for North American firms. By paying its employees rock-bottom Indian wages, the company is able to compete on par with top U.S. software firms. Thanks to the company's steady growth in earnings, Infosys stock reached nirvana-like levels during the height of the dot-com boom. That rise was helped along in large part by active traders in the United States, like Allan James.[1] James did some research on the stock and was impressed enough that he bought 80 shares at the then going price of about $270, paying out $21,680 in all. Within eight weeks, the stock ascended to $625 per share, giving James a better than $28,000 profit. "That was definitely one of my better trades," he remembers. A few months later, however, James found that losing money on high-flying stocks was just as easy. A bad bet on Internet service provider MainSpring (now a part of EarthLink) cost him $27,000.

If investing is anything like gambling, then trading Internet stocks during the late 1990s could be compared to Russian roulette. For several heady years prior to the April 2000 market meltdown Internet stocks witnessed the same wild gyrations that earlier high-flying categories of OTC stocks like computer and aerospace firms had experienced. Amazon's stock rose by a breathtaking 966 percent in 1998. But between August 31 and September 1, 1998, shares of the online book retailer plummeted 25 points, from about $105 to $80. And although the period was a rough one for the Nasdaq in general, Amazon's steep fall was hardly an unusual event.

Unknown to most casual stock market investors, day traders thrived on just these sorts of wild price swings. With a little luck, a day trader working in his pajamas at home could buy from a lengthy list of Internet stocks priced at around $180, wait for them to reach $200, sell, and then watch those stocks drop by 30 points, at which point traders could buy them once again. When it came to trading Internet stocks, rolling with the punches could make you rich. Tech stocks, such as Cisco, Dell, and Intel, may have set the Nasdaq on fire during the earlier part of the decade, but Internet stocks caused it to explode.

And that explosion had a lot to do with the symbiotic relationship that emerged between day traders and the Internet stocks they traded. The aggregate buying by day traders bolstered the prices of these stocks. Later, when the day traders headed for the exits, the prices fell. But for months throughout the late 1990s, each time Internet stocks fell, they managed to recover once again and subsequently achieve higher highs. The reason this happened was often because less savvy, buy-and-hold investors eagerly purchased the shares whenever day traders and other professional traders decided it was time to sell. The buy-and-hold investors continued to take supply off the market and thus created a new price plateau, which the professional traders could then build on once again. Look at a chart of the Nasdaq during the late 1990s, and this pattern becomes vividly apparent. Throughout the period, the market periodically rose, then fell, then rose again to even higher highs—a classic bull-market pattern.

The Precious Few

IN ANOTHER ERA, that pattern might have manifested itself with energy stocks or software stocks. But during the 1990s, the Internet was far and away the most volatile, fastest rising sector, which made it the most tradable—for several reasons. First, the floats of Internet stocks, or the number of shares available for trading, were deliberately kept small (see chapter 14). James O'Shaughnessy, author of the financial bestseller *What Works on Wall Street,* explains how this simple fact often fooled investors:

> They [investors] fail to understand the idea of marginal prices, and they fail to understand the reason that the Internet stocks went up in a vertical ascent is that there's no float. They become priced at what the last marginal buyer was willing to pay for those shares—even if it's six shares.[2]

O'Shaughnessy was one of a small group of investment advisers during the late 1990s who stuck to the traditional idea of buying quality stocks at reasonable prices and watching them grow over the long term—a strategy that at the time lagged far behind portfolios overloaded with dot-com companies. Lauded as a brilliant investment adviser just a few years earlier for his pioneering analysis of long-term stock trends, O'Shaughnessy found himself removed from the mainstream in the late 1990s, though many returned to his tried-and-true advice following the crash. "We go from being heroes to goats in a very short time," he joked.

This relates to the second reason that Internet stocks were so volatile. Far more than stocks in other sectors, their worth was tied directly to fickle public opinion. Unlike solid, stodgy, blue-chip stocks with hard assets like factories and machinery that accountants could quantify, Internet companies were not weighed down by anything other than expectations. With no history of earnings, few assets in the traditional sense, and even fewer models for their growth, Internet stocks could float like feathers in the wind. More precisely, they moved on rumor. To find a parallel for how readily Internet stocks responded to rumors, you need only look at gold stocks that trade on the Vancouver Stock Exchange. A gold stock priced for pennies could suddenly jump in value by 300-fold if a rumor surfaced that someone had struck it rich nearby—a phenomenon that gold traders call "closeology."

Similarly, with Internet stocks, if one company proved that it could grow revenues or attract visitors to its Web portal or business-to-business exchange, then why could the Internet not support a dozen or more competitors? Investors were all too eager to buy into this idea. After all, the Internet was growing by millions of users each month. If eBay could burst out of the initial public offering (IPO) starting gate, then another auction house, QXL.com, might well do the same. Indeed, in April 2000, SG Cowen analyst Thomas Bock reportedly predicted that QXL's stock would rise from its then-current split-adjusted price of $112 to $1,665. The stock more than doubled as a result.

"The Madness of Crowds"

AFTER THE DOT-COM crash of 2000, the title of a Sunday *New York Times* Business section editorial aptly summed up the delusion from which Wall Street had just recovered: "What were we thinking?" There was a prevailing belief that a handful of people, often with little business experience could somehow grow their online companies large enough to rule a market—in the same way that Coca-Cola or McDonald's had cornered their respective markets. If you were the first or second or third Internet company to carve out turf in the uncharted online world and were smart enough to hold on, you could own an industry. Whole empires could be built on air—overnight. Or so the thinking went.

Incredibly, this Internet myth held investors spellbound throughout the late 1990s. As *Red Herring* magazine editors Anthony B. Perkins and Michael C. Perkins explained in their book *The Internet Bubble,* which was published before the 2000 market crash, "The mania surrounding Internet companies has translated into too much venture capital, too many Internet startups, and too many Internet IPOs, driving both private and public company market valuations to insane levels."[3]

Manias of this kind had occurred before. During the 1920s, radio was widely seen as the hot new medium that would transform American life. And radio bandwidth, like cyberspace, appeared infinite. Wall Streeters believed that the company best poised to capture this infinite new market was Radio Corporation of America (RCA). In 1928, RCA stock sold for about $85.25. Immediately before the crash, it rose to a split-adjusted $573.10.[4]

However, a much earlier crash bears an even greater resemblance to the dot-com bomb: the so-called South Sea Bubble of the early 1700s. The South Sea Bubble began when one firm, the South Seas Company, devised a plan to monopolize British trade with South America. The trade privilege was to be in exchange for the South Seas Company's financing of some of Britain's national debt. This scheme (which is what it turned out to be) readily captivated the imagination of the investing public. As with radio in the 1920s, the possibilities for profit in South America appeared infinite to the investing public of that era. Untold amounts of gold and silver from mines in the Andes Mountains could be traded for British-manufactured goods. Numerous other companies also sprang up to exploit the possibilities. And like the dot-coms that mushroomed out of strategies sketched on napkins eons later, these 18th-century firms often debuted with only the vaguest of business plans. Here's how one business plan hoping to capitalize on the South American trade read: "A company for carrying on an undertaking of great advantage, but nobody is to know what it is." Incredibly, a line of investors emerged to buy shares out of fear that all the shares would be sold. After collecting the money, the company's promoter was never heard from again.

Meanwhile, stock in the South Seas Company rose to preposterous levels as expectations of its future profits spread like an urban legend. After the British Parliament clinched the company's financial plan by authorizing interest payments to the South Seas Company on the nation's debt at a rate of 5 percent, the South Seas Company's stock rose from £130 to £300. It would eventually rise to £1,000—even as some in Parliament protested that the company would bankrupt many in the nation. And they were right. Common people mortgaged their businesses and homes in order to buy South Seas Company stock. Or else they took out loans, pledged their inheritances, or hocked their jewelry. Spirited trading in South Seas Company stock took place not only in the coffee houses along Exchange Alley but also on street corners and in taverns. Britain's financial establishment, although late to join the melee, nevertheless placed huge bets on the company as well. One banker at the time described the phenomenon: "The more intense the craze, the higher the type of intellect that succumbs to it." In the end, the massive trade that the South Seas Company had foreseen did not materialize.[5] The stock plummeted to £135. And angry mobs marched on Westminster, demanding to know what had happened to their money. Parliament began investigating the company and discovered widespread corruption. Many of the South Seas Company's directors had their estates confiscated. Still others were forced to flee the country.

The Hypemeisters

FAST-FORWARD TO THE 1990s, where light-speed communications and an overabundance of capital came together and created a far larger bubble. The Internet rather than South America was the bold new arena for commerce. And on the Internet, space, if not opportunity, truly was infinite. Moreover, both seemingly could be exploited with near-infinite speed. Using off-the-shelf software or, more likely, a series of virtual online partners, it was possible to create an online store or service operation ("virtual company" was the popular term) literally within days. As one National Public Radio columnist, commenting on the launch of the online political magazine Slate.com by Microsoft Corporation, cynically explained, the Web allowed an entrepreneur to take the most mundane idea and make it sound ingenious simply by adding the words "on the Internet." So, if you said, Why don't we start a cigar store? everyone would think the idea unoriginal. But if you added the words "on the Internet," you could get millions in venture capital.

Of course, as with the South Sea Bubble, there were reasons why intelligent people bet their life savings on companies that existed only in the void of cyberspace. As everyone knew, Internet growth had become exponential. Predictions for future growth were astronomical. Some industry pundits said that revenues would top $1.2 trillion by 2002 and might someday reach $33 trillion worldwide. More important, real people had indeed made real money from Internet stocks. Anyone who had bought 1,000 shares of America Online at its 1992 opening price of $11.50 and held them until July 1998, would have received $125,000, 12 times their original investment in half as many years.

Other examples abounded. When Microsoft emerged as the clear winner in the Internet browser wars, Netscape stock fell to $20. But share prices more than doubled in price when analysts realized that Netscape's home page was one of the Internet's most visited sites.

For every Internet stock success story, there were also horrendous failures, stocks that reached $100+ share values that later sold for pennies. Nevertheless, with the prospect of vast riches awaiting anyone with a few thousand to invest, it is little wonder that an entire industry sprang up to track Internet companies—and, by extension, the Nasdaq's phenomenal rise. A new breed of newscaster, the financial anchor, became media superstars, notes *Washington Post* media reporter Howard Kurtz in his book *The Fortune Tellers: Inside Wall Street's Game of Money, Media, and Manipulation*. Each morning, before the market's opening bell, millions watched CNBC's Marie Bartiromo and David Faber handicap the coming day's trading action while throughout the day, coverage on CNBC followed the Nasdaq's every twitch. Some day traders claimed that they could make money on CNBC just by buying stock in a company whose chief executive officer was scheduled for an on-the-air interview, then sell the stock when it peaked during the actual interview.

Elsewhere in the cable universe, Lou Dobbs, CNN's *Moneyline* host, became as much a fixture of the airwaves as regular network news anchors with his postgame analysis of market action. Interestingly, Dobbs himself was impressed enough by the millions being made by Internet entrepreneurs that he decided to join them. Dobbs quit CNN in 1999 to help launch

Space.com, an online magazine covering space exploration, only to find his way back to CNN in the months after the dot-com bomb.

Pundits appearing on financial shows also became media superstars. When sharp drops in the market occurred, financial newscasters inevitably sought out comments from William Fleckenstein, perhaps the market's most famous bear and short seller. Much to the dismay of those who had tied up their 401(k)s in overvalued Internet stocks, Fleckenstein correctly pointed out that the Nasdaq during the height of the boom traded at about 90 times earnings. In contrast, the Nikkei traded at a maximum of 80 times earnings before the Japanese economic bubble burst in the late 1980s.[6] Portfolio manager O'Shaughnessy also warned of the coming downfall more than a year before it occurred. In 1998, he said:

> You start to see the cracks appearing right now. Articles in the *New York Times* on how the business models of Internet stocks don't make sense. You start to see reporters who are more cynical than the average person say "hey wait a minute this doesn't make a lot of sense."[7]

Likewise, Warren Buffett, perhaps the most successful investor in history, said in a famous quote that he would flunk any MBA student who could tell him the value of an Internet stock. Still, the returns of Buffett's company, Berkshire Hathaway, suffered during the height of the Internet boom, largely because Buffett was unwilling to join the buying frenzy.

Indeed, for every bearish profit in the wilderness, there were perhaps dozens who served as Internet stock cheerleaders, including Morgan Stanley analyst Mary Meeker, named "Queen of the Net" by *Barron's;* Merrill Lynch analyst Jessica Reif Cohen, whom *Fortune* magazine named "The Queen of All Media"; and Robertson Stephens analyst Dan Niles, whom one newspaper called the Michael Jordan of Wall Street.[8]

The Next Insanely Great New Thing

A COMMON THEME among many Internet stock cheerleaders
was that dot-com companies were really in the business of creating an entirely new species of economy—cutting out the middle-
man, speeding the flow of information, and aggregating buyers
and sellers into groups that would have been impossible to form
in the pre-Internet era. Priceline.com was often held up as an example of how Internet companies were said to be changing the
very dynamics of commerce. Priceline earned a patent for what it
called its reverse-auction market. People e-mailed in the price
they were willing to pay for a coast-to-coast airline ticket, for example. Then an interested airline with seats to fill, e-mailed back
either an acceptance of the offer or a slightly higher price. Pundits claimed the reverse-auction idea could be applied to everything from insurance to automobile sales to mortgages.

It was because of companies like Priceline that all the stuffy
old rules of investing no longer applied, or so pundits said. How
could one use traditional measures of the value of a stock when
the underlying company was reinventing capitalism on the fly?
Still, theirs was a tough argument to make because the numbers
posted by even the most solid Internet players blew out the normal performance measures used by fundamental analysts. Ama-
zon.com, following the August–September 1998 crash, was still
selling for about 16 times sales. Again, that is sales, not profits.
Amazon had yet to generate profits. If every business enjoyed
similar valuations, then a money-losing corner drugstore with an
annual gross of, say, $500,000 would be worth $8 million.

So the real question to Internet stock pundits became this: If
the traditional measures are too scary to use, how else could you
determine a new economy company's value? Michael Murphy,
editor of the *California Technology Stock Letter,* devised one solution for technology stocks, that he called the "price to growth
flow ratio." To find it you simply added earnings plus research
and development (R&D) expenditures, then divided it by the
company's market capitalization. Bargain stocks had growth

flow ratios of about 8. Correctly priced technology stocks had ratios between 10 and 14. Murphy's theory reportedly was that in a fast moving new economy the successful companies would be those that invested heavily in their future, which was the apparent reason R&D spending counted as heavily as profits.[9]

Other analysts came up with equally ingenious methods. Buyout value was one method used. Still other analysts sought to redefine the price-to-sales ratio, a traditional fundamentalist measure. This valuation method was based on the idea that all Internet companies were brand new. Most new companies lose money. Therefore, the important thing to focus on was not earnings but sales. If sales were growing steadily, profits were not as important since the company was capturing and holding market share. Amazon.com provides an illustration. At one point during the late 1990s, it had a sales growth rate of something like 838 percent, which meant that maybe the stock was was still a bargain. Nevermind the fact that it was selling for 16 times sales. Indeed, in 1998, star analyst Henry Blodgett, who was working for CIBC Oppenheimer at the time, announced that Amazon's price might hit $400.[10]

Another popular think-outside-the-box method used to predict an Internet's stock value was something called discounted future price. Analysts calculated it by taking current per-share earnings and compounding them by the company's projected growth rate. Multiply the answer by the current industry standard price-earnings ratio and you'd get the forecasted share price for whatever period in the future you were looking at. Of course, this assumed that current market multiples would hold. After the 2000 crash, most didn't.

From Bubbles to Suds

ACCORDING TO MARTIN Pring in his book *Investment Psychology Explained,* many such valuation methods devised during boom times, no matter how well thought out they might be, are really only justifications after the fact. They let investors who have bought the stocks sleep at night. And as such, they are a classic sign of a bubble market in progress.

Another clear sign of a market bubble is a perceived need to increase the supply of companies in order to provide fresh opportunities for investors who may have missed out on the first wave of miracle performers.

"Manias" Pring explained, "are eventually brought to a close as rising prices bring more marginal supply."[11] Which is a polite way of saying that when the boom climaxes a rush of poorly conceived companies with dim prospects appear, soliciting the investment dollars from an overeager public. Along the way, he says, even normally prudent financial institutions eventually rush in for fear of missing out. As you'll see in the next chapter, this is precisely what happened with investment-banking firms during the 1990s as they along with venture capitalists devised an assembly line to nurture and then market young Internet companies to hordes of investors—all with a frightening efficiency.

Once again, the incredibly strong synergies that existed between the Internet and the Nasdaq greatly aided this process. New companies, devoted to doing business on the Internet, were brought public via Internet brokers and then traded online via the Nasdaq. The result, for a time, would be an explosion of wealth such as the world had never seen.

CHAPTER 14

THE NEW-ECONOMY DREAM MACHINE

INTERNET AND OTHER technology stocks continued to fuel the Nasdaq's rise, causing ripple effects throughout the economy. Thanks to the rising markets, the average American household net worth grew by 14.1 percent in 1999.[1] Aggregate growth of household net worth climbed by a staggering $3 trillion just in the fourth quarter of that year.[2] Riding this wealth explosion, active traders continued priming Nasdaq tech stocks with vast reservoirs of liquidity, further driving the surge. As these traders watched their own earnings soar to undreamed-of levels, a kind of rapturous greed set in. After the 2000 crash, West Coast trader Tim Moss[3] remarked:

> Initially I wanted to make $200 per day. Then I got to the point where I was making $1,000 a day and maybe $2,000. During the beginning of 2000, when the market was going really crazy, I was averaging $10,000 or $12,000 a day. One thousand bucks a day didn't seem like that much any more.

Moss was far from alone. Average investors during the period eagerly opened their 401(k) statements each month and saw their net worth steadily grow. Many succumbed to the so-called wealth effect and found that their lives had changed astoundingly. As J. P. Morgan analyst Douglas R. Cliggott explained, the wealth effect "influences the size of the homes we live in, the type of cars we drive, where we go on vacation."[4]

It's easy to dismiss the huge rise in stock prices as merely an example of speculative frenzy. But that would gloss over the many forces—some of them unique to the times—that came together to produce that bubble. For example, some believe the new Internet-based Nasdaq itself was responsible for a part of the rise in stock prices. During the mid-1990s, for the first time ever, a single network seamlessly linked individual online investors trading from their desktops directly to brokerages and then to the exchanges and clearing firms. The result was vastly reduced shareholder costs. Federal Reserve Bank of Cleveland economists John B. Carlson and Edward A. Pelz studied the effects that efficiencies brought by Internet trading and other forms of automation had on the collateral costs of owning stocks. They found that even small declines in shareholder costs led to surges in stock prices.[5]

Other reasons for the markets' rise were more worrisome. By historical standards the markets had been overheated throughout the 1990s. Over a 67-year period between 1923 and 1993 the mean yearly performance of U.S. equities was a mere 7.2 percent, according to one analyst.[6] Year-over-year returns, even month by month returns on the Nasdaq had far exceeded that amount. A *Wall Street Journal* reporter studied the 33 largest firms by market cap that traded on the Nasdaq and found that 18 were full-blown technology companies, half of which had price-earnings levels (P/E) north of 100, and market-weighted P/Es of more than double that. By any reckoning this was well above historical norms.[7]

Stratospheric P/Es were in part fueled by record margin trading, that is trading using money borrowed from a broker in order to amplify returns. Margin debt, or the total amount of this borrowing, "is a greater share of total market capitalization than at any point" since the Crash of 1929, New York Democratic Senator Charles Schumer told members of the House Banking Committee in late March of 2000. In January and February of 2000, margin debt had climbed 15 percent, he said. "These numbers are an indication that margin borrowing itself may be fueling the market's rise. And that means speculation."[8]

Taking up the bully pulpit of his office, Federal Reserve Chairman Alan Greenspan made his famous prediction that the market was being moved by "irrational exuberance." Privately, he is said to have harbored worse fears. Late in 1998, Greenspan and his colleagues at the Federal Reserve reportedly saw grave parallels between the tech boom and the 1920s.

Speaking before the Economics Club of New York on January 13, 2000, just three months before the Nasdaq bubble burst, Greenspan remarked that years from now "We may conceivably conclude . . . that at the turn of the millennium, the American economy was experiencing a once in a century acceleration of innovation." That innovation would be reflected in corporate profits, output, productivity, and stock prices, he mused. Alternately Greenspan said the new economy might be seen as "one of the many euphoric speculative bubbles that have dotted human history."[9]

The More Things Change, the More They Remain the Same

MARKET ANALYST MARTIN Pring brilliantly describes how a bubble economy develops in his book *Investment Psychology Explained*. According to Pring, market bubbles typically play out over 12 steps—each successive step leading down a path of increasing delusion and then disillusion. Although the book came out in 1993, a couple of years before the Internet became a household word, the steps that Pring outlines uncannily apply to the Internet economy.[10] During the first phases of the bubble, he says, a new idea emerges. It is an idea that captivates the public's imagination and seems capable of generating unlimited wealth. The Internet was just such a powerful idea. Suddenly, the peoples of the world could talk directly with and buy directly from one another, reaping efficiencies undreamed of before. Never before had such opportunity existed. A relatively small percentage of the world's population were currently online. But growth rates were phenomenal. And economic growth rates could rise in tandem.

A bubble is reinforced, says Pring, if the idea is complicated enough that the average person cannot easily dismiss it. This also occurred. A kind of hip youth culture, flowing out from tech firms in northern California, in many ways pressured Americans to accept the new-economy credo. A generation before, baby boomers had rallied against the political establishment. This new generation's goals were far more defined and pragmatic: Dismantle the old capitalism system and replace it with a faster, cheaper, better version run via the Internet. If you were not on board, you did not get it. And if you hung on to the dreary old ways of doing business, you were a Luddite and deserved to be squashed. Some critics charge that a bit of this attitude rubbed off on the Nasdaq as well. "Nasdaq was the trailer park of Wall Street," wrote a commentator for the online political magazine Slate.com. In an article entitled "Nasdaq, the

Stock Market for the Smug Digital World," author David Plotz asserts that technology and the new economy reinvented the Nasdaq. "Like many Gen-Xers, Nasdaq was enthralled with computers, and tech stocks became its backbone." The result, Plotz says, "Nasdaq gloats over its transformation from penny-stock backwater to epicenter of cool."[11]

Human nature—not to mention the opportunity to profit—drives many of us to seek a spot in that "epicenter of cool." And for this reason, Pring says that during the early stages of a market bubble people from the financial establishment begin to join the early adopters. In the case of the Internet boom, the most important converts were often financial analysts. Increasingly, they went on record saying that they "got it," too. Their defense of the new economy and the lofty stock prices it engendered resulted in still more converts. Months after the 2000 meltdown, a *New York Times* article laid part of the blame squarely in the laps of these market analysts. "While the market sank to its worst performance in more than a decade, many of those analysts kept right on smiling and saying 'buy'" wrote reporter Gretchen Morgenson. [12]

The Silence of the Lambs

ANALYSTS, IN FACT, were widely blamed for talking up the market to the benefit of their firms and at the expense of everyday investors. The job of analysts was to provide studied, unbiased opinions on companies. But a potential for conflict is always present, since the companies covered by analysts are sources of revenue for the firm, whose brokers sell their shares. The potential conflict heightened greatly during the 1990s as more and more financial firms, seeking new sources of revenue, diversified into underwriting. Thus, an analyst might be charged with rendering an opinion on companies that their firms had brought public.

Financial firms try to avoid such conflicts by enforcing a strict church-state separation between the research department and the brokerage and underwriting division. But critics charged that subtle pressures exist within firms that encourage analysts to champion stocks of companies that have been IPOed by the firm. Normally, a group of firms might participate in an IPO (initial public offering), with one acting as lead underwriter and others offered a lucrative piece of the action. Thus, the temptation existed for analysts at all these firms to treat the recently IPOed company with kid gloves. Even when analyst reviews are less than favorable, critics charge they are released in a kind of code that less savvy investors are apt to miss. For example, if analysts believe a stock "is not worth buying" they label it "a market performer." And when they say investors should dump the stock it receives a "hold" or "accumulate."[13]

"Negative ratings lead to threats of lawsuits, loss of business and other forms of intimidation," writes Bruce Bartlett, a senior fellow with the National Center for Policy Analysis. At the very least, companies that receive a negative recommendation from an analyst might be less cooperative when he or she requests information in the future, he claims.[14] Companies and mutual funds issuing reports to shareholders are obliged to follow strict compliance standards mandated by the Nasdaq. The research reports, which often receive more credence from investors than a company's own statements, are essentially unregulated.

The sanctioning of the idea by experts alone is not enough for it to take flight, Pring says. There must also be an overabundance of capital—money that is sitting around, waiting to be spent. And this was precisely the case during the late 1990s as venture capital funds succeeded in raising vast amounts of capital year after year. A record $24 billion in fresh funding flowed from venture capitalists to start-ups during 1998 alone, according to the National Association of Venture Capitalists. Which prompted one journalist covering the venture capital field to proclaim that "The market right now is ridiculous. There are a lot of bad start-ups that are being funded."[15]

By contrast, in the early stages of a boom, venture funds can find only a few companies who are ready to take the idea and run with it. This in turn prompts investors to snap up the precious few shares that can be had, even as their prices steadily rise. So it was with the Internet in those early years when a few highly publicized companies went public.

Netscape, the company that brought the Internet to the masses and launched the boom, appropriately enough was the era's first parabolic initial public offering. In August 1995, shares of Netscape priced at $28 immediately jumped to $71 at the market open.[16] Anyone who had been lucky enough to receive shares before the open could have made a fortune. And the prospect of just such a fortune caused a flood of Internet companies to debut on the Nasdaq in the years that followed. As long as investors snapped up these shares, the boom might be allowed to continue. Investors proved amazingly eager to do just that. "During the first five months of '99, the average first-day return on IPOs was 68 percent," says Jay Ritter, a professor of finance at the University of Florida. "That is an aberration," he says. Although it is not unusual for IPOs to pop on the first day of trading, historical average first day returns are about 15 percent. These inflated returns leave "investors with the perception that it's easy to get rich on getting allocations of hot IPOs," says Ritter.[17]

During the latter phases of a bubble, as Pring describes it, "There is a feeling among investors that they must buy now before the opportunities disappear. This feeling is reinforced even as the boom lasts longer than anyone anticipates—and even as prices rise to ridiculous levels." eToys rose 160 percent in just a few months. Extreme Networks, up 175 percent, did likewise. Healtheon rocketed 979 percent in less than a year.

For those who cared to look, an entirely different story could be gleaned by taking a longer view. Thomson Financial

Securities Data reportedly analyzed 20 Internet firms IPOed by Merrill Lynch between 1997 and 2001 and found that three quarters of them were trading for less than their offering price. Two others shut down.[18] Merrill's most spectacular dot-com flameout was likely Pets.com Inc., which earned $66 million from its IPO and then ceased operating 10 months later. A hugely expensive TV ad campaign gobbled up much of the company's cash, as the company like other dot-coms discovered the enormous costs of acquiring customers. But the company's business plan, which called for customers to order their pet supplies online, leaves one to wonder, "What were they thinking?"

Fast-Lane Accounting

PETS.COM JOINED OTHER spectacular Internet flameouts that sold everything from gardening supplies to groceries online. In fact, when new companies begin to deluge the market, this is a sure sign that the bubble is about to burst, according to Pring. It happened with electronics and aerospace firms during the late 1960s. The Internet was history repeating itself.

So that they might better appeal to investors, many of these freshly hatched firms tried to push the envelope of generally accepted accounting principles. For example, one bookkeeping method popular with start-ups was called positive accrual. It enabled companies to denote expenses as bills are paid; while receivables were used to state earnings. By extending credit to customers, while stalling its own creditors, firms using positive accrual accounting could make it appear as if earnings surpassed cash flow.

Earnings misstatements were likewise common among technology and Internet firms. While studying for his doctoral degree at New York University, Min Wu reportedly found that the tech sector was responsible "for 39 percent of all the companies compelled to restate their earnings between 1999 and

2000."[19] As Wu remarked, "High-tech companies for the last few years have been trying to maintain at least the impression of growth for investors and Wall Street, and that has led to earnings management."

While recently IPOed companies struggled to live up to their hype, an avalanche of new Internet firms began trading on the Nasdaq. "Greed broke the system," Peter Elstom of *Business Week* wrote. Faced with the opportunity to earn billions "many leading U.S. financial firms threw out their business standards and started grabbing the loot."[20] During the late 1990s major U.S. commercial banks and financial firms saw a new gold rush in California's Silicon Valley and began acquiring smaller investment banks already tapped into the local deal flow. However, the long-term performance of the portfolios of dot-com start-ups these firms brought public was dismal at best. As of mid-April 2001, according to *Business Week,* the average of return of Merrill Lynch's Net IPOs was –87 percent. Robertson Stephens portfolio did only slightly better. It returned –65 percent to investors; While Credit Suisse First Boston's returns were –41 percent.[21]

The Automatic IPO

IN PRING'S SCHEMATIC of the boom and bust market cycle, when the market becomes saturated with less than prime companies, it defines the turning point between a run-up and a meltdown. In the short period before a crash, he says, "It is possible to lower investment standards because an increasingly gullible public is demanding new vehicles for instant wealth."[22]

The sad fact is that the public was indeed clamoring for IPOs whose shares would eventually decimate their savings. Because the number of shares released to the public was deliberately kept small in order to bolster prices, getting access to shares on their critical first day of trading was nearly impossible for the average investor. For this reason a handful of financial firms devised ways to automate and democratize the process using the Internet.

Indeed, the Web's new IPO marketplaces formed part of a bold revolution aimed at streamlining finance in the same way that online retailers and business-to-business exchanges tried to reform supply chains in other industries. The Internet financial revolution got its start when online brokerages cut commissions dramatically and eliminated the need for flesh-and-blood brokers to handle trades. In the next phase, direct-access brokerages had allowed more experienced investors (i.e., day traders) to function like Nasdaq dealers. Now these new IPO launching pads were attempts to supplant the traditional powerhouses in underwriting, namely, the investment banks. By making use of the Web, they promised to do such things as limit volatility in IPO prices, cut out middlemen, and speed up the distribution process. At least one, as you will see, promised to create online shareholder communities that might consist of a company's customers and suppliers. The approaches that these Web sites employed were at times as radical as their goals.

One of the first to promise his brokerage customers access to IPOs was Andy Klein. In 1995, Klein fielded the world's first Internet IPO when he took his microbrewery Wit Beer public. That small step evolved into WitCapital.com, an online financial services firm that included a brokerage and an investment-banking services firm. (The firm has since acquired an investment-banking firm called Soundview Technology Group and is now known by that name.) Klein's idea was to allow larger investment banks to serve as lead underwriter for an IPO. His task would be to market the IPO shares to the start-up firm's so-called affinity groups. These were people with a natural interest in the company, its customers, for example, or its suppliers. The Internet, a powerful one-to-one marketing medium, would make it possible to reach these diverse groups in a cost effective manner. And in Klein's view, everyone would benefit.

The ability to sell Barnesandnoble.com to the people who buy books on the Internet is great for the company. Because first, they get shareholders that really want to own the stock and they get customers that feel grateful for being able to buy in at the offering price. And they get a lot more people loyal to their company in a way they hadn't been before.[23]

Similarly, E*Trade, one of the nation's leading online brokerages, created an affiliated investment bank called E*Offering (it has since been absorbed into Soundview). And it devised a means to market IPO shares to a broad audience of both institutions and individuals, via online roadshows. Instead of sending executives around the country to tout the benefits of a soon-to-be IPOed company, online presentations would enable institutions to study that company at their leisure. Furthermore, these presentations could be precisely targeted or alternately mass marketed. "We look to reach not hundreds of institutional relationships and not 10,000s of individual accounts, but thousands of institutions and millions of retail customers in a largely self-service automated system," said a top executive. Broadening a firm's exposure would result in highly diversified share ownership once shares of the IPOed company actually went on sale. This in turn would limit volatility, since a diverse group of investors was less likely to sell in unison.

WR Hambrecht and Co. devised a far more radical means of marketing IPOs. The financial services firm was launched by Bill Hambrecht, who cofounded one of Silicon Valley's most respected investment banks, Hambrecht and Quist, when he split off to form the company bearing his name. Bill Hambrecht wanted to develop an entirely different model for an investment bank. To accomplish that, he used what is called a Dutch auction to allocate IPO shares. Investors enter a price and the number of shares they want. The collective bidding lets the company determine what offering price will enable it to allocate the greatest number of shares. Because the bidding for shares takes place prior to the IPO, share prices would theoretically stabilize once those shares actually become available. In other words, shares IPOed via a Dutch auction are less likely to experience an opening day pop. They are also less likely to decline in price, since speculators won't sell into the initial rise.

Multi-Level Marketing

THESE EXPERIMENTS AT delivering IPOs are noteworthy because they reveal the amazing amount of innovation that was occurring at the height of the Nasdaq boom. A revolution that had ironically begun with individual investors was attempting to spread to the traditional financial power structure. But it was there—thanks to the crash—that the revolution stalled. Online road shows did not uniformly replace face-to-face meetings with heavy-hitting institutional investors, Dutch auctions did not become the preferred method of allocating IPO shares, and affinity group investing so far has not become the norm. In the latter case, however, something approaching affinity groups did emerge. But it took a far different form. Stockholders formed voluntary associations of their own in chat rooms like Raging Bull and Silicon Investor. Many of these rooms were dedicated to discussions about a single stock.

Nevertheless, the online IPO markets were admirable attempts at counteracting many of the traditional tactics that had been used to bolster the prices of IPOs—tactics that had attracted the ire of the SEC as far back as the 1950s (see chapter 4). Those tactics included limiting supply, and pricing shares so that they would surge on the open. In a bull market environment one of the most successful tactics of all was to distribute shares via a system that spread rewards up and down the supply chain. "In a sense what investment banks are doing is they're giving kickbacks to investors," says Welch, and by that he means brokerages and institutions as opposed to retail investors. And so venture capitalists might receive shares as an incentive for them to bring more valuable deals to a particular investment bank. Other investment banks might also get large allocations, so that they might market future offerings on behalf of the lead underwriting bank. Certain brokerages that had a successful track record marketing an underwriting firm's shares in the past would likewise be rewarded. The shares would then be sold by that brokerage's best brokers, who would pass them on to their best customers. The effect of these carefully crafted share distributions was to take supply off the market, as a further means of bolstering price, or alternately as a way of allowing those receiving the shares to quickly flip them for a sizeable profit. The number of shares available for public trading at the onset was normally only a small fraction of the total float. But that did not prevent eager retail investors from clamoring for them, bidding up their prices to preposterous levels.

The system worked astonishingly well so long as that demand for IPO shares remained strong, and opening-day price surges were a virtual guarantee. By the time the April 2000 crash arrived, the market was saturated with supply. And the IPO market—both the traditional market and the experiments with Internet IPOs—slowed substantially.

Just before the bubble bursts, Pring says, "Anyone can cite an example of just how ridiculous prices have become." By the late 1990s examples were everywhere. "How can a company that doesn't have any earnings and has William Shatner for a spokesperson and nothing else be worth $15 billion?" asks UCLA professor of finance and IPO analyst Ivo Welch. Welch was speaking about Priceline.com, the high-concept reverse-auction e-commerce firm IPOed in March 1999. At the time, Priceline's $15 billion market cap roughly equaled the total market value of Delta, United, and American Airlines combined, Welch explains. "I would love to come up with a reason why this is rational," he says.

Meanwhile, at the Nasdaq, officials were acutely aware of what was happening, says former CEO Frank Zarb in an interview. "It was clear to a lot of us who had lived through a few [inflated markets] in our lifetime that the bubble was going to pop," he says. "The most frustrating thing was to watch the bubble build. And no matter what we did, no matter what we said, we could do nothing to discourage the participants from engaging in it. And the doors were wide open." Zarb says he and his colleagues at the Nasdaq discussed raising margin rates and maintenance rates as a possible solution. The Nasdaq also ran ads in the *Wall Street Journal* warning about the dangers of day trading. But in the end they felt their options were limited. "We couldn't as an exchange do anything to change the behavior of people." Zarb now says that the failure to halt the flood of dubious dot-coms from reaching the market was the biggest disappointment of his tenure at the Nasdaq.

According to Thomson Financial, Internet companies burned through a breathtaking $2.5 trillion of market capitalization following the April 2000 meltdown. Some 397 Internet companies that went public during the early days of the Internet boom in 1997 remained in business through the first quarter of 2001. However, three quarters of these had lost 75 percent of their share value, while only about 15 percent remained above their IPO price.[24]

Who suffered most as a result of the Internet stock debacle? In some cases those who ran the Internet companies or had large holdings of Internet company stocks handily escaped the debacle. And they had the derivatives market to thank for it. A popular—and perfectly legal—technique was to create something known as a collar to protect a large investor's profits and limit losses. With a collar, an investor buys a put option and sells a call option. The put gives the investor the right to sell a stock at a specified price, called the strike price, while a call, if sold, gives someone else the right to purchase the investor's shares at its strike price. A put will rise in value if the stock falls in price. A call works in just the opposite manner. It will rise more or less in tandem with the stock price rise. The price of the put the investor buys is offset by the money received from the sale of the call. This means that depending on where the strike prices are set, the two option contracts cancel each other out. The collar, may cost virtually nothing. As a result, if a stock rises astronomically in its first months of trading, investors who are company insiders can lock in their profits without selling their shares. In order for a collar to work, an options market has to exist for a company's stock. Which was usually not the case with recently IPOed firms. However, clever financial engineering could create something similar, using exchange traded funds (ETFs), some of which were designed to track specific sectors of the Internet, for example. They would therefore rise and fall in parallel with the stock of an individual company in that sector.

An article in the popular technology and finance magazine *Red Herring*[25] claims this is exactly what several corporate chieftains did to protect their stock holdings as the Nasdaq reached its high. These collars were at times created for them by the same investment banks that brought the insider's company public. By using a collar, they were able to retain their shares. In contrast, a sale of stock by a company insider would have been reported to the SEC. Such sales are posted on the Internet, so word that an insider was cashing in would inevitably leak out causing the shares to decline. According to *Red Herring,* the popularity of collars among corporate insiders may have deceived less savvy investors into believing that these executives were holding onto their stock, indicating their confidence in the company, even if the company was really a house of cards.

Individual investors for the most part neither knew about nor had access to complicated hedging techniques. Yet they were nevertheless the principal buyers of Internet stocks. According to one survey, investors with a net worth under $100,000 were the most likely buyers of freshly minted IPOed Internet stocks. Reportedly, most said they bought the stocks not because they liked a company's numbers, but because they liked its Web site.

CHAPTER 15

THE AMERICAN STOCK EXCHANGE AND THE "MARKET OF MARKETS"

ON NOVEMBER 6, 1998, Frank Zarb found himself standing before yet another large group of financial executives. The occasion this time was the Securities Industry Association annual conference, held that year in balmy Boca Raton, Florida. Zarb had been chief executive officer of the National Association of Securities Dealers (NASD) less than two years. Yet he had quickly managed to pull the organization out from the cloud of the market-maker scandal. Now he like everyone else in the room was riding an undreamed of wave of success. Since 1997, the Nasdaq Composite had made a near vertical ascent, starting at just over 1,500 that year. It would reach roughly double by the end of the following year. Facing his audience in Boca Raton, Zarb proclaimed that now was time to leverage that momentum and build something even grander. Nasdaq was poised to become the "Market of Markets," he said. In fact, it had just taken the first giant step toward this vision. Nasdaq's merger with the American Stock Exchange had been completed just days before.[1]

If Zarb and his cohorts could pull it off, the market of markets would become the single most significant financial trading arena on the planet. It would be the Microsoft Windows of the financial markets, a kind of branded universal online address within which a cornucopia of financial products could be bought and sold. Stocks, options, futures, mutual funds, and bonds—all could be traded by investors directly over the Internet and from anywhere in the world, 24/7. Ironically, the decision to push for the union reportedly had been made at the association's gathering a year before, when Zarb and then Amex Chairman Richard Syron had sat down for drinks.[2]

The way Zarb saw it, the Nasdaq had no choice but to evolve in this radical direction. "Forces like market globalization and technologies that cut trading costs while promoting a more direct investor access to the marketplace are challenging the way we do business,"[3] he told conference attendees. Drastic changes were in the winds thanks to the Internet. The Nasdaq could either lead the charge or wind up as roadkill.

To that end, Zarb and Syron had worked for months, building support for the Nasdaq-Amex merger. Still, not everyone saw the union as integral to Zarb's futuristic vision. Federal Reserve Board Chairman Alan Greenspan was on board. "This should have been done years ago," he said.[4] However, longtime Zarb friend, Securities and Exchange Commission (SEC) Chairman Arthur Levitt, refrained from praising the union. Although he did not criticize it, Levitt did predict that the Justice Department would elect to review the merger.[5] Syron would later describe the planned merger as being "like peace in Northern Ireland."[6]

That is because the two markets had feuded for years. Back in the 1970s, when the Nasdaq itself was still in its formative stage and plans called for it to include quotes of Amex-listed shares, the Amex had protested to the SEC. Moreover, the Nasdaq and the Amex had long competed fiercely with each other for listings, even as both markets had forever been in the shadow of the New York Stock Exchange (NYSE). To many growth-oriented firms, a listing on either market was merely a stopover on the road to the Big Board. A company might debut on the Nasdaq, then graduate to the Amex as it continued to grow, and finally move to the NYSE when it was able to meet the Big Board's more stringent listing requirements.

While staunch competitors, the Nasdaq and the Amex nevertheless differed significantly in the kind of trading environment they offered the companies whose shares they listed. The Amex had long ago evolved into an auction market, designed along the lines of the NYSE. That is, traders met in person, on a brick-and-mortar exchange floor. Just as they did on the Big Board, a cadre of specialists who were members of the Amex acted as auctioneers, overseeing trading for each of the exchange's listings. By contrast, the Nasdaq had begun as a loose network of brokers who were dispersed around the country and who traded shares over the phone to each other. The Nasdaq had clung to that decentralized model, upgrading itself as new technologies became available. And it had succeeded in attracting a long list of fast-growing, leading-edge companies.

But while the Nasdaq, thanks to its recent rise, was squarely in the limelight and was being praised as the nation's most dynamic stock market, the Amex could boast of traditions harking back to the earliest days of trading in New York. With its headquarters in the heart of Manhattan's financial district, the rise of the Amex paralleled that of the NYSE.

Streetwise Trading

LIKE THE NYSE, the Amex began as an informal gathering of traders in the open air. Many original Amex traders wore colored hats so they could be easily identified. In 1908, efforts began to organize Amex brokers into something more formal. The result, in 1911, was the New York Curb Exchange, formed as a voluntary association. The Curb Market would continue to hold its trading sessions outdoors until 1921, the year members moved into new digs behind the financial district's famous Trinity Church. In a bow to its roots, the trading posts on the exchange's new floor sported decorations that resembled street lamps. In 1929, it was officially christened the New York Curb Exchange.

The Curb Market's big advantage in those early years was its New York location. For that reason, perhaps, it was always perceived as a national stock market and not as a less visible regional exchange, such as those in Philadelphia, Chicago, and elsewhere. As a result, the Curb Market was able to garner listings of national companies. But it was destined to forever play second fiddle to the NYSE. During the 1930s it was even labeled the graveyard, by some of its listed companies. Throughout its history, the Curb Market was plagued by low membership and low liquidity. In the late 1930s and early 1940s, it had about an 11 percent share of trading volume at all the nation's exchanges. While a seat on the NYSE at that time cost over $250,000, membership in the Curb Market at one point could be had for under $1,000. Low fees and sparse listings caused the Amex to run deficits of around $100,000 annually. The NYSE was also running deficits at the time. And some Big Board members favored merging the two. Others suggested that the Curb Market be "downsized" to serve as a regional exchange, trading companies in the New York area that did not qualify for an NYSE listing.

The Curb Market's members fiercely held on to their autonomy, however, something they would always do. Rather than merging or downsizing, they sought other ways to attract business. For example, members were permitted to trade shares of companies not listed with the Curb Market. Thus, for years the New York Curb functioned as a parallel over-the-counter market. But the Curb Market members wanted to trade lucrative blue-chip stocks, too. During the late 1930s, the Curb Market allied itself with the Pittsburgh Stock Exchange in a plan to trade NYSE stocks.[7] A flowery statement filed with the SEC by the Curb Market explains the reasoning behind the move:

> The more issues dealt in on local exchanges, the wider the field of investment in securities concerning which information is on file with the local Exchange. The public within the radius of recognition of the individual Exchange will be thereby the more inclined to invest in Exchange securities which the New York Curb believes is one of the important provisions of the Securities and Exchange Act.[8]

In the 1940s and 1950s, exchange members devised more ways to increase business, trading monetary instruments and commodities, for example. By this time, the Curb Market had rechristened itself the American Stock Exchange, and it had acquired the reputation it maintains today as an innovative developer of new financial products. The Amex truly succeeded in defining itself in the mid-1970s, when it commenced trading options in addition to stocks. Other options/equities exchanges existed around the country, including notably the Philadelphia Stock Exchange. But the Amex was the only truly national equity market that traded in options as well as other products.

Then, in 1992, the Amex attempted to compete head to head with the Nasdaq when it formed something called the Emerging Company Marketplace. Reena Aggarwal and James Angel, professors of finance at Georgetown University, described the Emerging Company Marketplace as a kind of minor league for young companies. However, they noted, the Emerging Company

Marketplace was shut down three years after its launch—and for several reasons. For one, listing companies were not always screened carefully enough. This "resulted in several well-publicized scandals that tainted the image of the market and may have deterred other firms from listing."[9] Firms also tended to defect from the exchange as soon as they qualified for listing on the Amex proper or perhaps the NYSE. These defections were in marked contrast to the many large companies that had been launched via the Nasdaq and that had chosen to remain there, despite efforts by the Big Board to lure them away.

Aggarwal and Angel maintain that these larger firms—Dell, Oracle, and Cisco are examples—chose to stay with the Nasdaq while other growing firms defected from the Amex because the Amex's auction market environment is ill-suited to trading small-company stocks. Other attempts to create an auction-style small-cap market had likewise failed, the two say, among them the National Stock Exchange, launched in the 1960s, and several regional exchanges. In a nutshell, the reason auction markets are often a less desirable mechanism for trading in small-cap stocks is this: Auction markets funnel trading through a single specialist. Therefore, they do not furnish the kind of competitive bidding for order flow among dealers that you find in a dealer market. This competitive bidding tends to bolster the price of an otherwise lightly traded issue. In fact, dealers may trade stocks among each other, even in the absence of customer orders. Thus, a dynamic trading environment always exists, as does, at times, a volatile environment.

Many established companies prefer that their shares trade on an auction market because the intervention of a specialist tends to reduce volatility. Financial firms in particular often prefer to list with auction markets. For such firms, having a stable stock price is especially important since the stock value may be viewed as a reflection of the firm's stability. Who would put their savings in a bank whose share price careened wildly?

Two Systems, One Government

DEALER AND AUCTION markets possessed other pros and cons. Dealer markets might be faster and more liquid. But some believed that the on-the-floor human presence in auction markets made them more efficient. Specialists also acted as buyers and sellers of last resort. It was their responsibility to maintain an orderly market for the stock. Thus, in some cases, having a specialist come to the aid of a fledgling start-up was critical to supporting the stock price of companies in the absence of widespread buying interest, or alternately an attack by short sellers. When the Nasdaq and the Amex merged, Zarb imagined that some of Nasdaq's smaller firms would choose to migrate to the Amex for just this reason.

> There were probably 500 or more Nasdaq companies that were small enough to benefit from the tender loving care of an American Stock Exchange Specialist, because they were so small that they didn't have the necessary research following. And it would be logical for those companies to look in that direction.[10]

Studies done throughout the years had discovered another advantage of auction markets, which is that bid-ask spreads tended to be narrower in auction markets (see chapter 17). Whatever the case, no single type of market met the needs of all listing companies. Zarb told audience members in Boca Raton that the Nasdaq sought to merge with the Amex precisely so that it could recruit firms that preferred an auction market environment as an alternative to its electronic marketplace. The plan was to cobrand the exchanges and offer one-stop shopping for companies seeking a place to list. As he explained to his audience, "We won't be out there selling the gospel according to the auction market or according to the dealer market. We're going to be looking at shareholder value and suggesting that a company will trade better in this environment as compared to that environment."[11]

Options for Everyone

ZARB'S IDEA OF one-stop shopping went beyond services he hoped to offer listing companies. The Nasdaq-Amex merger would also furnish investors at every experience level with a supermarket full of financial products they could trade in addition to equities—all beneath the Nasdaq umbrella.

Chief among those products were derivatives, namely options, which were fast becoming popular even with some retail investors. Trading options usually required an Amex-styled auction market. That is because a single stock might have hundreds of options contracts written on it, each with different prices and expiration dates. And in many cases, only a small number of a particular contract are bought or sold. For example, less than a dozen people might have bought a single $20 January call option contract on XYZ stock. Such a contract would give them the right to purchase 100 shares of XYZ stock for $20, a price that was, say, $2 above XYZ's prevailing price. And they could exercise or trade the contract at any point up until its January expiration date. Another dozen March $20 contracts might have been sold, as well as another dozen January $22 calls, and so forth. Because volume in the case of each option is miniscule, it is unlikely that dealers or individual investors would trade directly with each other, as a dealer market encouraged them to do. Thus, to guarantee a market for individual contracts, there must be a guaranteed buyer and seller of last resort to serve as the nexus point for all trades—a service that the specialists on an auction market provide.

Recently, options markets were linked together via a single order display network. This in effect forced specialists working at all the major options exchanges to compete against each other. And it created something approximating a dealer market since options specialists would need to compete for order flow. But before that happened, Zarb and others appear to have had in mind creating just that sort of hybrid dealer/auction market for options. At the time of the Nasdaq-Amex merger, he hinted to a *Washington Post* reporter that the Nasdaq might entertain mergers with other regional options exchanges. "I'm not suggesting that we're on the hunt, but we would talk about the new world going forward," he said.[12] Though they would eventually be abandoned, talks were already under way between the Nasdaq and the Philadelphia Stock Exchange, a hotbed of options trading.

Mutual Funds on Steroids

WHILE OPTIONS CONTINUED to grow in popularity, the Amex was fast becoming known for another new investment product whose success was one of the great, if underreported, financial stories of the late 1990s: so-called exchange-traded funds (ETFs). The launch of many ETFs on the Amex was overseen by Gary Gastineau, who served as the exchange's senior vice president for new product development from 1995 to 2000.[13] Underwritten by financial services giants such as Barclays and Merrill Lynch, ETFs at first glance resemble garden-variety mutual funds in that they are made up of a basket of stocks. In addition, their values fluctuated in tandem with the stocks they hold. Like index funds, ETFs are not actively managed. (Although managed ETFs may be introduced.) That is, the individual stocks making up the funds are bought and held instead of being sold when the manager sees an opportunity to take profits. This passive management tends to cut expenses to the bone, which can give ETFs an edge over traditional mutual funds. However, unlike a typical mutual fund, ETFs trade just like stocks, which means that investors need not wait until the end of the day to buy or sell shares, as they normally must with mutual funds. Instead, they can trade them at any time during market hours.

In addition to providing investors with diversification within a single share of stock, many ETFs hold a powerful advantage over equities. They are exempt from the uptick rule, making them ideal for short sellers. If the market is sinking fast, traders need not wait for a transaction to go through at a price greater than the previous trade before selling short, as is required with stocks. By being exempt from the uptick rule, ETFs allow traders to readily capitalize on fast markets whether they were moving up or down.

For investors, ETFs offered an amazing range of ways to diversify. Some ETFs were created to track the Standard & Poor's 500 and the Dow. Others were baskets of the major stocks from places as diverse as Sweden and Hong Kong. Still others tracked sectors such as biotech and Internet stocks. Around the time that the Nasdaq-Amex merger took place, a highly popular ETF called a Cube, or QQQ, based on the Nasdaq 100 index, was launched. It offered a way for investors to buy into the rapidly rising market or alternately sell it short on particularly volatile days.

Eventually, investors could trade options on many ETFs as well. No surprise, throughout the late 1990s, millions flocked to ETFs, attracted by the low management fees and the ease with which they traded. Moreover, in a steadily rising market environment, ETFs, like index funds, often outperformed all but the best-managed mutual funds. As a result, the volume of ETF trading on the Amex nearly doubled from 14.6 billion shares in 1998.

By contrast, trading in stocks on the Amex hovered around 10 billion shares per year in 2000, and it had fallen by nearly 20 percent in just two years.[14] The relatively low volume, some money managers claimed, caused them to avoid trading Amex-listed shares because it hindered them from quickly exiting positions at an acceptable price. In the year prior to the merger, daily volume on the Amex was a scant 24.4 million shares versus more than half a billion on the Nasdaq.[15] (Volume has since more than doubled.)

Intense Lobbying

DESPITE DOING AN impressive amount of business in options and ETFs, the Amex appeared to some like a minnow and the Nasdaq like a whale poised to swallow it. What might have been equally scary to the Nasdaq, having just emerged from the market-maker scandal, was that the Amex, according to some, allegedly had some skeletons of its own. Admitting that since the late 1970s, the Curb Market's floor brokers had not been singled out for criminal indictment or major SEC investigation," *BusinessWeek* nevertheless began investigating the Amex during 1998 and focused a critical eye on the practices on its trading floor, particularly some Amex floor brokers and specialists involved in options trading. *BusinessWeek* charged that Amex regulatory officials as well as the SEC had turned a blind eye to the alleged abuses it claimed to have found.[16] In December 1997, a year before the Nasdaq-Amex merger was consummated, *BusinessWeek* reported that it found, for example, that an Amex specialist had been charged with making phony options trades by Amex's regulators. *BusinessWeek* charged, "the evidence is clear that the exchange has been too insular, too secretive, and too intent on protecting the status quo."[17]

During this period, the NYSE was also being investigated by the SEC over how it regulated its floor brokers.[18] With all three markets tainted, there was little reason why the Nasdaq should not plunge ahead. Also, as *BusinessWeek* noted, the NASD, which under the terms of the merger would be the ultimate regulator of the Amex, already had a proven track record of effective enforcement. And it was capable of reigning in any of the alleged abuses the magazine's investigators found.

A far bigger obstacle to any union of the two markets would prove to be the Amex's stalwart membership. Syron himself later said that in the early stages he privately gave the deal only a 50 percent chance of succeeding.[19] The reason was that Amex brokers feared that their best listings would abandon their trading floor in favor of electronic trading on the Nasdaq. The result would be declining seat prices.

Nevertheless, Zarb in an interview said that he and Syron believed that the Amex needed to partner with the far larger and better-capitalized NASD if it was to remain a viable exchange. According to Zarb, when the two had discussed the merger Syron voiced his concerns that "the Amex was being way overshadowed by the NYSE." Moreover, after many years of trying, the Amex's business model, "which was to be a small NYSE had generally failed. It needed a boost, but it didn't have the capital base to provide that boost."

Zarb says that he agreed with Syron that the Amex had enough going for it, that with some help, it would not only survive, but thrive. Also, the "NASD being an important institution, had some responsibility to look at the situation, and to the extent we could we should help an exchange like that to realize its objectives in a new world."

The merger talks took place at a time when markets throughout the world, but particularly in Europe (see chapter 16), were exploring the possibilities of partnerships. Zarb says that the strategy of creating a market of markets that would offer listing companies the chance to sign with either an auction or dealer market emerged as a logical way for the two organizations to join forces.

Syron and Zarb took their case directly to Amex's 25-member board. Zarb spoke before the board on March 19, 1998, finalizing details. Then late in the day, he and Syron traveled to New York's Waldorf Astoria to announce the merger, which would still require the approval of members of both organizations. Under the deal, both exchanges would retain their autonomy. Separate boards would oversee each market. Mean-while, four Amex representatives would receive NASD board seats. To further sugarcoat the merger, the NASD earmarked $50 million to support the price of Amex seats.[20] And the NASD promised an additional $110 million to revamp the Amex's trading systems. Under that plan, the Nasdaq would adapt its own limit order book to the Amex's auction market. When completed, the new system would offer the rules-based trading advantage of an auction market. And it would give traders a glimpse at the number of customer limit orders await-ing execution, the latter modeled on the Nasdaq's Level II dis-play.[21] Syron explained that the new order book would transform the Amex into an "advanced auction market." The NYSE would shortly debut a similar hybrid limit order book.

Following the announcement, Zarb spent months whipping up support among Amex members. He even traveled to Florida, where many retired Amex seat holders lived, for face-to-face meetings.[22] In the end, these efforts proved successful. The Amex membership voted 622 to 206 in favor of the deal.

Tomorrow the World

A MAJOR BENEFIT of the union would be an ambitious co-branding campaign, aimed at uniting the two exchanges in the public's mind. National Football League halftime reports on CBS became the *Nasdaq-Amex Halftime Show*.[23] And when visitors surfed the Web to Nasdaq.com or Amex.com, they reached a combined site that gave not only up-to-the-minute fi-nancial data on Nasdaq equities trading but also detailed infor-mation on ETFs and other Amex products.

The site was perhaps a proof of concept for Zarb's envi-sioned market of markets. Sometime in the future, the Nasdaq-Amex Web site might contain real-time data on markets in Europe and Asia. During the late 1990s, a golden opportunity existed for a brand as recognizable as the Nasdaq to establish itself as the preeminent global exchange. Markets in the rest of the world, with a few exceptions, were notably smaller than either the Nasdaq or the Amex. Some were fraught with corruption. Many suffered from poor liquidity. And attempts by these exchanges to unite had often fallen victim to internal squabbles. NASD executives were wracking up frequent-flyer miles to build a global alliance of financial exchanges. Now they were being joined by Amex executives in a department called Nasdaq-Amex International, which was charged with jointly developing opportunities overseas.

Zarb tried to explain just what he hoped would take shape as he faced the investment community in Boca Raton. "Our merger with Amex is the first big step in building a global market alliances—what we call the Market of Markets," he said. "It is going to connect firms and investors around the world through a common trading platform."[24] As Zarb saw it, market makers based in Japan and Europe would simply hand over their order books as the daylight greeted each region, creating vibrant 24-hour trading via the Internet. Indeed, Zarb speculated that the Nasdaq might test Internet trading overseas, where volume was lower, before bringing it to the United States. "The Internet allows for a new formula that will be in play abroad. We will then migrate that technology back to the U.S.," he said.[25]

CHAPTER 16

TOMORROW THE WORLD

STARBUCKS WOULD SEEM to be a natural initial public offering (IPO) candidate for the Nasdaq's new Japanese subsidiary. When shares of the ubiquitous coffeehouse chain began trading on October 10, 2001, Nasdaq-Japan had been open for just 16 months. That a U.S.-branded exchange had been able to open at all inside fortress Japan was maybe a small miracle. Yet Nasdaq-Japan had been able to railroad through the labyrinthine Japanese financial regulations with relative ease. In just months, it had managed to snare 71 listings. And that was no small miracle, given the sad state of the Japanese economy and the even sadder state of new issues worldwide following the April 2000 crash.

Nevertheless, the Starbucks IPO was in many ways special because here was a highly visible, successful, and cool U.S. company that marketed a kind of cultural behavior as much as a product. It was precisely the kind of company that trend-conscious Japanese consumers loved. "Japan is the best performing market for Starbucks in the world," boasted the company's chairman and chief global strategist Howard Schultz.[1] "And we accomplished this without advertising." Apparently, the Japanese liked their caffeine in infinite flavors as much as they liked breathing scented air through tubes in oxygen bars. As Schultz explained, "Starbucks became the Third Place between home and work for our Japanese customers."

Nasdaq-Japan's Chief Executive Officer Ted Saeki was equally effusive in his statements that accompanied Starbuck's trading debut. "Nasdaq-Japan is the market for companies that are changing the way we live," he proclaimed.

An astute student of business might see some powerful synergies at work. Here was one high-powered U.S. brand (the Nasdaq) that specialized in helping young companies secure equity financing on their home turf not only helping another freshly minted trend-setting American brand (Starbucks) reach more customers overseas but also helping that company tap into local financing. And tap into it directly. If the concept worked, the implications for U.S. business might be huge. American companies bent on expanding overseas would no longer need to traverse the steep learning curve of ferreting out local angel financiers and then convincing them to invest. Now they could go straight to the investing public. And they could do so through a medium the investing public already recognized and trusted. A couple of generations earlier, franchising had proved to be a powerful way for U.S. companies to expand overseas. But franchising was limited to certain kinds of businesses. A Nasdaq IPO could raise millions for virtually any type of company.

In many parts of the world, the Nasdaq's brand power appeared well up to that task. The companies it had bootstrapped to success in the United States were the stuff of legends, as were the fresh-minted billionaires who had invested in them. Thanks to its deep liquidity and its open-source online trading network, the Nasdaq had become the market of choice for active traders around the world. Active traders in China and Chile plied their craft on the Nasdaq each day via their home computers. As a result, it had built up a mammoth awareness. Back in the late 1990s, Response Analysis Corporation, a survey company, had asked people in the United Kingdom what U.S. stock market first came to their minds. Roughly 41 percent picked the Nasdaq, twice as many as had picked the New York Stock Exchange (NYSE).[2] For those launching a new company overseas, the Nasdaq represented a path to riches. It was Hollywood, a dream machine, and an American icon. For young upstart Internet entrepreneurs in Europe and Asia, a Nasdaq listing was the equivalent of a 1970s-era rock band scoring a cover story in *Rolling Stone*.

Direct Capitalism

IN FACT, THE idea of cloning a stock market from one nation to another was something radically new to the world of equities trading. For years, U.S. equities markets had adopted a very different tack. As they competed against each other for new listings, they sent their top brass abroad, scouting for companies that might want to list on a U.S. exchange. Even so, for a foreign firm, actually listing on a U.S. market was a cumbersome and little-understood process. Instead of buying shares in a foreign company directly, Americans purchase something called an American Depository Share (ADS). The term is often used interchangeably with American Depository Receipts (ADRs). In any case, the actual shares are held by an American bank. By the end of 2000, some 482 non-U.S. companies had shares trading on the Nasdaq versus 420 on the NYSE.[3]

It is possible for Americans to trade stocks directly on a foreign exchange. However, that process is complicated, too. Commission costs can run high. "There are no world trade organization and multilateral agreements and no bilateral agreements that allow you to buy French stock as easily as you buy French wine," says Nasdaq Vice Chairman, Alfred Berkeley.

In part because of that, if the foreign stock is not dual listed in a U.S. market, performing due diligence can be tough for a U.S. investor. The company's financial reports—quarterly earnings statements, notices of insider trading, and the like—might not be in English, for example. Worse, depending on the market, the accounting standards used to gauge the company's health might not be as rigorous as those followed by U.S. auditing firms.

So for that reason, trading in ADRs offers a measure of safety because the foreign companies that list with a U.S. stock market are required to furnish the same financial reports as their U.S. counterparts. And they are required to use U.S. accounting principles, even if regulations in their home country are less stringent. In addition, foreign companies must meet the same listing requirements as their U.S. counterparts as to their net earnings and so forth.

American investors, as evidenced by their outrage over the Enron scandal, expect that the companies they invest in will adhere to certain minimal reporting standards. Indeed, setting a high bar is vital to a stock market's credibility. A stock market will attract investors only if those investors believe that its practices are above board. "The one thing that United States markets have is tremendous self-regulatory organizations," said one former Nasdaq official. "The entire process is dedicated to protecting the investor."[4]

Compliance has its costs. A public company has to hire accountants and maintain an investor relations department, for example, and its management must be ever mindful of investor scrutiny. For a foreign company, these costs are in addition to whatever compliance costs it must pay out at home. But this may be a small price when weighed against the chance to tap into the flush U.S. equity markets. Important, too, a listing on a U.S. exchange lends a foreign company considerable prestige, particularly if that company markets its products in the United States. A listing is proof the company is committed to doing business in the United States and that its operations are an open book.

Laying Siege

DESPITE THESE ADVANTAGES, the Nasdaq and the NYSE had each managed to secure fewer than 500 foreign listings. Meanwhile, untold thousands of foreign companies existed beyond America's borders. More were being formed daily. They constituted a very rich prize. Stock markets gain revenues from listing fees and the like. In addition, the more companies they list, the more choices they give investors. More choices translate directly into higher volume, which benefits the market's member trading firms. Clearly, the old method of allowing foreign companies to trade shares in the United States via ADRs was reaching only a tiny fraction of future Oracles and Intels. To find more of these companies, the Nasdaq needed to take its show on the road.

In doing that, they had a good story to tell. As Zarb explained to a BBC reporter, a foreign-based Nasdaq "allows companies the ease of raising capital away from their home countries." At the same time, he said, it makes it easier for those investors to put their money into companies located beyond their borders. The net effect, Zarb proclaimed, was to energize an economy and create jobs.[5]

In other words, foreign Nasdaqs would give local companies in Japan, Belgium, or wherever a means to secure financing on their own turf. Eventually, these foreign Nasdaqs would give

U.S. investors a crack at trading the local company's shares. With the tech boom, the Nasdaq U.S. had already furnished a powerful model of just how quickly a vibrant stock market could create wealth. A Nasdaq Europe might fuel a similar boom there by serving as launching pad for a fast-paced German biotech firm or a Finnish company pioneering new wireless applications, while a Nasdaq-Japan might become the catalyst for those who felt stifled by that country's dominant large companies. The same might occur later when the Nasdaq opened an exchange in India, where start-up software firms were fast becoming a world force, and in Russia, where a young generation was steadily learning the ropes of capitalism.

Zarb and his leadership had to convince Nasdaq members back home that these overseas exploits were worthwhile. Some Nasdaq member firms had criticized Zarb for his global focus, saying that he was neglecting problems at home. "Before the locomotive starts moving forward, it has to be attached to the train," said the president of one prominent securities firm.[6] The counter-argument to these critics at home was basically this: An alliance of foreign Nasdaqs might pump up volume and liquidity at the mother exchange as well—to the benefit of U.S. member firms. That is because it would give investors outside the United States access to U.S.-listed Nasdaq stocks.

For a growing number of newly affluent peoples around the world, this represented a vast, hitherto untapped opportunity to invest. With a handful of notable exceptions, the exchanges in many countries are quiet backwaters. Only a few shares of major companies trade actively. As a consequence, perhaps, stock ownership by foreign individuals, even in Europe and Japan, is far lower than in the United States. And much of it is indirect through pension funds and the like. The Nasdaq could bring these people to the well.

And indeed, bringing new investors to the Nasdaq was critical to the total equation—whether that meant Americans putting their money into foreign growth stocks or the reverse.

Simply increasing the number of listings would tend to depress prices because it would overwhelm the market with supply. By contrast, increasing the number of buyers would raise prices by creating a sellers' market that would coincidently raise the wealth of buyers.

The net result of this vast world marketplace might be a boom like the tech rally being experienced in the United States, only global in scale. No better mechanism existed to create wealth than a dynamic stock exchange. A trade agreement yields benefits at a snail's pace. A sizable World Bank loan might take years to bear fruit. But a high-flying stock market could double its market capitalization in a year. All that might create a tidal wave of wealth for a nation—and out of thin air. As Zarb explained to a Senate Banking Committee hearing on the "Financial Marketplace of the Future:"

> Vibrant equity markets are important contributors to today's robust economy. Efficient and liquid equity markets help channel risk capital from investors to new and innovative companies who desperately need it. Equity shares allow investors to take part in the profit of firms while at the same time allowing firms to undertake the projects that lead to their growth. In addition to channeling capital to companies, equity markets produce a price for the equity of a company as a by-product of their trading operation, and that price is central to a market economy's allocation of capital.[7]

With that vision in mind, the Nasdaq set about quickly cloning itself around the world. Starting around 1998, Nasdaq officials fielded plans to link with stock exchanges in Australia and Hong Kong. And they were actively seeking ties to markets in Singapore and China. During April 1999, China's Prime Minister Zhu Rongji made a point of touring the Nasdaq's New York headquarters on a visit to the United States. And he and Zarb had several meetings.[8]

One of the leaders of the Nasdaq's overseas onslaught was John T. Wall. A fixture at the NASD, Wall had been named executive vice president of the Nasdaq in 1982. Prior to that, he had helped oversee the compliance and surveillance divisions. Wall was named president of Nasdaq International, Ltd., in December 1997, reporting to Alfred Berkeley, who at the time was Nasdaq Stock Market President. Nasdaq International would put Wall in charge of strategic development and international marketing of products and services as well as securing additional foreign listings.[9] With a team in place Nasdaq's first strategic coup occurred in Japan.

The Defeat of the Mothers and Other Markets

AS IT TURNED out, the Nasdaq had a fairly easy go of it expanding into Japan. The competition proved only halfhearted. The indigenous Japanese OTC market, for one, was languishing. Trading volume had dropped from ¥5.6 trillion in 1995 to under ¥2 trillion four years later. To help boost volume, the Jasdaq, as some called it, implemented a dealer-focused trading system modeled on the Nasdaq.[10]

The Godzilla of equities markets in Japan was the Tokyo Stock Exchange (TSE), which, depending on Japan's global fortunes at the moment, might exceed the NYSE or the London Stock Exchange in clout. Yet the focus of trading on the TSE was on monster-sized Japanese companies and on stocks of foreign companies. Still, officials at the TSE were mindful that a vibrant American stock exchange focusing on new companies could deal a blow to their business. It had happened in the United States as the Nasdaq successfully challenged the NYSE. And it was also happening in Europe, where Frankfurt's Neuer market had become one of the fastest-rising stock markets in the world. Thus, in April 1999 the TSE followed the trend of many European stock exchanges and replaced its polite, neatly dressed floor traders with an electronic system. It also announced plans to create its own growth-company exchange, called the "Mothers," because it was designed to nurture these young companies. The Mothers would be modeled after the Neuer.[11] Many claimed that the listing requirements were not stringent enough, meaning that it would attract low-quality firms. As a result, the exchange was slow to succeed.

For the Americans, meanwhile, owning a premier stock market in the world's second-largest economy represented a rich prize indeed. The Japanese economy, more than any other, was driven by technology. And while the number of Internet users was less than in the United States, growth was phenomenal. By some estimates, more than 30 million Japanese would be online by 2002, while millions more might connect to an electronic market via cell phones and personal digital assistants (PDAs). The Japanese were notably ahead of the Americans in both areas. Most important, the Japanese were renowned throughout the world for their prodigious savings rate despite that country's anemic interest rates. Nasdaq-Japan could offer them a high-profit alternative. And it might even bootstrap the country out of its economic malaise.

Zarb spoke of exactly that when he addressed a group of Japanese business executives in Tokyo roughly a year before the Nasdaq-Japan's debut. "Darkness begins just in front of you, yet suddenly the view ahead seems clear and bright," he said, quoting a well-known Japanese saying. Zarb went on to explain that, yes, the Japanese economy was a mess but that the Japanese were taking prudent steps to clean it up through deregulation, bank reform, and better corporate governance. But, Zarb said, readying the sales pitch, "I believe that equity financing—as opposed to debt financing—must play a more prominent role in financing Japanese business growth. Venture capital firms and entrepreneurs must be able to enter the public market to succeed." Elaborating, Zarb explained that in a vibrant market, an

IPO was likely the most lucrative exit strategy for VC-funded companies. Venture capitalists needed such rich incentives in order for them to fund risky start-ups. Nasdaq-Japan was destined to be that exit strategy, Zarb said. Methodically, he then recited the Nasdaq's lengthy list of U.S. accomplishments, in particular how it had printed money for scores of start-up companies.[12] "Our goal must not be to follow old ways of doing things, but to take bold, innovative steps to create a better marketplace," he lectured.

On one level, the speech represented a truly astounding turn of events in the state of U.S.-Japanese relations during the previous two decades. In the past, prominent U.S. executives, like Chrysler Chairman Lee Iacoca, sought ways to hold the Japanese economy in check. Now, here was Zarb, an equally high-profile U.S. business leader, preaching to the Japanese on how they could recover from their economic quagmire. It was like the 1950s postwar U.S.-Japan relationship all over again.

Rising Son

PROBABLY NO ONE in Japan understood Zarb's message better than Masayoshi Son, president and chief executive officer of Softbank, an Internet incubator and venture capital firm run along the lines of CMGI in the United States. It had been Son who persuaded Zarb to partner with Softbank in launching the Nasdaq. Perhaps fearful of Japan's legendary regulations against foreign financial firms, Zarb had previously planned to open the first Asian Nasdaq in some other country, probably Hong Kong.

Zarb and Son appeared to be natural partners. On the one hand, there was Zarb, the new-thinking American financier who was spearheading the financial revolution in the United States. As for Son, he too had proven that he could break down barriers and accomplish great things—and at Internet speed. In very un-Japanese fashion, Son had built a highly individualized empire virtually from scratch. Low key, a casual dresser at work, he had adopted the shoot-from-the-hip, gambler's approach to business that was more typically American than Japanese. In fact, Son was the offspring of Korean immigrants. His first millions came to him in the 1970s, when he sold Japanese arcade games to the University of California at Berkeley. At the time, he was enrolled as a student there. Son's next venture was a lightweight electronic translator—his own invention. He followed up that success with Softbank, which began as a software distribution firm in 1981. Over the years, Son funneled Softbank's growing profits into a mixed bag of technology firms, among them U.S. tech publisher Ziff Davis. The really big bucks came with the Internet IPO boom. Son's early investments in companies such as Yahoo, E*Trade, and Buy.com led many to believe that his $76 billion net worth at the height of the Internet boom would eventually top that of Bill Gates.[13]

Better, perhaps, than any of his Internet-mogul peers, Son had devised a formula to leverage his wealth globally. For example, a U.S. Internet firm such as E*Trade, funded early in its growth stage, could then be brought to Japan to essentially repeat the process. Likewise, a Swedish or Indian start-up could be cloned in China, Japan, or the United States. To accomplish his plan, Son set up immense venture firms that scoured the world for ripe companies to fund—and this even after the 2000 crash lobbed a breathtaking $140 billion off Softbank's market cap. Toward the end of 2000, he commanded Europe's largest Internet venture fund. Separate funds searched out Internet opportunities in China. Son even allied himself with the World Bank, creating a fund to search out promising new-economy start-ups in developing nations.[14]

In an interview, Zarb recalled the evening he and Son discussed the Nasdaq merger. Learning that Zarb was going to appear at the U.S. embassy in Tokyo, Son extended an invitation to dinner at his home. Zarb remembers touring the palatial

Tokyo mansion. The lower floor contained a computer-animated golf course that not only let players dial up and compete on major links throughout the world, moving platforms duplicated the ball's lie, and an elaborate climate-control apparatus actually mimicked weather conditions of golfing shrines such as Scotland, Phoenix, or Maui. During the remainder of that evening Zarb says that he and Son talked at length about Asia's future. Son insisted that Japan's fundamentals were sound and that an economic turnaround would come eventually. Zarb found himself agreeing. And while he had been in Tokyo only to give a speech and had found that the Japanese were polite "as only Japanese can be," Zarb had a feeling that he had not gotten through to the business leaders he had spoken with. Certainly during his talk and his subsequent appearance at the U.S. embassy, there was no serious talk of partnering with the Nasdaq. As Zarb and others at the Nasdaq sought to open a franchise in Hong Kong, he had encountered similar reticence. Oddly enough it was Chinese Premier Zhu Rongji, a man who came of age under Communism, who had truly grasped the enormous impact that a vibrant equities market could have on an economy. He had called the Nasdaq the crown jewel of American capitalism. And he saw such a market as essential if China were to develop not only a class of entrepreneurs, but also of venture capitalists who would fund them. The prospect of a rich IPO would be their reward. Rongji had gotten it. But so had Son, Zarb thought. "Here was a guy who represented a different part of the Japanese society that I still think represents the next generation of real builders in Japan. He had a Nasdaq mentality," Zarb concluded.

The seed money that Son allocated to Nasdaq-Japan, added to the NASD's own contribution, reportedly amounted to a scant $5.7 million, enough to give Son and the NASD each a 50 percent ownership.[15] However, for Son in particular, the money carried with it an awesome degree of leverage. Indeed, the likely motives for Son's interest in Nasdaq-Japan illustrate how the Internet was radically changing the process of capital formation. Nasdaq-Japan would create remarkable synergies with the bevy of Internet companies that Softbank had already funded, giving him an end-to-end revenue stream within the financing food chain. Softbank venture funds could provide seed money to firms that would IPO on Nasdaq-Japan, yet another Softbank subsidiary. Those trading the IPOs shares could do so via E*Trade.[16] As for the NASD, it would acquire a for-profit exchange that would garner revenues from listings and fees associated with trading. It could provide a model for future international Nasdaq exchanges. If it succeeded, Nasdaq-Japan would become one of three anchors in Zarb's bid to create the world's preeminent exchange—not bad for an investment of a few million.

Some in Japan criticized the way the Nasdaq had gone about entering the Japanese market, which was in typical American fashion. Hard-driving higher-ups in an organization set a course and then left it to underlings to work out the details. In consensus-conscious Japan, the more acceptable approach is to allow those midway up the organization chart to slowly build support for a project, then present it to the leadership when it was near completion. On a practical level, consensus building is a necessary fact, at least in regulation-burdened Japan. The Japan Securities Dealers Association, which was the NASD's counterpart there and overseer of the Jasdaq, had good reason to feel threatened and might move to block the Nasdaq. While no law prevented the launch of a competing exchange, laws did require that at least six brokerages sign on in support of a newcomer. As late as the fall of 1999, none had.[17] To smooth over these and other regulatory hurdles, Nasdaq-Japan was eventually launched as an arm of the Osaka Securities Exchange. (Ironically, this was essentially the same strategy followed by the Archipelago electronic communication network [ECN] in the United States when it allied itself with the existing Pacific Exchange.) Nasdaq-Japan opened on June 19, 2000.

Some 680,000 shares changed hands. Those shares came from eight companies coming from sectors in technology, pharmaceuticals, and multimedia.[18]

Plans called for the 100 top U.S. Nasdaq-traded shares to trade on Nasdaq-Japan. More U.S.-listed companies would follow—but not quickly, as it turned out. Japanese laws required that all financial statements be printed in Japanese, an expensive proposition. Nevertheless, Nasdaq-Japan proudly proclaimed itself a success following one year of operation. Some 56 companies had listed with the exchange, and a quarter of Japanese IPOs during the period had debuted on Nasdaq-Japan. E*Trade Japan, one of those firms, raised $85 million in its September IPO. Shares, which at one point traded at the lofty price of $14,151 each, subsequently fell to $7,441.[19] In October 2000, just months after trading commenced, a private placement to further fund Nasdaq-Japan attracted 13 prominent Japanese and foreign brokerages.

The European Theater

ROUGHLY FIVE MONTHS after trading on Nasdaq-Japan commenced, the Nasdaq opened its Canadian branch in Montreal. The move gave Canadian investors access to 42 local companies that traded on Nasdaq U.S., in addition to Canadian start-ups that had listed solely with the Canadian franchise. Canadian investors would also be able to trade the full gamut of Nasdaq companies directly through an affiliate local broker.

Europe had yet to be conquered. And that effort would prove somewhat more difficult. The Continent was already rife with fiercely combative exchanges. Like Central Asian warlords, these exchanges alternately fought each other or formed byzantine alliances. Like the long-held dream of European unification, these alliances were aimed at creating a pan-European stock exchange to rival competitors in the United States and Japan.

Midway through 2000, these alliances fell into three basic categories. The first group, called iX, attempted to link the powerhouse Deutsche Borse and London Stock Exchange. Meanwhile, exchanges in Amsterdam, Brussels, and Paris formed something called EuroNext, with an aim toward creating a single trading platform. The third group consisted solely of the Swedish-based OM Group, a company that developed trading software. In addition to its aim of uniting the European stock markets,[20] the OM group was also actively exploring overseas partnerships. In the United States, the American Stock Exchange, a NASD subsidiary, eventually opted for OM Group software in revamping its options trading platform. Adding to the confusion were a number of conflicting clearing systems that had long slowed down fund transfers and record keeping once trades were completed.

Just as the Tokyo Stock Exchange ruled Japan, the London Stock Exchange (LSE) lorded over the rest of Europe. Its roots went back to 1760. When 150 brokers at the Royal Exchange were kicked out for "rowdiness," they set up trading at a coffeehouse instead. In 1973, the LSE admitted its first female members. In 1995, it launched a subsidiary called AIM, which was designed to nurture growing companies. By the turn of the century, AIM had secured a respectable 500 listings. Ally with the LSE, many believed, and the other competing bourses would fall before you like dominoes. A fledgling partnership between the Deutsche Borse and the LSE garnered a lot of attention. But it ran into trouble when LSE shareholders reportedly balked at the deal, fearing that Germany's powerful banks would exert too much control over trading in London. The Nasdaq also apparently saw the LSE as an easy on-ramp to Europe and tried to join the attempted merger between the LSE and the Deutsche Borse. Nasdaq International Chairman John Hilley reportedly told the *Financial Times* that "it makes profound business logic for the LSE and Nasdaq to do a deal."[21] Sweden's OM Group made a bold attempt to buy out the LSE at the onset of the millennium but was rebuffed by the exchange's shareholders. The EuroNext alliance also made overtures. Meanwhile, the LSE and the NYSE were exploring ways to create a global exchange of their own, a partnership of equals that would eventually include bourses in Latin America and Asia.

Rife with Competition

EUROPE'S MYRIAD EVER combative exchanges had long hampered small companies from raising money on their home turf. And therein lay the Nasdaq's opportunity. No European exchange could raise money for a company as readily as the Nasdaq U.S. And for years, this fact of life had led better-funded European companies to IPO on the U.S. Nasdaq. However, high costs prevented many smaller companies from doing the same. The *Financial Times* once reported that a Nasdaq listing might increase a small firm's legal and auditing costs by a crippling 30 percent. One French software maker reportedly spent $1.2 million, or 20 percent of its quarterly revenues, on preparations for its Nasdaq-U.S. listing. Most worrisome of all to small European firms: Nasdaq-U.S. listings increased the chances of investor lawsuits.[22] In lieu of a Nasdaq-U.S. listing, some small European firms opted to list on several European Union exchanges. But this was also costly since it might require the firm to report its results in several languages and pay multiple listing fees.

For the Nasdaq, the goal was clear. If it could enter Europe as a recognizable brand, with an end-to-end trading platform that efficiently handled everything from quote dissemination to clearing operations, the Continent would be ripe for the taking. The Nasdaq appeared uniquely suited to the task. It had integrated a dozen or more ECNs into its order book, along with hundreds of market makers and numerous clearing firms. Meshing its trading platform and clearing systems with European brokerages and exchanges might be easy by comparison.

But the Nasdaq was not alone in recognizing that opportunity. Several Nasdaq-like markets were already in place. Besides London's AIM, the Paris Stock Exchange created a subsidiary in 1996 called Le Nouveau Marche (LNM).[23] However, the Nasdaq's most formidable competitor lay to the north. It was Frankfurt's Neuer market. An offshoot of the Deutsche Borse, the Neuer was conceived as a Nasdaq-like trading arena for growing companies. And it had its eye on becoming a pan-global exchange right from the start. Conceived in the backrooms of German financial powerhouses, it also enjoyed instant credibility with institutional investors in Germany and elsewhere, thanks to its strict standards. Listing companies were required to publish earnings reports in both German and English and to adhere to U.S. accounting standards. To ensure liquidity of newer issues, investment banks sponsoring a new listing had to sign up at least two market makers before trading could commence.

When launched in 1997, the Neuer quickly lived up to expectations by besting every other major exchange in the world. In 1998, a shaky year, especially for European markets thanks to Asian contagion and the Russian meltdown, the Neuer rose by an astounding 175 percent. New issues were said to be 100-times oversubscribed. Like their American counterparts gazing through the windows of the Nasdaq's Times Square Market-Site, Germans crowded a Frankfurt sidewalk to watch Neuer-market ticker prices stream past at a nearby bank.

To its backers, the Neuer's success represented a major change in the traditionally conservative way German and other European companies raised money. In the past, seed money had come mainly from wealthy individuals, while money to finance a company's growth had come from bank loans. Conservative German banks had long insisted on steady and consistent earnings. This naturally limited the kinds of companies able to receive loans. With the Neuer's heady IPO market came a realization that these old rules could not apply to an economy propelled by leading-edge technology. By the time a small company's earnings qualified it for further debt financing, its competitors could have left it in the dust.[24]

This same thinking could be found in Brussels, home to another one of the Nasdaq's potential competitors in Europe, the EASDAQ. Launched in 1995, the name was an acronym for European Association of Securities Dealers Automated Quotation System, meaning that it was designed as a Euro counterpart of the Nasdaq, with a screen-based, dealer-market trading system to match. In addition, like the Nasdaq in the United States at the time, it was a quote delivery system and not an exchange. The EASDAQ nevertheless geared itself toward companies with $80 million market cap or IPOs looking to raise $8 million.[25]

The German Connection

AFTER MERGER ATTEMPTS by the Deutsche Borse and the LSE broke down, the Nasdaq, which had hoped to join the deal, was forced to find a new partner. In late March 2001, it did. The Nasdaq announced that it had reached an agreement to purchase 58 percent of EASDAQ. Zarb commented that the agreement formed the third leg of the Nasdaq's planned global trading platform, the other two legs being Nasdaq-Japan and Nasdaq U.S. The deal, he said, "moves us closer to achieving our strategic vision of an international Nasdaq."[26] Although terms of the deal were not disclosed, one of the Nasdaq's partners was Knight Trading Group,[27] the powerful U.S. market-making firm that was poised to profit as trading volume grew. The Nasdaq announced that it would change EASDAQ's name to Nasdaq Europe. Just weeks after the acquisition, Nasdaq Europe debuted something called the ETS (European Trading System), modeled after the Nasdaq's U.S. limit order book along with some enhancements that would form part of the Nasdaq's upgraded platform SuperMontage in the United States.[28] "We want to begin as a wholly local market in Europe, doing IPO listings and cross border trading," said one Nasdaq official. In time, the exchange would expand its horizons. But for the start, it would tap into European companies that Nasdaq U.S. was liable to miss.[29] And this was a substantial number. Unification would inevitably lead to a deluge of spin-offs, privatizations, and mergers as many large firms there faced Continent-wide competition for the first time. In addition, a new generation of European entrepreneurs was bent on bringing their companies public. In the months following the 2000 crash, underwriting in Europe was double the IPO activity on Wall Street. During the first quarter of 2001, some 25 offerings raised $7.6 billion on the Continent.[30]

The Nasdaq chose Michael Sanderson to head up its fledgling European exchange. Sanderson had previously served as chief executive officer of MarketXT.com, an ECN that at first focused on after-hours trading. It was later sold to Tradescape Corp., a company that also owned a direct-access brokerage. Before heading up MarketXT.com, Sanderson served as chairman and chief executive officer of Reuters America Holdings, where he helped grow Instinet.

In mid-November 2001, less than a month after Sanderson took the job, he announced a major coup: an alliance with the Berlin Stock exchange. A staunch rival to the Deutsche Borse, the Berlin Stock Exchange had nevertheless focused much of its trading activity on U.S. and non-German, European stocks. Its total listings numbered 10,000, more than any other exchange in the world. Under the deal, each exchange took a minority ownership interest in the other. But the union would bring other benefits as well. Germans, for both regulatory and cultural reasons, were known to favor trading in German markets. Thus, the alliance would allow Nasdaq Europe to capture German order flow. As for the Berlin Stock Exchange, it would enjoy eased access to U.S. equities and greater liquidity.

As occurred in Japan, the Nasdaq had found a European partner with a strong desire to compete with the region's dominant exchange. And that partner had smoothed over many of the issues of regulations and acceptance by the financial community that might have arisen had the Nasdaq made a go of it alone.[31]

Futures Trading

OTHERS AT THE Nasdaq were working on similar deals. But they did not necessarily concern equities trading. In March 2001, Nasdaq officials announced an agreement with the London International Financial Futures and Options Exchange (LIFFE) to trade single stock futures.[32] The Nasdaq Liffe Market would be the first U.S. market allowed to trade them. Single stock futures would give investors a high degree of leverage over a particular stock, greatly multiplying any gains or losses. And those gains and losses could be realized even in relatively slow markets. Single stock futures were also more liquid and potentially more risky than options. Many in the financial community saw them as the next big thing.

Thus, at the end of 2001, the Nasdaq had positioned itself with all three legs of its grand strategy in place. Fledgling exchanges were open for business in Japan and Europe, while the mother exchange plodded toward recovery after its low following the terrorist attacks of September 11. In addition, it had one of America's largest options exchange in the Amex, which also did a brisk business in exchange-traded funds. At the onset of 2002, no other stock market on the planet had as many pieces in place. Though the NYSE and the European stock exchanges had themselves worked toward similar ends, it was the Nasdaq that reached critical mass first. Now the challenge would be to keep this fledgling empire together and also to fund it. The Nasdaq had two strategies in the works for accomplishing these goals. One was a new global trading system called SuperMontage; the other was privatization.

CHAPTER 17

GOING PUBLIC

DURING 2000 AND 2001, while Nasdaq officials set about building an integrated global market, they faced several potentially dangerous brushfires at home. The millennium had begun with the April 2000 crash. And from there, markets had stair-stepped relentlessly downward. From its high of over 5,000 in the first quarter of 2000, the Nasdaq Composite fell as low as 1,387 on September 21, days after the terrorist attack on the World Trade Center.

Many of the challenges the Nasdaq faced could be traced back to that 18-month decline. The market that had become a legend now saw its image severely tarnished. As it searched for a bottom, the Nasdaq was increasingly being seen by both investors and listed companies as the market that could pump up a company's stock price but also send it crashing downward. Some listed firms openly revolted against the Nasdaq's volatility by defecting to the New York Stock Exchange (NYSE), where it was the job of trading-floor specialists to maintain an orderly market. *BusinessWeek* reported that between January and April 2001, nine firms had announced moves to the rival Big Board, including previous Nasdaq trophy companies like E*Trade and Krispy Kreme Doughnuts. One clothing firm, Chicos FAS Inc., announced that it was moving its listing to the NYSE and that it did so in the hopes of reducing volatility and increasing liquidity, both of which, the company said, would help it "achieve our long-term goal of increased shareholder value."[1]

Adding to the insult, during the Nasdaq's late 1990s run-up, it had been unable to recruit firms from the Big Board. A 1939 NYSE edict known as Rule 500 forbade NYSE-listed companies from defecting to another exchange unless two-thirds of its shareholders supported the decision. In July 1999, the Securities and Exchange Commission (SEC) approved the NYSE's less stringent reversion of Rule 500 that required a company's board of directors to approve the decision to jump ship.[2] Meanwhile, the NYSE had set up an office in Silicon Valley to fatten the ranks of tech firms that had already made the switch, among them BMC Software, Gateway Computer, and America Online. And the NYSE was prepared to make the case that trading on the Nasdaq potentially cost investors money. A much-quoted report by the SEC, released in January 2001 (before the phase-in of decimalization), had found that Nasdaq spreads were often wider than those on the NYSE.[3]

The Harder They Fall . . .

THE NASDAQ'S OWN regulations threatened it with the loss of still more companies. Chief among them were the high-flying tech stocks that had once propelled the Nasdaq skyward. Now, with their share prices beaten down, these firms risked being delisted from the Nasdaq National Market. One such company was the Midwest telecom firm McLeod USA. At the start of 2001, its shares had topped $20. By year's end, it had succumbed to many of the same problems plaguing the telecom sector. By the last days of January 2002, they had fallen to 19 cents. Nasdaq rules normally required companies to maintain a minimum bid price and minimum public float or market value to maintain their listing on the Nasdaq's National Market. Companies that fell short of the mark for 30 consecutive days were given 90 days to regain compliance by meeting the minimum requirements for 10 trading days or else face delisting. Once delisted, the stock was transferred from the Nasdaq National Market and traded on the less liquid Nasdaq SmallCap Market. Such a demotion could hurt a company. Analysts all too often stop giving coverage, volume drops, and the stock languishes.

As share prices reached new lows following the attack on the World Trade Center, the Nasdaq's board of directors realized they needed to take action or risk losing more companies from the National Market. On September 27, the board announced a moratorium on some of its listing requirements until the following year.[4] A month later, after the NYSE reduced some of its listing fees,[5] the Nasdaq announced sweeping proposed cuts as well.[6]

The Demise of Fractions

IF NASDAQ-LISTED companies with mutilated share prices were hurting, the Nasdaq-member dealers making a market in those shares were also feeling pain. Volume on the Nasdaq was holding up. But the spreads, which were the source of much of their profits, were being cut to the bone. However, the fact that spreads had narrowed had nothing to do with the market meltdown. The culprit was decimalization. At the end of the 1990s, the U.S. markets were the only ones in the world still quoting shares in fractions. Congress held hearings on the matter in April 1997. But it was not until the start of 2000 that the SEC first ordered U.S. markets to phase in decimalized pricing, even in the face of many critics.

Some believed that decimalization would overload trading systems. They said that it would compel market participants such as dealers, specialists, and traders to constantly update their quotes in response to their competitors' minute price moves. Volatility might also increase as a result. Stocks would rise up and down as trades took place in 1-cent intervals.

Neither in fact occurred. Instead, as the NYSE and the Nasdaq phased in decimalization during the opening months of 2001, both saw dramatic decreases in the size of spreads, something not everyone had anticipated. On the NYSE, spreads crumbled by nearly 20 percent,[7] while on the Nasdaq, the average spread dropped by roughly 51 percent and in some cases by as much as 71 percent.[8]

Theoretically, the decline in spreads is supposed to mean a savings to investors. However, the truth is not as simple as that. Proponents of dealer markets such as the Nasdaq say that constant back-and-forth trading activity among dealers themselves tends to pump up a stock's valuation, which benefits shareholders over the long term. The downside is wider spreads. Back-and-forth dealer trading creates more volatility. Faced with volatility, so the argument goes, dealers protect themselves by quoting wider spreads.

It is a debatable point. But what is certain is that while traders may have benefited from narrowed spreads. They were hurt by a decline in the number of shares made available to trade—called size—by both specialists and dealers. On the NYSE, quoted size declined by as much as 70 percent during the phase in of decimalization. Across the board declines in size on the Nasdaq were somewhat less, but Nasdaq dealers also tended to display fewer quotes. The effect was a little like learning a supermarket was holding a sale on milk, but that quantities at the sale price were sorely limited. One possible explanation for the reduced size is that dealers and specialists—already smarting because of narrowed spreads—reacted cautiously to decimalization at the onset. By offering to trade fewer shares, they protected themselves from sudden adverse price moves.

However, at least one broker, allied with an electronic communications network (ECN), learned to profit from the very thing that was starving out dealer firms. If the Nasdaq could quote shares in 1-cent increments, an ECN could file down the spread even more. That is exactly what Datek, a brokerage catering to active traders, and its affiliate ECN, Island, did in June 2001, when Datek allowed traders to enter bids and offers in increments of just one-tenth of a penny.[9] For active traders, these razor-thin levels offered a clear advantage. By making a minimal adjustment in the price they were willing to accept when buying or selling shares, they could place themselves at the head of the line, awaiting execution. ECNs profited from the transaction fees they received. Thus, unlike dealers, the spread was of no consequence. By allowing finer increments, an ECN could divert more order flow from dealers. The more flow, the more fees that poured in.

Smaller and more nimble than the Nasdaq and unburdened by the vested interests of members and the degree of oversight by the SEC, ECNs were increasingly demonstrating that they could innovate faster than the mother market. More and more, they were becoming a threat to the Nasdaq.

Changes at the NYSE

THANKS TO COMPETITION from ECNs (and also to the new order-handling rules instituted in 1996; see chapter 9), the Nasdaq was becoming more like an order-driven market, akin to the NYSE. In an order-driven market, individual participants set the bid and ask prices by the limit orders they post.

Meanwhile, the NYSE was fast morphing into something more like the Nasdaq and radically changing its staid centuries-old traditions. These changes, too, were reactions to challenges posed by the Nasdaq and ECNs and by something called Rule 390.

For years under an NYSE edict called Rule 390, Big Board member firms had only been allowed to trade NYSE-listed securities on a national securities exchange—which is to say, if you were an NYSE member broker and you wanted to trade an NYSE-listed company such as IBM, you generally could do so only via the NYSE or one of the regional exchanges. But at the start of the millennium, ECNs were poised like barbarians at the gates of the Big Board. By the NYSE's own admission, they threatened to steal a large share of trading volume from the Big Board floor. An NYSE report noted that ECNs had captured up to one-third of the Nasdaq volume. "It has been suggested that ECNs could capture a similar share of NYSE-listed stock order flow."[10] One way ECNs could steal orders from the NYSE floor was to go through the arduous process of themselves becoming exchanges and setting up their own in-house self-regulatory organizations. Several were in the process of doing just that.

Meanwhile, Rule 390 was increasingly being seen by some as an anticompetitive anachronism. As the SEC commented:

> Off-board trading restrictions such as Rule 390 have long been questioned as attempts by exchanges with dominant market shares to prohibit competition from other market centers. . . . In an age when advancing technology and expanding trading volume are unleashing powerful forces for change and new competitive challenges for the U.S. securities markets, both at home and abroad, the continued existence of regulatory rules that attempt to prohibit competition can no longer be justified.[11]

Perhaps seeing the handwriting on the wall, the NYSE itself proposed rescinding Rule 390 in a filing with the SEC in December 1999. In May 2000, the SEC approved the request. As a result, NYSE-listed shares began appearing on ECNs like Island and Brut, although the amount of order flow they lured away was in single digits. Nevertheless, in a flash, it mattered a good deal less whether you traded shares of a company on the floor of an exchange or via a distributed network such as the Nasdaq.

What mattered more was the trading platform people used, namely, the actual display that traders viewed on their computer monitors that showed how many buyers and sellers were in the market at that moment as well as the prices they were fielding. The Nasdaq had reached its astronomical volume levels thanks in part to its legendary Level II display screen that showed quotes from all market participants competing for trades. The NYSE, by contrast, had long hidden its limit order book from public view. Only the specialists who oversaw trading for a particular stock knew how many limit orders might be awaiting execution should the stock's price move in their direction. Thus, only each individual specialist knew the true picture of supply and demand.

Remember that ECNs were now trading Big Board stocks, too. And in order to attract users, they provided order books that were modeled after Nasdaq Level II. However, rather than charging rental fees, ECNs made their limit order books available free to anyone with an Internet connection. If the NYSE was to compete in a world where ECNs could trade shares of Big Board–listed companies, it had to make its own order book more transparent. Thus, in 2000, the exchange began implementing a series of innovations that were intended to do just that. In December 2000, the Big Board began testing something called NYSE Direct+, which was an internal matching system designed to automatically link buy and sell orders—just like an ECN. An even more radical innovation was something called

OpenBook, which received SEC approval on December 12, 2001.[12] OpenBook would display customer limit orders for all to see.

Such fundamental changes are difficult to implement when they go against the vested interests of exchange members. OpenBook and NYSE Direct+, while they might have been necessary for the NYSE's long-term competitive survival, nevertheless threatened the livelihood of the Big Board's specialists. They would lose some of their trading edge as a result of Open-Book and some of their order-handling responsibilities as a result of NYSE Direct+. And their votes could block any changes. For that reason, the NYSE was wrestling with the process of becoming a for-profit company. Privatization promised to streamline management decision making. No longer would exchange leaders have to rally majority support from members each time they instituted changes. If those members could be converted into owners, they would profit from the overall gains made by the exchange.

Under New Management

AT THE NASDAQ, a similar rush was in progress to revamp trading systems and transform itself into a private company. However, the Nasdaq's situation was made perhaps more complicated by the fact that it was not an exchange in the formal sense,[13] nor was it an ECN.

As the Nasdaq grappled with its unique position within the U.S. financial markets, it was also undergoing a transition of sorts and a significant change in leadership. In April, the Nasdaq moved its business offices from Washington to Manhattan, where its glittery Times Square MarketSite became the market's spiritual headquarters. Nasdaq officials said that the move north from D.C. was a prelude to privatization and was meant to distance itself from the National Association of Securities

Dealers (NASD), still located in Washington.[14] In late June 2001, with the markets remaining in the doldrums, management announced layoffs of 140 persons.[15] Bigger changes came the following month, when it was announced that Robert Glauber and Hardwick "Wick" Simmons had been tapped to replace Frank Zarb. Glauber would take over the chairmanship at the NASD. while Simmons would chair the Nasdaq. Simmons, who before joining the Nasdaq as CEO the previous year had served as president and chief executive officer of Prudential Securities, assumed his new post on September 26, less than two weeks after Nasdaq trading resumed following the September 11 tragedy.[16]

While they laid the groundwork necessary to take the Nasdaq private, NASD insiders were also at work on a new trading platform called SuperMontage to compete with the NYSE and ECNs. Nasdaq officials claimed that both moves were critical to the future of over-the-counter (OTC) trading. During a hearing before the Senate Banking Committee in late September 1999, Zarb said that the rise of the Internet demanded drastic changes. "To fully realize the benefits that the Internet can provide to the capital formation process, Nasdaq must be reinvented for the digital age,"[17] he said.

The decision to go public had received NASD board approval just two months before. Several compelling reasons prompted it, Zarb told the Senators. Privatizing would provide the capital needed to keep Nasdaq's trading technology up to par. Indeed, some expected a private placement to raise $1 billion,[18] a conservative estimate at a time when upstart Internet firms commanded market caps in the billions of dollars. Moreover, said Zarb, a privatized for-profit Nasdaq responsible to its shareholders would be better able to move quickly in response to the rapid changes the Internet was bringing to the financial markets. As with the NYSE, one of the chief reasons for privatization would be to recapture some of the revenue lost by its members, in this case Nasdaq's dealer firms. Having already lost as much as a third of their order flow to ECNs, those dealers would likely lose even more if SuperMontage came online. Thus, like their counterparts at the NYSE, it was in their short-term interest to oppose the new platform. On the other hand, if SuperMontage lived up to its promises, it would be a mammoth, fee-generating machine—the largest pool of liquidity on the planet, and one that earned a tiny commission each time a trade took place. Privatizing Nasdaq would give its dealers an ownership stake in that machine.

But privatization was also a risky move for its would-be owners. Once unhinged from the NASD, the Nasdaq from a regulatory standpoint would become just one among many exchanges and ECNs or just one more route investors might choose when directing their trades. It would face stiff competition in the same way that a once public utility faced competition when privatized. To counteract this risk, a privatized Nasdaq needed a means if not a mandate to continue in its role as the nexus point for all market participants, that is, ECNs and dealers. Zarb may have been hinting at this goal when he told the Senate Committee:

> We expect this new [Nasdaq] structure will allow us to build a consensus for offering, in one place, the transparent price discovery needed by the market to address a continually increasing trend toward market fragmentation that creates a market structure that combines the best elements of a deal-based and aggregate display market.[19]

In other words, the Nasdaq wanted to remain the central switching facility for all trades, whether they originated from its dealers, the traditional liquidity providers, or the new liquidity providers, namely the ECNs. In Internet parlance, Nasdaq hoped to become something like the quote aggregator for the financial world. SuperMontage, as you'll see, was intended to make that happen.

A second component of the spin-off, Nasdaq Regulation Inc., was equally crucial in planners' eyes. Nasdaq Regulation also had been partially spun off from the NASD in 1996 as part of the initial SEC-mandated restructuring that had separated the Nasdaq from the NASD.[20] Now, under the privatization plan, Nasdaq Regulation would continue as the body charged with overseeing market performance. But its future role might grow.

Like the Nasdaq stock market, NASD Regulation's role also faced a long-term threat from ECNs. Each ECN that cared to become a registered stock exchange had to create its own enforcement arm, similar to NASD Regulation. Therefore, the argument went, a danger existed that oversight might become fragmented by the proliferation of exchanges, just as some claimed that multiple ECNs caused fragmentation of order flow. In the future, instead of dealing with two dominant equity market, self-regulatory bodies—the NYSE and the Nasdaq—the SEC might face dozens.[21] Zarb hinted that NASD Regulation could play an increasing role in the marketplace of the future:

> The time may . . . be right to consider whether it makes sense for the regulatory units of all institutions choosing to register as exchanges to be combined into a single SRO governed by market participants and public representatives. Such an entity could be given the primary financial, sales practice and market rules examination, surveillance and enforcement responsibility for all broker-dealers.[22]

Regardless, in the near term, Zarb promised that a substantial portion of the profits from privatization would go toward financing NASD Regulation. All in all, it was an ingenious arrangement. Privatization would transform the Nasdaq into the "market of markets," the mother exchange where dealers and ECN traders met. And NASD Regulation might become the single regulatory body overseeing all Nasdaq market participants.

Trouble was, interests both inside the NASD and without did not like the idea.

Identity Crisis at the American Stock Exchange

AMONG THE FIRST to cry foul were American Stock Exchange (Amex) members. Some Amex seat holders reportedly claimed that they had been led to believe new listings would result as companies seamlessly moved from the Nasdaq's dealer market to the Amex auction platform. And that, they said, is what had prompted them to vote in favor of the Amex-Nasdaq merger. There was even talk of a lawsuit despite the fact that by some reports the Nasdaq had promised to give the Amex $215 million from proceeds of its private placement, $40 million more than the original $175 million to upgrade and promote the exchange promised when the merger took effect.[23]

In fact, just months after the Amex merger occurred, it looked as if it might be sidestepped by the Nasdaq's restructuring. As Zarb explained to Senate Committee members in 1999:

> The current recapitalization plans do not include the American Stock Exchange. Since the acquisition of the Amex last fall, we have begun a series of initiatives to strengthen that market. We are making good progress and hope to be in a position to recapitalize the Amex in the next few years.[24]

Yet when the merger took place in the fall of 1998, an intense effort had been made to cobrand the exchanges, through both Web sites and advertising campaigns. National Football League fans used to watch the *Nasdaq-Amex Halftime Show*.[25] Three years later, Web sites of the two markets were notably separate. Moreover, on October 29, 2001, Amex President Salvatore F. Sodano announced a multimillion-dollar branding campaign aimed at creating a distinct identity for the Amex. While Americans were glued to their televisions for news of the "War on Terrorism," separate commercials for both the Nasdaq and the Amex aired on news and financial cable-TV networks.

Both campaigns made ample use of catchy music and pleasing graphics. Yet each carried a markedly different message. The Nasdaq spots featured 1970s-era symphonic rock—coming-of-age music for baby boomers—and showed the familiar names of Nasdaq-listed companies flashing across the giant electronic marquee of the Nasdaq's Times Square MarketSite. The implied message: The companies that trade on the Nasdaq will be the ones that drive the country out of its recession and will propel the nation forward to a bright future. The Amex message was more subtle. The Amex slogan, "Opportunity, made fresh daily," appears aimed at acquainting people with that market's more exotic products, such as exchange-traded funds (ETFs) and options.

Whatever the intent of the two campaigns, with the Nasdaq moving aggressively toward privatization, the Amex appeared back in the position it had long occupied among America's financial markets. It was more than a regional exchange, but it was still a distant third behind the NYSE and the Nasdaq. CNN, Fox News, and CNBC all monitor real-time performance from the NYSE and the Nasdaq but omit the Amex.

Meanwhile, Amex members, like their counterparts elsewhere, were hurting from narrowing spreads and competition from other markets. While the Amex had long established itself as powerful player in options trading, it faced tough rivals, like the Chicago Board Options Exchange (CBOE). Newly instituted quote reporting practices had linked the exchanges tightly together, cutting spreads to levels normally seen with stocks. This was severely hurting specialists' profits. The Amex's other profitable product, ETFs, were being increasingly traded on other exchanges, including the NYSE and the CBOE and, ominously, on ECNs, like Island. In late October 2001, Island placed full-page newspaper ads boasting that it had become the dominant QQQ[26] trading venue the previous week, besting Amex by 110.9 million to 129.2 million shares.[27]

True to its heritage, the Amex continued to launch new products, including single stock futures and a debt/stock hybrid known as SPARQS (Stock Participation Accreting Redemption Quarterly-Pay Securities). Still some in the financial community pointed to the Amex's new branding campaign as evidence that it would be spun-off as a separate entity, once the Nasdaq became fully privatized.[28]

All of this begs the question: Why did the merger, which took so much work and seemed to hold so much promise, appear in danger of shattering? An article in *Wall Street & Technology* magazine explored two possible reasons: technology and regulation.[29] In the article, an unnamed Nasdaq source admitted that the two markets began pursuing separate courses in the final months of 1999 and that the catalyst indeed had been the NASD member decision to privatize the Nasdaq market. In an interview Zarb told a different story. One of the things he and others promoting the merger hadn't counted on, he said, "was the enormous interest in the Nasdaq and its huge brand name growth." Because of that growth, firms that might have been expected to switch from the Nasdaq to the Amex had stayed put. The acquisition had in part been an attempt to bolster the Amex and the millions spent to upgrade its trading systems had done that, he insisted. Indeed, if the Amex, helped by an infusion of cash, could reinvent itself as a market for derivatives and other cutting-edge financial products, then its eventual spin-off would produce nice profits for members.

Whatever the outcome, the fact that the Amex and the Nasdaq were going in separate directions meant that, in the near term, both markets were compelled to develop separate trading systems. The Nasdaq focused on SuperMontage as a way of positioning itself as the nation's central trading hub, while for its part, the Amex needed to quickly upgrade its options trading platform. Options trading on the Amex had increased from roughly 200,000 to 820,000 contracts per day over a three-year period ending in 1999, while equities trading levels on the exchange remained at roughly the same levels.[30]

Finally, the Amex was not in a position to privatize as quickly as the Nasdaq. Amex's members had to be brought on board first. Also, the Amex was classified as an exchange, necessitating more regulatory hurdles that might add months if not years to the Nasdaq's strategic timetable.

Raining Money

ON MARCH 9, 2000, the Nasdaq Composite topped 5,000, having gained nearly 150 points on the day. It was the 15th record high for the new millennium[31] and an auspicious time for the market to launch its privatization drive, which began just four days later. Roughly half the Nasdaq's 5,500 participating member firms participated in the private placement.[32] The Nasdaq would raise something like $516 million from the two-phased offering. An additional $627 million was expected to follow in the years ahead as warrants that had been sold were actually exercised.[33] Plans called for the NASD to retain control of the shares until it received SEC approval to become an exchange.[34] At that point, if the market climate appeared right and the SEC sanctioned the move, the Nasdaq would field an initial public offering (IPO).[35] The public not only would trade shares on the Nasdaq but could own a piece of it as well.

Some of the NASD's smaller broker-dealer firms reportedly complained about the lack of information that accompanied the Nasdaq's private offering. Others feared that a few large brokers that had traditionally exerted a strong influence over the market's direction would now be in complete control. What had been a democratic association of theoretical equals was now a corporation controlled by its major shareholders. Still, more than 80 percent of NASD members voted in support of privatization.[36]

The Nasdaq's next challenge was to go through the hassle-ridden process of becoming an exchange, even though the label was little more than a formality. The Nasdaq had functioned as a de facto exchange for decades. While the Nasdaq had begun as a quote delivery mechanism, its refinements over the year, including the small-order execution systems (SOESs) and Select-Net, facilitated trades, just as did the various electronic networks employed by the Big Board and other exchanges. In years past, an exchange designation would have smoothed the way for the Nasdaq to trade listed shares. Those listed shares were already being traded by Nasdaq dealers through a network called the Nasdaq InterMarket.[37] But it was slow in comparison to the kind of network Nasdaq planners envisioned.

And so the Nasdaq filed the application with the SEC on November 9, 2000, and at some risk. The required SEC review process would give competitors the chance to lobby for their own changes in the Nasdaq's governance. And this is exactly what happened.

The Nasdaq's critics voiced concerns that as a privatized exchange, it would be less responsive to investors. They were also wary that the Nasdaq would create a monopoly for itself in the trading of OTC securities. Specifically, the Nasdaq's critics were upset with its next-generation trading platform: Super-Montage as well as the order execution network linked to it called SuperSOES.

A Brand-New CLOB

DESPITE ALL THE hype and controversy surrounding it, SuperMontage on the surface would seem a fairly straightforward idea. Basically, it was an add-on to the Nasdaq's long-standing Level II window. Level II displayed the best bid and ask price from each market participant. But it did not show the depth of market from each participant—a significant drawback. For example, a market maker might display a bid of 500 shares of XYZ at $10.52. However, no one but the market maker for XYZ would know that another order to buy 20,000 shares at $10.51 in that market maker's own order book. The same situation might exist on the Island ECN. Someone might wish to buy 1,000 shares of XYZ at $10.52. And if that were the best bid residing on Island, it, like the market maker bid, it would appear on Level II. But again, a 10,000-share buy order might also reside on the Island book, at a price of $10.50.[38] And traders watching the Level II book would never know it. They could surf over to the Island order book. But in a fast market, this is cumbersome and time consuming. Yet knowing the depth of the market within certain price ranges is vital to active traders—whether they are professionals or day traders. Supply and demand dictate price in securities trading, just as in anything else. And they dictate it profoundly in the short term.

SuperMontage's solution: incorporate the best bid from each market participant in the Level II window as before. Traders could still see the familiar four-letter symbols for each market participant, whether dealer or ECN. But SuperMontage would also include a second window, which would be an enhancement of the Level I display showing the current best bid and offer and the corresponding size of each. The SuperMontage version of that window would aggregate the five best bid and ask prices for a stock regardless of where they appeared. For example, if the second-best bid price for 10,000 shares of XYZ was buried in the REDI ECN book and an identical bid for 5,000 XYZ shares was buried in the Island book, SuperMontage would combine both bids and show that 15,000 shares were available at that price. And it would do the same with the three next best prices on each side of the market. Even more important, it would allow users to access that well of liquidity.

SuperMontage incorporated other bells and whistles. Market participants could enter orders anonymously or tie them to their dealer ID. And they could choose the priority they wished to give an order before sending it to the market, say, by price/time or price/size/time. As a software application, none of this was exactly rocket science. Nevertheless, to planners at the Nasdaq, SuperMontage would be a little like the Windows operating system, a common platform through which all other applications, in this case trades, needed to pass, that is if they hoped to access SuperMontage's huge market share. The ungainly technical term for this aggregated display was CLOB (central limit order book). CLOB was essential to stemming fragmentation from ECNs, its supporters claimed. That is because ECNs, while highly efficient, execute trades only when prices match. They do not incorporate market makers who have committed to maintaining liquidity in a stock (risking their own capital to do so). In a fast-dropping market, such as occurred during the crash of 1987, there might not be buyers to take stock from the panicked sellers. Thus, a serious meltdown might occur.[39]

Trouble was, ECNs like Archipelago and third-party Web developers like 3Dstockcharts.com had devised their own quote displays that incorporated limit orders from rival ECNs. ECNs had also incorporated software algorithms called smart order routing that automatically searched markets for the best price and then directed customer orders there. Critics charged that SuperMontage might stifle these innovations. More important, these critics said, any CLOB must by definition incorporate certain rules governing the order by which trades occur. By owning the quote display, the Nasdaq was in a position to set the rules to its benefit. As officials at Bloomberg Tradebook, an ECN used by institutions, noted, "The NASD . . . has not ever made clear exactly how the order-routing algorithm would work or what design features have been built into the proposed SuperMontage ECN Nasdaq has been constructing for itself."[40] As a result of criticisms like these, SuperMontage went through several revisions before receiving SEC approval in January 2001.[41] Reacting to the Nasdaq's critics, the proposal version that received SEC approval allowed market participants to bypass SuperMontage and use alternate networks of their choosing to process trades. And it required the NASD to construct an alternate version of SuperMontage that would show quote data but not facilitate executions. But even the final proposal failed to satisfy all of SuperMontage's critics. Noting that the SEC-approved SuperMontage proposal was an improvement over previous versions, Instinet President and Chief Executive Officer Doug Atkin nevertheless warned the financial community:

> Nasdaq continues in many ways to put its interests above those of investors, especially in regard to the concerns of mutual funds, pension funds, consumer groups and others who urged that the order matching priorities of SuperMontage itself be amended in a way that is more fair to investors.[42]

The Nasdaq announced that SuperMontage would be up and running early in 2002, though some wondered if the system would come online that quickly. Nasdaq's critics had often charged that it was slow to incorporate technological changes and that rather than innovating, it supplanted ideas from others. In an interview Nasdaq Vice Chairman Alfred Berkeley who had guided much of the market's technology development, admitted that the Nasdaq incorporated outside innovations, but for sound reasons:

> SuperMontage is mutualizing the ECN functionality and making it available for everyone cheap. What Nasdaq has always done is to take technological innovation and to mutualize it, build it into the system and let everyone have it. Therefore we've always been criticized by technology innovators who say here comes Nasdaq stealing my idea. We're not stealing their idea . . . If it's a public domain idea we're going to build it into the Nasdaq if that's what the customers want. This is the difference between us and the other exchanges. We have invited the other exchanges to display on the Nasdaq.

What was even more likely to delay SuperMontage's implementation, was the arduous exchange registration process. The comment period gave the Nasdaq's critics another opportunity to influence the rollout of SuperMontage. This time, critics voiced fears of the combination of SuperMontage and something called SuperSOES, the Nasdaq's own execution-enabled routing network. SuperSOES replaced two Nasdaq execution networks: SOES and SelectNet. SOES was designed to allow retail traders to send orders directly to market makers, while SelectNet was typically reserved for larger trades, often between market makers themselves. In the past, the two networks had forced dealers to doubly expose themselves to orders.[43] And this led many to reduce the size of shares they offered in trade. SuperSOES was, among other things, designed to prevent that double liability.

But its critics feared that it would divert order flow from their own rival trading networks. Not only would the Nasdaq possess a monopoly on how quotes were displayed and disseminated (via SuperMontage), but, thanks to SuperSOES, it would possess a clear advantage in the way actual orders were routed. The liquidity that resulted from combining the Nasdaq's dealers and ECNs would render insignificant the matching capabilities of ECNs. In other words, they might go out of business.

The criticisms voiced were strong enough that in November 2001, the Nasdaq requested an extension of its exchange application so that it would have more time to devise a response.[44] If becoming a for-profit exchange was integral to the Nasdaq's grand vision of creating a unified global marketplace, then that vision, at least for the short term, now appeared temporarily on hold.

All these events were overshadowed by the tragedy of September 11 and the war in Afghanistan that followed. The vicious terrorist attack exposed many vulnerabilities in America, among them the financial markets. But as with many other aspects of American society, the attacks also revealed the markets' unique and unrecognized strengths.

EPILOGUE: WILL EXCHANGES MATTER IN THE FUTURE?

WHATEVER DIFFERENCES THE NASDAQ AND THE NEW YORK Stock Exchange (NYSE) may have had over the years were put aside on September 17, 2001. Nasdaq Chief Executive Officer Wick Simmons stood beside his NYSE counterpart Dick Grasso on the balcony above the NYSE. Other prominent politicos and VIPs also crowded into the cramped space in order to witness the reopening of the NYSE for the first time since the September 11 terrorist attacks. The list included then New York Mayor Rudolph Giuliani and the U.S. senators from the state, Charles Schumer and Hillary Clinton. They were joined by several New York firefighters and police officers.[1]

The opening bell, when it rang, was both somber and celebratory. The destruction of the World Trade Center towers had put the nation's financial community on the front lines of a new and little understood war. In an instant, the attack revealed that no American and no American institution was safe. And yet the opening bell, coming the Monday following the Tuesday morning attack, also proved that two of the nation's most important institutions had been able to recover within a relatively short time, even from a direct hit.

All weekend long, Nasdaq officials had worked feverishly testing their network to make sure it was ready. A steep drop in stock prices was forecast when trading resumed. If the market was to function effectively, the dealers, day traders, institutions, and retail investors required unhindered access to the markets' order-processing systems. The markets needed as broad a constituency as possible to ensure that enough liquidity existed to weather the waves of expected selling. This was no small matter. If a problem arose and traders perceived that there was no liquidity behind the market, the odds favored a calamitous meltdown at least on par with what had occurred on Black Monday 1987.

But the weekend testing had proved hopeful. Nasdaq technicians had discovered that 2,400 of the 2,700 servers at its dealer firms were online and ready for Monday's trading.[2] Many of the network connections that did not respond were no doubt destroyed in the attack. When the World Trade Center towers collapsed, they had damaged a switching facility operated by Verizon where 350,000 voice and 3.5 million data lines converged. These lines had been among the principal conduits of financial information to Wall Street. Rerouting them would take roughly one week.[3] The good news was that the traffic on the Internet was only minimally affected following the attack. The reason harked back to the Internet's origins as a Defense Department project. If a portion of the Internet was destroyed, the self-healing design would allow for traffic to be automatically rerouted.

Despite weeklong, round-the-clock television coverage, few Americans outside the New York metro area could truly grasp the degree of destruction—and particularly the deep wound it left in the financial community. The new chief executive officer of the National Association of Securities Dealers (NASD), Robert Glauber, relayed the grim facts when he spoke before the Senate Banking Committee just three days after the markets reopened. Some 31 main offices of broker dealer firms had been located in the World Trade Center towers, he said. Another 30 firms had maintained branch offices there. In all, 350 Nasdaq member firms were located in the area south of 14th Street that was now a de facto war zone. For the thousands with jobs in the financial district, simply getting to work now meant breathing hazardous dust and smoke and reliving the tragedy each day as they watched rescue crews search for survivors.

Untold hundreds in the financial industry had been among the attack's victims, including several hundred people who had worked for the mammoth trading firm Cantor Fitzgerald. NASD officials were in possession of information such as dental records, and they performed the sad task of locating and passing these records along to families, law enforcement, and employers. Nasdaq officials also worked the phones, helping displaced member firms locate office space.[4] In some cases, competitors shared temporary quarters. The American Stock Exchange (Amex) headquarters, for example, lay just a few hundred feet from the disaster site. And although the building itself was undamaged, it was impossible for traders to reach it easily. As a result, options traders were relocated to the rival Philadelphia Stock Exchange, while the Amex's equity traders moved into space at the NYSE.[5]

As for the Nasdaq, its lower Manhattan administrative office building was close enough to ground zero to serve as a staging area for disaster workers. But its critical computers were miles away in Trumbull, Connecticut. Nothing would have prevented the Nasdaq from remaining open during the week following the attack. Most of the 120 clearing firms regulated by the NASD were likewise located outside lower Manhattan, meaning that trades would have been seamlessly processed. (Although if the NYSE specialists were not at their jobs, trading of

Big Board shares might have suffered liquidity shortfalls.) However, in a show of unity, all three major equity markets had elected to resume trading together. The end result was that the systems functioned as needed when trading resumed, even as volume soared above pre–September 11 levels. It was one of the new war's first victories. "Make no mistake, these attacks were an assault on our financial markets as well as our nation," Glauber told the senators. By keeping markets running, he said, "we will ensure their ultimate failure."[6]

Glauber's comments underscored the importance of institutions such as the NASD and the NYSE in times of crisis. Trading had resumed without problems thanks to the NASD's and the NYSE's long-standing relationships within securities industry and their ability to organize and rally their memberships when needed. No other organizations likely could have achieved the same result in so short a time.

A New National Market

ALL OF WHICH called to question the many sweeping changes affecting securities trading. Even as the Nasdaq and the NYSE proved themselves impervious to acts of war, other forces threatened their long-term survival. Thanks to the success of electronic communications networks (ECNs) at grabbing market share from the Nasdaq and the brick-and-mortar exchanges, it was now theoretically possible, for example, to construct a kind of confederation of ECNs that would possess a larger pool of liquidity than the Nasdaq. Moreover, such an alliance might execute trades faster, more intelligently, and at a lower cost than the Nasdaq. The Nasdaq's answer to this challenge was SuperMontage (see chapter 17), which was meant to be the central nexus point for all trades. But fierce resistance from ECNs made it clear that SuperMontage would likely compete with several similarly designed platforms in the years ahead. During 2000–2001, academics, ECNs, and think tanks fielded numerous proposals on what shape the market of the future should adopt.

For example, two ECNs, Island and Archipelago, suggested changing the way that share prices were broadcast from one exchange to the next. The original network designed to accomplish this had been around since the mid-1970s. Dubbed the National Market System (NMS), it was mandated by Congress to ensure that all traders could access the best-quoted prices currently available, regardless of the exchange utilized for trading. However, after more than a quarter century of operation, some charged that the NMS was too slow, that it was further encumbered by rivalries between exchanges, and that it stifled innovation.

In a white paper published in April 2001,[7] Island ECN claimed in particular that the mandatory linkages between exchanges slowed down trading. Auction markets, even when augmented by automation, could not match the lightning speed of an ECN like Island. Speed up trading, and you deepen liquidity. Instead of mandatory linkages, Island proposed voluntary ones. Exchanges still would have the incentive to offer the best price if they hoped to attract order flow.

Archipelago had a different idea. It said that quotes should be aggregated to ensure that one locale existed that displayed the best price but also that the quote data should be sold to third-party firms who could then devise competing ways of displaying it. This proposal allowed brokers to add value for their customers; namely, they could invent ways to direct trades that were most in the customers' interest.[8] And indeed, the Nasdaq network had evolved into something very similar to Archipelago's proposed revamping of the NMS. Numerous direct-access brokers had devised innovative trading software that let traders either manually or automatically scan the market for the best prices.

These proposals suggested, in other words, that a plethora of competing exchanges could be tied together via a number of different trading platforms. In this scenario, brokers would be the ultimate value-added agents. They would compete with each other on the basis of their ability to get customers the best price.

The Liquidity Factor

IN AN INTERVIEW, former Nasdaq Chief Executive Officer Frank Zarb said that someday dealers, ECNs, and other market participants also might compete on the basis of the amount of liquidity they could provide and that they might charge for that liquidity:

> What will happen is that dealers will more and more find a way to be compensated for the liquidity they provide. It will look like a fee. If I ran a broker dealer now and made a market in every Nasdaq stock and I agree that I am going to buy 1,000 shares of every Nasdaq stock whenever you hit me, that's my promise to you to provide liquidity. To have me standing there all the time I'm going to take a fraction of a penny.

The situation is similar to shopping at a grocery store with low prices but bare shelves or paying slightly more to shop at a store where supplies are guaranteed. The reason for this sea change, Zarb said, had everything to do with decimalization, which had narrowed spreads to razor-thin levels that market makers might no longer find profitable to trade. When spreads were wide enough for dealers to earn handsome profits, they had paid brokers to send customer orders in their direction. Now that spreads had narrowed, the opposite was true. ECNs had become important liquidity providers for the Nasdaq, and they charged fractional commissions for executing trades. SuperMontage, through its order-execution networks, would do the same. And dealers offering sufficient liquidity might find this something that investors, particularly large institutions, would pay for.

In fact, liquidity promises to become an increasingly critical issue as markets fragment and spreads wither. By the Nasdaq's own admission (see chapter 17), the size of transactions declined significantly following decimalization. While day traders in the postcrash environment often complained about size shortfalls, institutions, wishing to trade blocks of shares, have been especially affected. OptiMark (see chapter 11) was likewise an attempt to charge fees for creating a pool of liquidity—although investors were reluctant to learn how to use it. A newer alternative that had attracted some buzz was called Liquidnet.

Liquidnet was launched in 1999 by Seth Marrin and Eric LeGoff. Both had previously worked together developing software for institutional investors. Liquidnet aimed to serve those same customers by helping them execute their large orders discretely so as not to upset the market. Indeed, citing research from the Plexus Group, Liquidnet's founders claim that growing market fragmentation costs these traders roughly 39 cents per share. The total cost is a staggering $100 billion per year. The company's solution is something the founders call a decentralized automated trading system (ATS) that is accessible online to participating institutions. An ATS is basically a peer-to-peer network. If one member wants to sell 50,000 shares of Wal-Mart, notice of the sale gets sent to prospective buyers that are signed on to the network. If someone's interested, the two parties can negotiate a price online—but again, anonymously. Because the transaction occurs on a private network, it does not create news, nor does it suddenly swamp retail traders with shares. As a result, the price of the stock tends to hold steady. Liquidnet profits from two-cent-per-share commission.[9] A similar process of uniting people on both sides of a trade already takes place on the NYSE, where specialists have been known to put floor brokers in contact with people interested in similarly sized trades.

Another way to create liquidity is via a form of trading known as a call auction. Robert A. Schwartz, a professor of finance at Baruch College, suggested it as an alternative to the auction and dealer trading venues that dominate the markets today. With a call auction, sell orders are batched together, and the bidding of buyers sets a consensus price. The consensus price may be superior to the price arrived at through regular trading because it involves all the active participants and is immune to short-term supply and demand that characterizes continuous trading. Call auctions have already been incorporated into the Paris Bourse and Deutsche Bourse. Something like a call auction also occurs at the open of the NYSE.[10]

Some see the falloff in liquidity and other pressures brought about by competition among exchanges as leading to consolidation. Noting that the U.S. markets have been littered with dead and long forgotten exchanges over the years, among them the Intermountain Exchange in Salt Lake City and the Consolidated Stock Exchange in New York, a Georgetown University professor predicts that in the future even national exchanges may die. "Eventually the question will not be 'Does Germany need three stock exchanges?' but 'Does Europe need three stock exchanges?'" Exchanges, after all, are expensive to operate, and throughout their history they have traversed through long periods of annual losses. That being the case, Angel believes that "global equity markets will continue to be molded by the twin forces of technology and regulation."[11] Technology affects markets on several key fronts. On the one hand, it reduces costs, which lowers the barriers to entry. It also allows for fast linkages, increasing transparency almost to the point where markets themselves cease to have distinct identities. In a sense, they become just what the over-the-counter (OTC) market was in its earliest days: a loose affiliation connecting participants to pools of liquidity.

The effects of regulations are more difficult to predict since they take into account the politics and passions of the moment. In the wake of the Enron debacle, Congress and others will no doubt push for some form of increased market regulation. Meanwhile, some have proposed changing not simply the regulations but also the fundamental way exchanges are regulated, that is, the self-regulatory organizations (SROs).

As Dale Arthur Oesterle, a professor at the University of Colorado School of Law, points out in a paper published by the conservative Cato Institute, SROs had long played a contradictory role in regulating financial markets. All too often, the enforcers were the same people in need of enforcement. Such was the crux of the 1990s market-maker scandal. This conflict will likely be exacerbated as exchanges follow through with plans to go public. According to Oesterle, market forces might do a better job. "Individual stock markets and exchanges have a strong self-interest in monitoring internally the honesty and integrity of their traders," he says.[12] Just as gamblers would not walk into a casino if they knew that the dice were loaded, neither would traders likely frequent an exchange if the rules were blatantly rigged against them. That argument assumes that people are aware the dice are loaded. Further, says Oesterle, the SROs stifle competition since they force markets and exchanges to jump through lengthy and involved regulatory hoops mandated by the Securities and Exchange Commission (SEC) whenever they make changes. And yet in the end, the SEC oversight does not focus on areas where it is truly needed. "The SEC has a tendency to meddle too much in the formal, written operational mechanics of the systems regulated by the SRO and a tendency to rely too much on the SRO for policing of floor trading practices." Like Zarb and others at the Nasdaq, Oesterle suggests that one solution might be creating a super-SRO and that Nasdaq Regulation (NASDR) might fill that role.[13]

The Ultimate Pipeline

TAKING INTO ACCOUNT all these proposed changes, in the future we are likely to see not just one way of trading stocks but many, from hybrid specialist-dealer marketplaces to peer-to-peer networks similar to Liquidnet, to ECNs turned exchanges and Dutch auctions such as W. R. Hambrecht's OpenIPO (see chapter 14). Competitive forces will forever search out innovations. And those forces are strongest in the financial markets, which have always been quick to adopt new technologies and new ways of doing business.

How will the Nasdaq fare in the face of these changes? Better than the great majority of its competitors, most likely, thanks to several key components of its culture that go back to the OTC market's earliest days and have formed the basis of its grand strategy since the 1930s. For one thing, it has consistently maintained a policy of inclusiveness. While the brick-and-mortar exchanges functioned as clubs, the NASD inherited a large amorphous group of nonaffiliated brokerages. By necessity and by its mandate, the NASD needed to create a place for them. The Nasdaq's Vice Chairman Alfred Berkeley explains:

> Look at the difference between our business model and the other exchanges. On a traditional bourse there are a limited number of seats. And to get a place at the table you have to buy somebody else out. If it were not for the Nasdaq there would be no way for people to enter the business over and above the number of seats available on these limited exchanges. That's a profoundly important thing.[14]

Indeed, as an organization, the Nasdaq has three decades experience at creating liquidity for companies where none existed before. "Think of the Nasdaq model as building pipelines to different pools of liquidity,"[15] explains Zarb. Nasdaq's SuperMontage proposal was designed to create the largest pipeline of all. Whatever competition it faces should only improve it. But in any case, the beneficiaries will be not only investors but also the small companies that Nasdaq has traditionally incubated to success.

While the exchanges barred small companies from listing their shares, the Nasdaq likewise has a long tradition of aggressively seeking them out. "Elevating the status of younger companies searching for capital and making capital more available to them was a wonderful phenomenon," said former Nasdaq Chief Executive Officer Gordon Macklin. "Working to create capital for the next generation of growth companies was nearly a religion" among he and his colleagues.[16]

That tradition of discovering and then nurturing small companies lies at the core of the Nasdaq's brand image. And it will likely be critical to attracting the growth companies in the years ahead. In the end, the details about the technological hurdles that are needed to provide smooth executions and best prices are of little concern to most of us as long as we have reasonable assurance that they work in our favor. What is important is the Nasdaq brand and that, like the Good Housekeeping Seal of Approval, it provide some reassurances that the company's listing on the exchange are worthy of it. If that is the case, then the allure of those companies will keep the Nasdaq vibrant for years to come.

There's kind of a forward edge of what Nasdaq represents," says Zarb:

> If it doesn't make the same mistake it made five or six years ago and forget to challenge itself and to look at the markets and ask itself if it's continuing to serve them the way it should be, then it will continue for some time to be a market leader. And I wouldn't be surprised to see a global Nasdaq in the next several years that really is going to be the largest integrated pool of liquidity by far. And I wouldn't be surprised to see one or two of the other major stock exchanges of the world be part of the Nasdaq circuit.

NOTES

Chapter One

1. "Building the Global Digital Stock Market" (prepared remarks by Frank G. Zarb at the National Press Club, Washington, D.C., June 13, 2000), p. 7.
2. Hal Lux, "Frank Talk from Zarb," *Institutional Investor*, February 1, 1999, accessed online.
3. Personal interview.
4. Personal interview.
5. "Nasdaq in Black and White" (online document published by the Nasdaq).

Chapter Two

1. *New York Times,* March 18, 2001, national edition.
2. Nasdaq online market data.
3. The Nasdaq has applied to the SEC to become an exchange, at press time that application was still pending, see chapter 17.

Chapter Three

1. Encyclopedia Britannica Online *(www.britannica.com)*.
2. B. Mark Smith, *Toward Rational Exuberance* (New York: Farrar, Straus and Giroux, 2001), pp. 80–81.
3. John Kenneth Galbraith, *The Great Crash* (Boston: Houghton Mifflin Company, originally published in 1954, cited version reprinted in 1988), pp. 40–50.
4. Ibid., p. 51.
5. Smith, *Toward Rational Exuberance,* p. 81.
6. Galbraith, *The Great Crash,* p. 79.
7. Defined here as anyone who makes more than 50 trades per month.

8. Martin Pring, *Investment Psychology Explained* (New York: John Wiley & Sons, Inc., 1993), p. 109.
9. "The Basics of Business history," online document published by TheStreet .com.
10. Ibid.
11. Galbraith, *The Great Crash,* pp. 108–127.
12. Online at *www.sec.gov/about/whatwedo.shtml.*
13. Smith, *Toward Rational Exuberance,* p. 23.
14. Smith, *Toward Rational Exuberance,* p. 81.
15. Marshall E. Blume, Jeremy J. Siegel, and Dan Rottenberg, *Revolution on Wall Street: The Rise and Decline of the New York Stock Exchange* (New York: W.W. Norton & Company, 1993), p. 30.
16. James Angel, "Consolidation in the Global Equity Market" (draft paper), p. 13.
17. Smith, *Toward Rational Exuberance,* p. 123.
18. Mary Clare Fitzgerald, "Recommendations for a Regulatory Paradigm in the New Millennium—'Electronic Commerce' . . . Policing Only the 'Sub-marginal Fringe,'" (online document, EcomForum, 2000, *www.ecomforum .org/submarginal.html).*
19. See *A.L.A. Schechter Poultry Corp. v. United States,* 295 U.S. 295 (1935).
20. Online at *www.law.uc.edu/CCL/34Act/sec15A.html.*
21. Mary Clare Fitzgerald, "Recommendations for a Regulatory Paradigm in the New Millennium."
22. Jeffrey W. Smith, James P. Selway, III, D. Timothy McCormick, The Nasdaq Stock Market, "Historical Background and Current Operation," NASD Working Paper No. 98-01, 1998.

Chapter Four

1. "The Poker Game That Ross Perot Won," *Business Week,* March 27, 1971, p. 74.
2. John Brooks, *The Go-Go Years: The Drama and Crashing Finale of Wall Street's Bullish 60s,* (New York: John Wiley & Sons, 1973, 1999), p. 17.
3. "The Poker Game That Ross Perot Won," *Business Week,* p. 74.
4. Jacob O. Kamm, *The Decentralization of Securities Exchanges,* (Boston: Meandor Publishing, 1942), p. 76.
5. Securities and Exchange Commission, *Special Study of the Securities Markets* (Washington, D.C.: SEC, 1963), chapter VII, p. 541.
6. Ibid., p. 548.
7. Ibid., p. 555.
8. Ibid., p. 563.
9. Ibid., p. 597.

10. Ibid., p. 596.
11. Ibid., p. 631.
12. Brooks, *The Go-Go Years,* p. 56.
13. Ibid., p. 28.
14. Jacob O. Kamm, *The Decentralization of Securities Exchanges,* p. 81.
15. SEC, *Special Study of the Securities Markets,* p. 10 (back).
16. Brooks, *The Go-Go Years,* p. 28.
17. SEC, *Special Study of the Securities Markets,* p. 499.
18. Ibid., p. 498.
19. Ibid.
20. Ibid., p. 513.
21. Ibid.
22. Ibid., p. 502.
23. Brooks, *The Go-Go Years,* pp. 19–21.

Chapter Five

1. "The Street Won't Be the Same Again," *BusinessWeek,* May 23, 1970, p. 97.
2. "Casey: An SEC Chairman Wall Street Loves," *BusinessWeek,* October 16, 1971.
3. "The Rank-and-File Brokers' Revolt," *BusinessWeek,* January 31, 1970, p. 90.
4. NASD Web site *(www.nasd.com/corpinfo/co_ove_histr.html#ceo).*
5. "The Tussle over Automatic OTC Trading," *BusinessWeek,* January 30, 1971.
6. Securities and Exchange Commission, *Special Study of the Securities Markets* (Washington, D.C.: SEC, 1963), p. 669.
7. *www.britannica.com/eb/article?eu=74291&tocid=0&query=stock%20ticker.*
8. SEC, *Special Study of the Securities Markets,* p. 657.
9. Ibid., p. 667.
10. Ibid.
11. Ibid., p. 665.
12. Ibid., p. 658.
13. "Casey."
14. NASD Web site *(www.nasd.com/corpinfo/co_ove_histr.html#ceo).*
15. Ibid.
16. Personal interview.
17. Marshall E. Blume, Jeremy J. Siegel, and Dan Rottenberg, *Revolution on Wall Street: The Rise and Decline of the New York Stock Exchange* (New York: W.W. Norton & Company, 1993), pp. 13–17.

18. "Casey."
19. "Regional Exchanges Come Out of the Sticks," *Business Week,* January 3, 1970, p. 74.
20. "The Tussle over Automatic OTC Trading."
21. As quoted in ibid.
22. Ibid.
23. Jeffrey W. Smith, James P. Selway III, and Timothy McCormick, "The Nasdaq Stock Market, Historical Background and Current Operation" (NASD Working Paper No. 98-01), August 24, 1998.
24. Ibid.
25. Ibid.

Chapter Six

1. Robert X. Cringely, *Accidental Empires, How the Boys of Silicon Valley Make Their Millions, Battle Foreign Competition, and Still Can't Get a Date* (Reading, MA: Addison-Wesley Publishing, Inc., 1992), pp. 93–94.
2. Gary Rivlin, *The Plot to Get Bill Gates: An Irreverent Investigation of the World's Richest Man . . . and the People Who Hate Him* (New York: Three Rivers Press, 1999 & 2000), pp. 224–227.
3. Robert X. Cringly, *Accidental Empires,* pp. 171–172.
4. Ibid., p. 196.
5. Ibid, pp. 220–221.
6. Ibid, p. 8.
7. Personal interview.
8. *www.wired.com/wired/archive/6.12/redmond.html.*
9. Jeffrey W. Smith, James P. Selway III, and D. Timothy McCormick, "The Nasdaq Stock Market: Historical Background and Current Operation," NASD Working Paper No. 98-01, August 24, 1998.
10. Marshall E. Blume, Jeremy J. Siegel, and Dan Rottenberg, *Revolution on Wall Street: The Rise and Decline of the New York Stock Exchange* (New York: W.W. Norton & Company, 1993), p. 147.
11. General Accounting Office, "Financial Crisis Management: Four Financial Crises in the 1980s," May 1997.
12. Hal Lux and Jack Willoughby, "May Day II," *Institutional Investor,* February 1, 1999.
13. John Greenwald, "The Secret Money Machine," *Time,* April 11, 1994, accessed online.
14. Ibid.
15. National Center for Policy Analysis, "Bad Policies Triggered 1987 Market Crash" (available at *www.ncpa.org*).
16. General Accounting Office, "Financial Crisis Management."
17. General Accounting Office, "Securities Market Operations: The Effects of SOES on the Nasdaq Market," August 1998, p. 18.

18. Ibid., p. 3.
19. Ibid.
20. Ibid, p. 15
21. Ibid., pp. 9–10.
22. Ibid., p. 18.
23. Harvey Houtkin, with David Waldman, *Secrets of the SOES Bandit* (New York: McGraw-Hill, 1999), p. 177.

Chapter Seven

1. Dwight Garner, "Rooting for the Crash," Salon.com, Oct 2, 1998.
2. *Fortune,* September 1998.
3. He currently serves as vice chairman.
4. "Investors First" (prepared comments of Alfred R. Berkeley III, president, Nasdaq Stock Market, ISI Money Show, Orlando, Florida, February 8, 1997; available at *www.nasd.com/news/sp/ppl_04.html*).
5. William Christie and Paul H. Schultz, "Why Do NASDAQ Market Makers Avoid Odd-Eighth Quotes," *Journal of Finance* 49, no. 5 (December 1994), p. 1813.
6. Remembering, of course, that their study preceded decimalization by a decade. The postdecimalization equivalent is $0.25.
7. Gretchen Morgenson, "Fun and Games on Nasdaq," *Forbes,* July 29, 1996.
8. Christie and Schultz, "Why Do NASDAQ Market Makers Avoid Odd-Eighth Quotes," p. 1814.
9. *Securities Week,* May 30, 1994, cited by Christie and Schultz, "Why Did NASDAQ Market Makers Stop Avoiding Odd-Eighth Quotes," *Journal of Finance* 49, no. 5 (December 1994): 1851.
10. Securities and Exchange Commission, "Report Pursuant to Section 21(a) of the Securities Exchange Act of 1934 Regarding the NASD and the Nasdaq Market" (hereafter 21[a] Report), May 7, 1998, p. 39.
11. *Securities Week.*
12. William Christie and Paul H. Schultz, "Why Did NASDAQ Stop Avoiding Odd-Eighth Quotes," p. 1853.
13. Shobo Narayan, "Pension Sponsors React Slowly to SEC Investigation of NASDAQ Spreads," *Plan Sponsor,* December/January 1995, accessed online at *assetpub.com.*
14. *Investment Dealers Digest,* May 22, 1995, cited at *fisher.osu.edu/fin /journal/jfidd.htm.*
15. Lucy F. Ackert and Bryan K. Church, "Competitiveness and Price Setting in Dealer Markets," Federal Reserve Bank of Atlanta *Economic Review* (Third Quarter 1998), p. 10.
16. Ibid.
17. Ibid, p. 8.

18. Ibid.
19. Gretchen Morgenson, "Fun and Games on Nasdaq."
20. 21(a) Report, pp. 2–3.
21. Susan E. Woodward,, "Price Fixing at Nasdaq? A Reconsideration of the Evidence" (paper prepared for the Congressional Budget Office, Washington, D.C., Contract No. 96-0228).
22. 21(a) Report, pp. 26–27.
23. Ibid., pp. 29–30.
24. Ibid., p. 19.

Chapter Eight

1. Lucy F. Ackert and Bryan K. Church, "Competitiveness and Price Setting in Dealer Markets," Federal Reserve Bank of Atlanta *Economic Review* (Third Quarter 1998), p. 10.
2. "Report Pursuant to Section 21(a) of the Securities Exchange Act of 1934 Regarding the NASD and the Nasdaq Market" (hereafter 21[a] Report), p. 35.
3. "Appendix to "Report Pursuant to Section 21(a) of the Securities Exchange Act of 1934 Regarding the NASD and the Nasdaq Market" (hereafter 21[a] Appendix) p. 28.
4. Ibid., p. 31.
5. Ibid., pp. 30–36.
6. 21(a) Report, p. 38.
7. 21(a) Appendix, p. 22.
8. Ibid., p. 34.
9. 21(a) Report, p. 39.
10. The Rudman Committee's other blue-ribbon panel members included A. A. Sommer Jr., a securities lawyer; Jean W. Gleason, a former SEC regulator; Stephen L. Hammerman, general counsel for Merrill Lynch; Robert H. Mundheim, general counsel for Salomon Brothers; and Irving M. Pollack, a one-time SEC enforcement officer. *The Wall Street Journal, Who's Who and What's What on Wall Street* (New York: Ballantine Books, 1998), p. 396.
11. "NASD to Sharply Increase Public Representation" (NASD press release, September 19, 1995).
12. 21(a) Report, p. 10.
13. Rudman Report at IV-6, quoted in 21(a) Report, p. 11.
14. Rudman Report at IV-5 and III-25, quoted in 21(a) Report, pp. 11–12.
15. NASD press release.
16. Rudman Report at IV-6, quoted in 21(a) Report, p. 12.
17. NASD press release.
18. Patrick J. Healy, "Nasdaq Reform: Take Another Look," *Chief Financial Officer,* March 1996, accessed online.

19. Michael Schroeder, "NASD—Your Habits Will Have to Change," *BusinessWeek*, August 26, 1996, accessed online.
20. NASD press release.
21. "Justice Department Charges 24 Major Nasdaq Securities Firms with Fixing Transaction Costs for Investors" (Department of Justice press release, July 17, 1996).
22. *Who's Who*, p. 397.
23. Department of Justice press release.
24. *Who's Who*, p. 398.
25. Ibid., p. 397.
26. 21(a) Report, p. 41.
27. Ibid., p. 43.
28. Ibid., p. 42.
29. Ibid., p. 50.
30. Schroeder, "NASD."
31. *Who's Who*, p. 391.
32. Schroeder, "NASD."
33. Brett D. Fromson, "Make-Over for a Tarnished Stock Market," *Washington Post*, March 17, 1997, p. F12.
34. Schroeder, "NASD."
35. David Henry, "More Nasdaq Stocks Defect to Big Board," *USA Today*, October 22, 1996.
36. Financial Economists Roundtable, "Statement on the Structure of the Nasdaq Stock Market," September 18, 1995, (available at *www.luc.edu /orgs/finroundtable/statement95a.html*).
37. Ibid.
38. Susan E. Woodward, "Price Fixing at Nasdaq? A Reconsideration of the Evidence" (paper prepared for the Congressional Budget Office, Washington, D.C., Contract No. 96-0228), p. 13 (available at *www.netecon .com/nasdaq.pdf*).
39. Ibid., p. 4 (footnote).
40. Ibid., p. 15.
41. Ibid., p. 13.
42. Financial Economists Roundtable, "Statement on the Structure of the Nasdaq Stock Market."

Chapter Nine

1. Lucy F. Ackert and Bryan K. Church, "Competitiveness and Price Setting in Dealer Markets," Federal Reserve Bank of Atlanta *Economic Review* (Third Quarter 1998), p. 10.
2. Securities and Exchange Commission, "Final Rules" (Release No. 34-37619A), p. 51.

3. Ibid., p. 33.

4. Ibid., p. 28.

5. Jeffrey W. Smith, "The Effects of Order Handling Rules and 16ths on Nasdaq: A Cross-Sectional Analysis" (NASD Working Paper No. 98-02).

6. "To Trade, or Not to Trade," *Van Kasper Review,* summer 2000, p. 3.

7. Ibid.

8. *Economic Review,* p. 10.

9. *The Wall Street Journal, Who's Who and What's What on Wall Street* (New York: Ballantine Books, 1998), p. 401.

10. Gretchen Morgenson, "Fun and Games on Nasdaq," *Forbes,* July 29, 1996.

11. David Henry, "More Nasdaq Stocks Defect to Big Board," *USA Today,* October 22, 1996.

Chapter Ten

1. Hal Lux, "Frank Talk from Zarb," *Institutional Investor,* February 1, 1999.

2. Editors of the *Wall Street Journal, The Wall Street Journal Guide to Who's Who and What's What on Wall Street* (New York: Ballantine Books, 1998), p. 390.

3. Statement by Chairman Arthur Levitt (U.S. Securities and Exchange Commission press conference regarding the NASD, Washington, D.C., August 8, 1996).

4. Federal Reserve Bank of Atlanta *Economic Review* (Third Quarter 1998).

5. Editorial staff, "The Chairman as Headhunter," *Institutional Investor,* January 1, 1998.

6. Brett D. Fromson, "Make-Over for a Tarnished Stock Market," *Washington Post,* March 17, 1997, p. F12.

7. Personal interview.

8. Lux, "Frank Talk from Zarb."

9. Editors of the *Wall Street Journal, The Wall Street Journal Guide to Who's Who and What's What on Wall Street,* p. 416.

10. Ibid., p. 415.

11. NASD Corporate Information (available at NASD.com).

12. Paula Dwyer, "Tough Love at Nasdaq," *BusinessWeek,* November 3, 1997 (available at *www.businessweek.com/1997/44/b3551129.htm*).

13. Statement by Chairman Arthur Levitt.

14. Securities and Exchange Commission, "Order Instituting Public Proceedings Pursuant to Section 19(h) (1) of the Securities Exchange Act of 1934, Making Findings and Imposing Remedial Sanctions" (Release No. 37538, August 8, 1996).

15. Editors of the *Wall Street Journal, The Wall Street Journal Guide to Who's Who and What's What on Wall Street,* p. 392.
16. "NASD Regulation Fines J. P. Morgan $200,000 for Limit Order Violations" (NASDR press release, June 6, 2000).
17. Fromson, "Make-Over for a Tarnished Stock Market."
18. Ibid.
19. Statement by Chairman Arthur Levitt.
20. Rethinking Equity Trading at Nasdaq (conference at the Zicklin School of Business, Baruch College, City University of New York, October 8, 1997) (available at *http://newman.baruch.cuny.edu/digital/nasdaq/deafult.htm*).
21. Dwyer, "Tough Love at Nasdaq."
22. "NASD Announces Plan For Restructuring Boards to Streamline Decision Making" (NASD press release, June 26, 1997).
23. Fromson, "Make-Over for a Tarnished Stock Market."
24. Interview with Al Berkeley, The Motley Fool, 1996 (available at *www.fool.com/Features/1996/sp0802d.htm*).
25. Editors of the *Wall Street Journal, The Wall Street Journal Guide to Who's Who and What's What on Wall Street,* p. 418.
26. Interview with Al Berkeley.
27. Fromson, "Make-Over for a Tarnished Stock Market."
28. "Investors First" (prepared comments of Alfred R. Berkeley III, president, Nasdaq Stock Market, ISI Money Show, Orlando, Florida, February 8, 1997; available at *www.nasd.com/news/sp/ppl_04.html*).
29. Hal Lux, "Building the Ultimate Deal Toy," *Institutional Investor,* May 1, 1998.
30. Fromson, "Make-Over for a Tarnished Stock Market."
31. Editors of the *Wall Street Journal, The Wall Street Journal Guide to Who's Who and What's What on Wall Street,* p. 416.
32. Fromson, "Make-Over for a Tarnished Stock Market."
33. "Shifting Focus—NASD Turns Its Attention to Individual Investor" (prepared statement by the NASD Office of Individual Investor Services, February 1997).
34. Editors of the *Wall Street Journal, The Wall Street Journal Guide to Who's Who and What's What on Wall Street,* p. 417.
35. "NASD Announces SEC Approval of Proposed Code of Procedure and New Membership Rules" (NASD press release, August 7, 1997).
36. "NASD Regulation, Inc. Bars 20 More Registered Representatives Suspected of Using an Imposter to Take Qualification Examination" (NASD press release, July 23, 1997).
37. "NASD Regulation Sanctions Olde Trader for Anti-Competitive Harassment of a Nasdaq Market Maker; Firm Also Fined" (NASDR press release, November 3, 1998).
38. Alfred R. Berkeley, "Nasdaq Market Is at Forefront of Technology," *Atlanta Business Chronicle,* October 9, 1998.

39. Ibid.
40. Personal interview.

Chapter Eleven

1. Carrie Coolidge, "Wait Until Dark," *Forbes Global,* February 21, 2000.
2. Nasdaq statistics (available at *www.nasdaq.com).*
3. Michael Peltz, "Instinet's Identity Crisis, *Institutional Investor,* November 1, 1995.
4. Carol Bere, "Reuters' Electronic Trading Cash Cow," *Global Custodian,* summer 1997.
5. Marc Friedfertig and George West, *The Electronic Day Trader: Successful Strategies for On-line Trading* (New York: McGraw-Hill, 1998), p. 17.
6. Hal Lux and Jack Willoughby, "Technology and Regulatory Reform Are Turning the Over-the-Counter Market on Its Head," *Institutional Investor,* February 1, 1999.
7. *www.island.com/about/future.htm.*
8. Hal Lux, "Make That e-CNBC," *Institutional Investor,* January 1, 2000.
9. "Archipelago and REDIBook to merge, combining the two fastest growing ECNs," Archipelago press release, November 29, 2001.
10. "Archipelago Exchange Approved by SEC, Archipelago press release, October 25, 2001.
11. Personal interview.
12. Personal interview.
13. Personal interview.

Chapter Twelve

1. Personal interview.
2. Personal interview.
3. Cited in *Forbes,* June 12, 2000.
4. See *www.sec.gov.*
5. Number based on the author's conversations with the editors of one such site.
6. Number based on various interviews by the author with online brokers.
7. Personal interview.

Chapter Thirteen

1. At the person's request, this name is a pseudonym.
2. Personal interview.
3. Anthony B. Perkins and Michael C. Perkins, *The Internet Bubble* (New York: HarperBusiness, 1999), p. 3.

4. "The Basics of Business History" *(www.thestreet.com)*.
5. "Net Stocks and the South Sea Bubble," *The New Australian,* February 21–27, 1999.
6. William Fleckenstein and Dave Kansas, "Dialogues," Feb. 8, 1999, TheStreet.com.
7. Personal interview.
8. Nina Munk, "In the Final Analysis," *Vanity Fair,* August 2001, pp. 100–113.
9. Scott Burns, "Call Him Mr. Technology," *Dallas Morning News,* January 25, 1998, accessed online.
10. Nina Munk, "In the Final Analysis."
11. Martin Pring, *Investment Psychology Explained* (New York: John Wiley & Sons, Inc., 1993), pp. 115, 120–123.

Chapter Fourteen

1. Floyd Norris, "With Bull Market Under Siege, Some Worry About Its Legacy," *New York Times,* March 18, 2001, p. 1.
2. John H. Makin, "America's Destabilizing Wealth Explosion," *Economic Outlook,* American Enterprise Institute, May 2000.
3. Personal interview. At the person's request, this is a pseudonym.
4. Norris, "With Bull Market Under Siege, Some Worry About Its Legacy."
5. "John B. Carlson and Eduard A. Pelz, "A Retrospective on the Stock Market in 2000," *Economic Commentary,* pp. 1–2, Federal Reserve Bank of Cleveland, January 15, 2001.
6. Asset International Inc., "Is the party over?" December–January, 1995, accessed online at *www.assetpub.com.*
7. Jeremy J. Siegel, "Big-Cap Stocks Are a Sucker Bet," *The Wall Street Journal,* March 13, 2000, p. A30.
8. Testimony of Senator Charles E. Schumer, House Banking Committee, Subcommittee on Domestic and International Monetary Policy, March 21, 2000.
9. Excerpt from speech given to the Economics Club of New York on January 13, 2000, cited by John B. Carlson and Eduard A. Pelz, "A Retrospective on the Stock Market in 2000." p. 1.
10. Martin Pring, *Investment Psychology Explained* (New York: John Wiley & Sons, Inc., 1993), pp. 115, 120–123.
11. David Plotz, "Nasdaq: The stock market for the smug digital world," Slate.com, April 20, 2000.
12. Gretchen Morgenson, "How Did So Many Get It So Wrong?" *New York Times,* December 31, 2000. Section 3, p. 1.
13. Patrick McGeehan, "Market Place: Study Questions Advice From Brokerage Firms," *New York Times,* May 29, 2001, accessed online.

14. Bruce Bartlett, "Financial Analysts Often Biased," National Center for Policy Analysis, December 17, 1997.
15. Personal interview.
16. David Plotnikoff, "Internet Born with Netscape, SiliconValley.com," *Mercury News*, December 24, 1999 (available at *www.siliconvalley.com/news/special/orchards/seven.htm*).
17. Personal interview.
18. Cited in "The Great Internet Money Game, How America's Top Financial Firms Reaped Billions from the Net Boom, While Investors Got Burned," Peter Elstrom, *Business Week*, April 16, 2001, p. EB 16.
19. John T. Mulqueen, "Tech Companies Play Numbers Game," *Interactive Week*, June 18, 2001, p. 11.
20. Peter Elstrom, "The Great Internet Money Game," p. EB 18.
21. Ibid., pp. EB 18–EB 19.
22. Martin J. Pring, *Investment Psychology Explained*, p. 122.
23. Personal interview.
24. Peter Elstrom, "The Great Internet Money Game," p. EB 18.
25. Eric Moskowitz, "Choke Hold: Collars Can Cloak Insider Bearishness," *Red Herring*, March 6, 2001, p. 142.

Chapter Fifteen

1. "The Market of Markets: Delivering Bottom-Line Value to Companies, Firms, and Investors," prepared remarks by Frank G. Zarb, Chairman and Chief Executive Officer, National Association of Securities Dealers, Inc., Securities Industry Association Annual Conference, Boca Raton, Florida, November 6, 1998.
2. Sharon Walsh, "NASD, Amex Vote to Combine Markets," *Washington Post*, March 19, 1998, p. C1.
3. "The Market of Markets."
4. Hal Lux, "Frank Talk from Zarb," *Institutional Investor*, February 1, 1999.
5. Walsh, "NASD, Amex Vote to Combine Markets."
6. Richard Syron profile, *Institutional Investor*, April 1, 1998.
7. Jacob O. Kamm, *The Decentralization of Securities Exchanges* (Boston: Meandor Publishing, 1942), p. 73.
8. Ibid., p. 72.
9. Reena Aggarwal and James J. Angel, "The Rise and Fall of the AMEX Emerging Company Marketplace," July 1997, research paper, p. 1.
10. Personal interview.
11. "The Market of Markets."
12. Walsh, "NASD, Amex Vote to Combine Markets."
13. Lori Pizzani, "The Fast Track: Along Came a Spider and Made a Bundle," *Investment News*, March 27, 2000.

14. Robert Sales, "NASDAQ and AMEX: Divided They Stand," *Wall Street & Technology Online,* March 12, 2001.

15. "Amex-Nasdaq Marriage May Not Lower Trading Costs—Yet: Investment Managers Hope Liquidity, Technology Make Needed Strides," *Investment News,* March 23, 1998.

16. "The American Stock Exchange: Scandal on Wall Street," *BusinessWeek,* April 26, 1999.

17. "The Flaws in Self-Policing," *BusinessWeek,* April 26, 1999.

18. "The American Stock Exchange."

19. Hal Lux, "Zarb of the 1,000 Deals," *Institutional Investor,* January 1, 1999.

20. Ibid.

21. Sales, "NASDAQ and AMEX."

22. Lux, "Frank Talk from Zarb."

23. Sales, "NASDAQ and AMEX."

24. Frank G. Zarb, "The Market of Markets."

25. Katherine Cavanaugh, "Nasdaq Chief Reveals His Global Game Plan," *Wall Street & Technology,* December 7, 1999.

Chapter Sixteen

1. "Starbucks Coffee Japan Lists IPO on Nasdaq-Japan" (Nasdaq press release, October 10, 2001).

2. *Nasdaq in Black and White* (online document published by the Nasdaq, pp. 3–8).

3. Ibid., p. 6.

4. Personal interview.

5. "Nasdaq-Japan Begins Trading in Osaka" (interview transcript from BBC World Service, June 19, 2000).

6. Ian Rowley, "Yokoso Nasdaq," *Institutional Investor,* International Edition, October 1, 1999.

7. Senate Banking Committee Hearing on the "Financial Marketplace of the Future" (prepared testimony of Frank Zarb, chairman and chief executive officer, National Association of Securities Dealers, New York, February 29, 2000).

8. Rowley, "Yokoso Nasdaq."

9. John T. Wall Appointed President of Nasdaq International, Ltd.

10. Rowley, "Yokoso Nasdaq."

11. Ibid.

12. "Partnership for Japan's Economic Recovery" (prepared remarks by Frank G. Zarb, chairman and chief executive officer, National Association of Securities Dealers, Inc. Nikkei Business Publications, Inc., 30th Anniversary Seminar, Tokyo, April 7, 1999).

13. The net worths of both men have suffered following the 2000 crash.

14. John Boyd, "Staking His Claim," *The Industry Standard,* April 24, 2000.
15. Rowley, "Yokoso Nasdaq."
16. James Christie, "E*Trade Cautiously Enters Japan," *Red Herring,* September 25, 2000.
17. Rowley, "Yokoso Nasdaq."
18. Anthony Guerra, "Nasdaq-Japan Opens for Trading," *Wall Street & Technology Online,* June 23, 2000.
19. Christie, "E*Trade Cautiously Enters Japan."
20. Robert Sales, "The Incredible Shrinking Europe," *Wall Street & Technology Online,* June 12, 2000.
21. "Alone Again?," Economist.com, November 16, 2000.
22. "Flirting with the Nasdaq," *Financial Times,* February 15, 2001.
23. Nicolas Bornozis, "Exchanges Nouveau Marche," *Global Custodian,* summer 1996.
24. Fleming Stewart, "The Neuer Market's Wild Ride," *Institutional Investor,* April 1, 1999.
25. Christopher Stokes, "EASDAQ: A Truly European Exchange?" (available at *www.lawdepartment.net/scripts/article.asp?Article_ID=579*).
26. "Nasdaq Strikes Euro Deal," CNN.com Europe, March 27, 2001.
27. "Three More Major Market Participants Agree to Invest in Nasdaq Europe" (Nasdaq Europe press release, November 13, 2001).
28. Robert Sales, "Nasdaq Plunges into Europe with Launch of ETS," *Wall Street & Technology Online,* June 8, 2001.
29. Ibid.
30. Julie Watson, "Europe Outpaces U.S. Underwriting," Forbes.com, March 13, 2001.
31. "Nasdaq Europe and Berlin Stock Exchange Announce Partnership" (Nasdaq Europe press release, November 14, 2001).
32. *www.nasdaqnews.com/news/pr2001/ne_section01_246.html.*

Chapter Seventeen

1. "What Else Can Go Wrong with the Nasdaq? Well . . . ," *BusinessWeek,* April 30, 2001.
2. "NASD Opposes SEC Approval of NYSE's Anti-Competitive Amendment to Rule 500" (NASD press release, July 22, 1999).
3. Office of Economic Analysis, *Report on the Comparison of Order Executions Across Equity Market Structures,* Securities and Exchange Commission, January 8, 2001.
4. "Nasdaq Takes Actions to Help Companies Remain Listed" (Nasdaq press release, September 27, 2001).
5. "What Else Can Go Wrong with the Nasdaq?"
6. "Nasdaq Announces Proposed Changes in Services and Listing Fees" (Nasdaq press release, October 26, 2001).

7. "Decimals Cut Spread Between Bid, Ask Prices," *Investment News,* January 8, 2001.

8. Nasdaq Economic Research, Nasdaq Stock Market Inc., "The Impact of Decimalization on the Nasdaq Stock Market" (final report to the SEC, June 11, 2001).

9. "Datek Introduces Trading in One-Tenth-of-Cent Increments" (Datek press release, June 18, 2001).

10. Alex Trotman and Clifton R. Wharton, Jr., et al., "Market Structure Report of the New York Stock Exchange Special Committee on Market Structure, Governance, and Ownership," New York Stock Exchange, April 6, 2000, p. 3.

11. "NYSE Rulemaking: Order Approving Proposed Rule Change to Rescind Exchange Rule 390" (Release No. 34-42758), Securities and Exchange Commission, May 5, 2000.

12. "NYSE Receives Approval from SEC on NYSE OpenBook" (NYSE press release, December 12, 2001).

13. Officially, the Nasdaq was a quote delivery system, while the parent NASD was a member-supported self-regulatory body.

14. "Nasdaq Leaves D.C. for New New York Home," *Washington Business Journal,* April 16, 2001.

15. "Nasdaq Implementing Workforce Reduction in Response to Market Conditions" (Nasdaq press release, June 27, 2001).

16. "Robert Glauber and Wick Simmons Named to Replace Frank Zarb as Chairman of NASD and Nasdaq" (NASD press release, July 26, 2001).

17. Senate Banking Hearing on Public Ownership of the U.S. Stock Markets (prepared testimony of Frank G. Zarb, chairman and chief executive officer, National Association of Securities Dealers, September 28, 1999).

18. Jon Birger, "Irate Amex Members Pose Threat to Nasdaq's Spin-Off," *Investment News,* January 24, 2000.

19. Senate Banking Hearing on Public Ownership of the U.S. Stock Markets.

20. Nasdaq Regulation corporate profile (available at *www.nasdr.com/2220 .asp*).

21. The nation's regional exchanges already had their own regulatory bodies in place.

22. Senate Banking Hearing on Public Ownership of the U.S. Stock Markets.

23. Birger, "Irate Amex Members Pose Threat to Nasdaq's Spin-Off."

24. Senate Banking Hearing on Public Ownership of the U.S. Stock Markets.

25. Robert Sales, "NASDAQ and AMEX: Divided They Stand," *Wall Street & Technology Online,* March 12, 2001.

26. An ETF representing the Nasdaq 100.

27. Sarah Gordon, "Island, Amex Duke It out for Supremacy in QQQ Trading," *Institutional Investor,* October 28, 2001.

28. Eric Baum, "AMEX Planning Marketing Campaign to Promote New Logo, Branding Image," *Institutional Investor,* June 6, 2001.

29. Sales, "NASDAQ and AMEX."
30. Ibid.
31. "Nasdaq Composite Index Tops 5000" (Nasdaq press release, March 9, 2000).
32. Bruce Kelly, "Nasdaq Stock Deal Confounds Members," *Investment News,* January 8, 2001.
33. "Nasdaq Completes Private Offering and Expands Board" (Nasdaq press release, January 25, 2001).
34. Senate Banking Hearing on Public Ownership of the U.S. Stock Markets.
35. "Nasdaq To Become a Public Company" (Nasdaq press release, April 26, 2001).
36. "Fact Sheet on the Proposed NASD Restructuring (NASD online publication, March 13, 2000).
37. Nasdaq InterMarket PDF presentation.
38. Island, working with certain brokerages, allows trading in tenth-of-a-penny increments.
39. Bruce Kelly, "Nasdaq Hits ECNs in a Letter to the SEC," *Investment News,* August 14, 2000.
40. "Bloomberg Tradebook LLC comment Re: SEC File No. SR-NASD-99-53," September 12, 2000.
41. "NASD Rulemaking: SuperMontage" (Release No. 34-43863; File No. SR-NASD-99-53), Securities and Exchange Commission.
42. "Statement from Instinet CEO on SEC Formal SuperMontage Approval" (Instinet press release, January 23, 2001).
43. Robert Sales, "SuperSOES Is Finally Here, but Will Investors Benefit?" *Wall Street & Technology Online,* August 15, 2001.
44. "SEC Grants Extension of Time on Nasdaq's Exchange Registration Application" (SEC press release, November 14, 2001).

Epilogue

1. "The Nasdaq Stock Market and the New York Stock Exchange Unite as Trading Commences" (Nasdaq press release, September 17, 2001).
2. "Nasdaq's Weekend Testing Is Successful—Ready for Monday" (Nasdaq press release, September 15, 2001).
3. Reed Hundt, "Keeping the Net Secure," *Atlantic Monthly,* January 2002, p. 26.
4. "Testimony of Robert R. Glauber, President and CEO of the National Association of Securities Dealers, Inc., Before the Senate Committee on Banking, Housing and Urban Affairs Hearing on the Condition of the U.S. Financial Markets," September 20, 2001.
5. "The American Stock Exchange Resumes Trading on Monday, September 17, 2001" (American Stock Exchange press release, September 17, 2001).

6. "Testimony of Robert R. Glauber."
7. Island ECN, "Strengthening the National Market System: Unleashing Innovation and Competition" (report prepared by the Island ECN, April 2001).
8. Archipelago, "Archipelago Proposal to Modernize the National Market System (white paper published by Archipelago, February 28, 2001).
9. Jonathan Burton, "To Make More Money, Cut the Noise," *New York Times,* September 26, 2001 (available at *www.liquidnet.com).*
10. Robert A. Schwartz, "Building a Better Stock Market: New Solutions to Old Problems" (revised draft of paper prepared for the American Enterprise Institute Conference on ECNs and the Future of the Securities Markets, February 3, 2000), pp. 1–26.
11. James J. Angel, "Consolidation in the Global Equity Market, an Historical Perspective" (draft paper, February 19, 1998).
12. Dale Arthur Oesterle, "Securities Markets Regulation: Time to Move to a Market-Based Approach" (paper prepared for the Cato Institute, June 21, 2000), p. 1.
13. Ibid., p. 15.
14. Personal interview.
15. Ibid.
16. Ibid.

SELECTED BIBLIOGRAPHY

Books

Blume, Marshall E., Dan Rottenberg, and Jeremy J. Siegel. *Revolution on Wall Street: The Rise and Decline of the New York Stock Exchange*. New York: W. W. Norton, 1993.

Brooks, John. *The Go-Go Years: The Drama and Crashing Finale of Wall Street's Bullish 60s*. New York: John Wiley & Sons, 1973, 1999.

Cringely, Robert X. *Accidental Empires: How the Boys of Silicon Valley Make Their Millions, Battle Foreign Competition, and Still Can't Get a Date*. Reading, MA: Addison-Weslcy, 1992.

Friedfertig, Marc, and George West. *The Electronic Day Trader: Successful Strategies for On-Line Trading*. New York: McGraw-Hill, 1998.

Galbraith, John Kenneth. *The Great Crash*. Boston: Houghton Mifflin, 1988 (originally published in 1954).

Houtkin, Harvey, with David Waldman. *Secrets of the SOES Bandit*. New York: McGraw-Hill, 1999.

Kamm, Jacob O. *The Decentralization of Securities Exchanges*. Boston: Meandor Publishing, 1942.

Kurtz, Howard. *The Fortune Tellers: Inside Wall Street's Game of Money, Media, and Manipulation*. New York: The Free Press, 2000.

Perkins, Anthony B., and Michael C. Perkins. *The Internet Bubble*. New York: HarperBusiness, 1999.

Pring, Martin. *Investment Psychology Explained*. New York: John Wiley & Sons, 1993.

Rivlin, Gary. *The Plot to Get Bill Gates: An Irreverent Investigation of the World's Richest Man . . . and the People Who Hate Him*. New York: Three Rivers Press, 1999, 2000.

Securities and Exchange Commission. *Special Study of the Securities Markets*. Washington, D.C.: Securities and Exchange Commission, 1963.

Smith, B. Mark. *Toward Rational Exuberance.* New York: Farrar, Straus & Giroux, 2001.

Wall Street Journal. *Who's Who and What's What on Wall Street.* New York: Ballantine Books, 1998.

Reports, Academic Papers, and Articles

Ackert, Lucy F., and Bryan K. Church. "Competitiveness and Price Setting in Dealer Markets." Federal Reserve Bank of Atlanta *Economic Review* (Third Quarter 1998).

Aggarwal, Reena, and James J. Angel. "The Rise and Fall of the AMEX Emerging Company Marketplace." Research paper, July 1997.

Angel, James J. "Consolidation in the Global Equity Market, an Historical Perspective." Draft paper, February 19, 1998.

Archipelago. "Archipelago Proposal to Modernize the National Market System." Comment paper prepared for the Securities and Exchange Commission, February 28, 2001.

Christie, William, and Paul H. Schultz. "Why Did NASDAQ Market Makers Stop Avoiding Odd-Eighth Quotes." *Journal of Finance* 49, no. 5 (December 1994).

———. "Why Do NASDAQ Market Makers Avoid Odd-Eighth Quotes." *Journal of Finance* 49, no. 5 (December 1994).

Fromson, Brett D. "Make-Over for a Tarnished Stock Market." *Washington Post,* March 17, 1997.

General Accounting Office. "Financial Crisis Management: Four Financial Crises in the 1980s," May 1997.

———. "Securities Market Operations: The Effects of SOES on the Nasdaq Market," August 1998.

Island ECN. "Strengthening the National Market System: Unleashing Innovation and Competition." Report prepared by the Island ECN, April 2001.

McCormick, Timothy, James P. Selway III, and Jeffrey W. Smith. "The Nasdaq Stock Market: Historical Background and Current Operation" (NASD Working Paper No. 98-01), August 24, 1998.

Morgenson, Gretchen. "Fun and Games on Nasdaq." *Forbes,* July 29, 1996.

Nasdaq Economic Research, Nasdaq Stock Market Inc. "The Impact of Decimalization on the Nasdaq Stock Market." Final report to the Securities and Exchange Commission, June 11, 2001.

Nasdaq Stock Market. "Nasdaq in Black and White." Online document published by the Nasdaq.

Oesterle, Dale Arthur. "Securities Markets Regulation: Time to Move to a Market-Based Approach." Paper prepared for the Cato Institute, June 21, 2000.

Schwartz, Robert A. "Building a Better Stock Market: New Solutions to Old Problems." Revised draft of paper prepared for the American Enterprise Institute Conference on ECNs and the Future of the Securities Markets, February 3, 2000.

Securities and Exchange Commission. "Appendix to Report Pursuant to Section 21(a) of the Securities Exchange Act of 1934 Regarding the NASD and the Nasdaq Market," May 7, 1998.

———. "Final Rules." Release No. 34-37619A.

———. "Order Instituting Public Proceedings Pursuant to Section 19(h) (1) of the Securities Exchange Act of 1934, Making Findings and Imposing Remedial Sanctions." Release No. 37538, August 8, 1996.

———. "Report Pursuant to Section 21(a) of the Securities Exchange Act of 1934 Regarding the NASD and the Nasdaq Market," May 7, 1998.

Securities and Exchange Commission, Office of Economic Analysis. "Report on the Comparison of Order Executions Across Equity Market Structures," January 8, 2001.

Smith, Jeffrey W. "The Effects of Order Handling Rules and 16ths on Nasdaq: A Cross-Sectional Analysis." NASD Working Paper No. 98-02.

Trotman, Alex, and Clifton R. Wharton Jr. et al. "Market Structure Report of the New York Stock Exchange Special Committee on Market Structure, Governance and Ownership." New York Stock Exchange, April 6, 2000.

Woodward, Susan E. "Price Fixing at Nasdaq? A Reconsideration of the Evidence." Paper prepared for the Congressional Budget Office, Washington, D.C., Contract No. 96-0228.

INDEX